Our Money Our Lives

Our Money Our Lives

Women and Microcredit in Cross-Cultural Perspective

Edited by
Bidyut Mohanty
Victor Faessel

AAKAR

Our Money Our Lives: Women and Microcredit
in Cross-Cultural Perspective
Edited by Bidyut Mohanty and Victor Faessel

First Published 2018

ISBN 978-93-5002-555-0

Published by
AAKAR BOOKS
28 E Pocket IV, Mayur Vihar Phase I
Delhi 110 091 India
aakarbooks@gmail.com

Laser Typeset at
Arpit Printographers, Delhi 110 032

Printed at
D.K. Fine Art Press, Delhi 110 052

Contents

Preface

Years ago when I was a graduate student studying in India my life was transformed by a remarkable incident in a famine. I heard about the drought in the state of Bihar that was imperilling millions of lives, and wanted to help. So I left my comfortable situation at Punjab University and travelled to Patna where for a time I was part of an international aid team distributing sacks of food products from the UN and America—powdered milk, wheat, and soy—which was made into a porridge and distributed free at massive outdoor areas.

Then I noticed a different group of relief workers, Indians who had the same resources of sacks of free food. But they were not giving the food away free at the edge of villages. They went into the heart of the hamlets and organized workers into teams, and then paid them in portions of food. The work projects that they organized were aimed at helping the whole village: they built roads and schools and constructed dams and tube wells that would ensure that water resources, when the rains returned, would last longer.

"This is smart," I said to myself. "Who are these people?"

Gandhians, it turned out, was the answer. They were volunteers with the Sarvodaya movement, men and women who believed in the philosophy of village uplift and self-help advocated by Mohandas Gandhi and led by the former socialist-turned-Gandhian, Jayaprakash Narayan (JP).

So I left the international aid group with which I had been working, and came to JP to offer myself as a volunteer. He welcomed me into his cadres even though I was the only foreigner in the group and my Hindi was only marginally adequate. But there was work to be done, and I helped recruit Indian student volunteers to go into the villages and organize food-for-work projects. It was an extraordinary year, and I learned much from the creativity of the villagers with whom I worked, as well as imbibing ideas of Gandhian social change from JP and his staff. Gandhian ideas and non-violent conflict resolution remained a focus of my writing and teaching for much of my career, and I owe it all to that chance meeting with Gandhians in the Bihar famine.

What I learned from this incident is that people want to work. They want to work not only to survive but to bring the dignity of labour and accomplishment to themselves and those around them. Work need not be a dirty word, nor a dirty task. It can be a means of ennoblement and empowerment.

This is what Muhammad Yunus discovered some years ago in Bangladesh when he found that people wanted to work, that they had innovative and creative ideas about how to raise their living standard, and could realize them if only they had a small amount of money to get the projects going. But they needed that money. This is where Yunus's small-loan banking system came into the picture. He had faith that with small loans to the right people—usually women who were not prone to squander the money but to invest it wisely in local projects—they would be able to repay the loans with interest in a timely way, and thus allow the people's bank to thrive.

Microcredit was born in Bangladesh. And like the Gandhian food-for-work projects in which I participated in the Bihar famine, the projects supported by these ventures not only provided for the economic and social development of rural areas, but also enhanced the human spirit. These projects allowed people to experience the dignity and sense of accomplishment that comes with engaging in projects that may involve risk, but also offer the possibility of success; and even when the projects fail the participants are usually given other chances to succeed.

The world's attention turned to Yunus's modest venture in Bangladesh, in part because it soon became an enormous venture, one that involved tens of millions of loans. Still the return rate on the loans was remarkably high, some 95 to 98 per cent. Yunus became a world-wide figure, and in 2006 he received the Nobel Prize for Peace for his efforts.

With success comes diversity and criticism, and microcredit as a development strategy has received both. Some question whether it really alleviates poverty, or simply shifts the burden of debt to a different kind of institution. Others see it as socially disruptive, since it privileges women as recipients of the loans. Still others wonder if it is equally as effective outside Bangladesh, in other parts of the world.

That's where this volume comes in. The editors of this book have looked at microcredit not just as a regional approach but as a global one. They have brought together an impressive assemblage of expertise to focus on the diverse settings in which microcredit has been conducted—not only in Bangladesh, India, and Pakistan, but also in Peru, Iran, Vietnam, and the United States. It shows that although the basic approach is the same, the diverse settings each have their own limitations on how microcredit is administered, and what can be achieved through its efforts.

Some contributions in this volume also take a critical stance. Though they appreciate some of its accomplishments, they take a realistic look at the dark side of the microcredit industry. They raise questions about its impact on economic development, impoverishment, political democracy, and gender relations. What these contributions prove is that microcredit may not be a panacea for all kinds of development, and that it needs to be a part of a larger social and economic strategy that is supported by the democratic structures of society.

This volume shows that there is much to be learned by looking at microcredit from a global perspective. It also shows that there is a remarkable resilience in the human spirit that allows people in the most dire circumstances to think creatively and participate in their own solutions. As I discovered many years ago in a famine in Bihar, sometimes the most desperate situations can become the fertile ground for opportunity and social change.

Mark Juergensmeyer
Professor of Sociology and Global Studies
University of California Santa Barbara

Acknowledgements

The workshop that formed the genesis of this volume brought together social science scholars and members of civil society organizations involved with microcredit efforts on the ground, to examine present realities and future challenges of microfinance as it moves from the margins of the financial system to the mainstream. Assessing progress towards the twin goals of poverty alleviation and the empowerment of women, workshop participants considered these complex issues from the ground-level perspective of the providers and recipients of microfinance programmes in India, Bangladesh, Pakistan, the Philippines, Vietnam, Iran, Egypt, Haiti, Peru and the US. Their analyses examined the ways in which local and global exigencies influence outcomes in the context of social and economic processes that are both increasing global integration and weakening social safety nets.

The May 2010 workshop, titled "Revisiting Microcredit/ Microfinance as a Development Strategy for an Inclusive Growth: A Global Perspective," was sponsored by the Orfalea Centre for Global & International Studies at the University of California in Santa Barbara and was conceived and principally organized by Bidyut Mohanty, who at the time was a visiting professor in UCSB's Global Studies Department. Victor Faessel at the Orfalea Centre was logistical lead for both the workshop event itself and the assembly of the manuscript that forms the basis of this volume.

Many hands contributed to our successful undertaking. Of numerous people to be thanked for their involvement in this project, the first word goes to the workshop participants themselves who in some cases travelled a great distance in order to share their experience. The discussions were enriched by several UCSB faculty colleagues who participated either as panel chairs and respondents, or as an engaged audience that also included members of Santa Barbara's community of activists. Special thanks go to Mark Juergensmeyer, director of the Orfalea Centre at the time, who provided the material support that made this project possible. Important contributions at UCSB came from workshop rapporteur Patricia Taber, and Mary and Thomas Jacobas. The Orfalea Centre staff supported the project in various ways, including graduate students Kendra Sarna, Lori Frisbie, and Linda Khoury, and undergraduate assistants Alex Ling and Cory Baker. Berkeley Sanjay is thankfully acknowledged for visually documenting the event. We also thank Ms. Joya Roy for editorial assistance.

We are gateful to the contributors for staying with the project and finalizing their chapters in response to the suggestions from reviews.

The Preface by Mark Juergensmeyer and the Foreword by M.A. Oommen introduce this work in their unique ways. Our deep gratitude to them.

Editors

Foreword

Towards a Dynamic Micro Credit Regime

Micro-finance is a much debated concept, yet a widely accepted policy tool to fight poverty since the 1970s following the inauguration of the Grameen Bank project in Bangladesh. Micro finance which initially covered only a few thousand people has today reached over 211 million across the globe. Its unique salience is the dominating presence of women who admittedly constitute a deprived and vulnerable category. Indeed, its rapid spread and popularity is indicative of the pervasiveness of poverty and signals the crying need for reform for human progress. In geographical terms this is a developing world phenomenon accounting for over 97 per cent of the client members. To avoid confusion of the term microcredit with microfinance, the former is to be understood as a subset of the latter, confined to credit. To put the discussion in perspective, I would define microfinance (a chapter in this volume even uses the term 'nano' finance), as the arrangements of financial services such as loans, savings, insurance, money transfers and so on offered to the lower income groups or any vulnerable categories its conceptualization and practice, it is much more than an income enhancing poverty alleviation project. It is widely characterized as a women empowering programme banking on social capital or if we choose a less loaded but more relevant expression, an instrument for equitable social change. It is to be noted that the project presents itself as a powerful narrative that proclaims the need for greater gender justice, financial inclusion and widening of people's choices and enhancing their freedoms. *Our Money, Our Lives* is a gripping narrative of women and credit in a cross-cultural perspective. Bidyut Mohanty's comprehensive introduction provides a fitting backdrop to the theme as well as to the presentations, besides raising a wide range of pertinent issues.

The chapters in this volume are the outcome of a project of the Orfalea Centre for Global and International Studies at the University of California, Santa Barbara with a view to revisiting microcredit as an inclusive development strategy in a global perspective. Nine case studies covering countries as diverse as USA, Peru, India, Pakistan, Iran, Vietnam and Bangladesh provide a wealth of information regarding the ground realities about the impact of microcredit on women, their well-being, besides their agency role in social transformation. The Women's Economic Ventures (WEV) from USA stands out as an initiative of a different genre and does not easily mesh with the rest. As well exemplified in the concluding chapter by Patricia Taber in this volume, the contributions are scholarly and insightful. To be sure, the 'frontline experience' of professionals like Jean Weidemann with over 35 years in 30 countries captured by Taber have added depth and sagacity to the deliberations.

It is instructive to note that the authors of the volume are not a unanimous voice for microcredit. By and large, the contributions are in the best academic traditions and are generally dialectical and evidence-based. The very first chapter, a refreshing piece, theoretically-oriented, but empirically grounded goes beyond the phenomenal form of Micro Finance Institutions (MFIs) and tries to get at the essence. Along with Lamia Karim's findings from the very home of Grameen Bank, which *inter alia* highlights the pathology of the family of the first woman loanee of the Grameen Bank are stimulating. What Mahlyah Laila Fahimuddin noted about Pakistan, viz: "The studies that have been conducted on microfinance and microlending institutions in Pakistan, lead to conflicting and unclear conclusions reporting the efficacy of microfinance in reaching the poorest of the poor and empowering women" could be true for several other country cases as well.

For the market fundamentalists, MFIs open up a new market segment. This reductionist approach goes against the very grain of all avowed notions of microfinance. Here social goals are kept out and left out as redundant pursuits. For the neoliberals who want to avoid any structural change in society, MFIs are welcome tools that may mitigate the potential threats and embarrassments of a poverty-ridden world. They are but easy antidotes to whatever market failures that happen. Mohanty while aware that the MFIs are not the harbinger of structural transformation acknowledges that the microcredit experience "produces a kind of social bonding among women to work in a united fashion to champion the cause of women." Along with the 50 per cent reservation for women that has become common in the local government in most states in India it is important to underscore the potential of microcredit to be used as a political weapon for changing social structures.

Now what are the important takeaways? One, almost all the studies testify that the poorest of the poor do not benefit and this must be taken as an *obiter dicta,* a reminder for remedial reform. Of course this reality defeats the social philosophy and idea of justice that motivates the formation of self-help groups. That ego clashes can kill even a project of long-standing history is shown when the more educated and richer group of bee keepers in Iran fought against the old and less educated women. The Iran case study and several others in the volume tell us unequivocally the need for building capabilities (in education, skills, health, etc) as a precondition for poverty eradication. Poverty is a multi-dimensional deprivation and microcredit however important could not go beyond a limited space. This has created serious handicaps in making headway in improving the quality of human life unless and until the actors assume political empowerment. Kerala's Kudumbashree is a classic case and stands out as a monumental lesson.

Two, the major message of the book is that there is no standard model that fits all times and regimes. Success is contextual and considerably influenced by culture, tradition, mutual trust and collective power.

Three, microcredit *per se* cannot alter social relations and norms that govern gender relations. Micro credit can be a potent force of change only when economic and social paradigms of development itself also change. Even so the MFIs can keep alive the social issues where they did succeed and this is no small achievement. Endemic cases of failure however can send out negative signals in the present-day world where patriarchal values continue to dominate.

Four, *inter alia* the success of a microcredit project depends (a) on the nature of the organization (a bank, NGO, government or whatever) from which a women's group borrows money and (b) on the nature of beneficiary group dynamics. Passive beneficiaries can seldom become active agents of change.

Five, if Bangladesh, a country much below India and Pakistan in terms of per capita income and economic development has acquired a higher female HDI (Human Development Index) and GDI (Gender Development Index) and have several women empowerment indices in their favour (see table below), the credit for this should go to Grameen Bank, the pioneer of microfinance and to BRAC, an equally major NGO in the state. The table below compares Bangladesh with India and Pakistan. It tells a long transformative story briefly as it highlights how women have acquired a clear advantage over men. Imagine what would have been the fate of Bangladesh if these institutions were not there. This is a great lesson not only for all developing countries, but for all who want proof about the transformative potential of microcredit.

Country	*Gender Development Index*	*Human Development Index (HDI) Value (2015)*		*Life Expectancy at Birth Years*		*Mean Years of Schooling Years*		*Estimated Gross National Income Per Capita 2011 ppp($)*	
	Value (2015)	*Female*	*Male*	*Female*	*Male*	*Female*	*Male*	*Female*	*Male*
Bangaladesh	0.927	0.556	0.599	73.3	70.7	5	5.6	2,379	4,285
India	0.819	0.549	0.671	69.9	66.9	4.8	8.2	2,184	8,897
Paksitan	0.747	0.452	0.61	67.4	65.4	3.7	6.5	1,498	8,376

Source: Table 4 Gender Development Index in *Human Development Report 2016*, p. 212.

Our Money, Our Lives is an inclusive title and conveys more than it connotes. Poverty and gender inequity continue to yawn wide and deep. The UN, the lending agencies, the policy makers, media and development thinkers round the world have to see this as a colossal social failure. Many have enlisted the myth of neoclassical economics to logjam human progress. Will the MFIs acquire strength to counter this? This book can be a telling pointer towards the mission of social transformation.

Thiruvananthapuram
October 5, 2017

M.A. Oommen
Honorary Fellow
Centre for Development Studies

Introduction: Women's Empowerment and Microcredit

Bidyut Mohanty

All over the world, the subordinate position of women cuts across class, caste, race and ethnicity, and has multiple manifestations. It is more pronounced in South Asia than many other regions of the world. This status is reflected, for example, in women's limited voice in the political system, their disproportionately high share of employment in the low paid, insecure, informal sector of the economy with harsh working conditions failing to meet the norms of 'decent work' and certain kinds of work such as caregiver responsibilities in the family not being recognized as work. In addition, they not only face many forms of social harassment and are treated with low self-esteem, they have very few or no assets of their own, physical or otherwise to rely upon. Thus we sit up and reflect when we confront a piece of reality that the financial exclusion of women exceeded 80 per cent of the total level of such exclusion according to the 2005 *Human Development Report of India*.[1] To address this situation, which was especially grave in South Asia, there were some initiatives both at the civil society level and at the governmental level in the 1980s. This quickly acquired global relevance as similar conditions obtained in many other countries. Providing credit to women and enabling them to organize themselves in small groups to use that fund to improve their economic opportunities and socio-political status was the key idea which drove some visionaries and policy makers in South Asia to launch this initiative. So much so that the total number of clients particularly in South Asia spread rapidly. Most of the clients are women and also from the poor class. (Please see Tables 1 and 2 at the end). However, the peak was achieved in 2010 after which the numbers declined because of a crisis in the microcredit sector. The underlying philosophy was that once women had not only access to but also control over money, they would have a greater say in family affairs and enjoy a higher status in their environment. This would be a significant contribution to the process of women's empowerment. It is interesting to note that a number of poor women in Asia-Pacific countries became members of the microcredit groups (Table 1). Alas, little was it realized that patriarchy's tentacles were too strong and widespread to allow this to succeed easily. The neo-liberal policy makers had other priorities such as economic growth, profit and financial sustainability rather than working towards women's empowerment. Through this story in South Asia and some countries from other parts of the world, we try to focus on how the struggle for making microfinance an instrument of women's upliftment continues. Let us first of all grasp the context of this discussion before we explain the basic dynamics of the microcredit experience.

Table 1: Number of Poor Borrowers All Over the World

Years	*Total Borrowers (millions)*	*Total Poor Borrowers (millions)*
2010	205	138
2011	195	124
2012	204	116
2013	211	114

Source: Figure 1: Growth of Total Clients and Total Poorest Clients (December 31, 1997 to December 31, 2013)
https://stateofthecampaign.files.wordpress.com/2015/11/figure-1_growth-of-total-and-total-poorest-borrowers_en-full.png

The UN and the Microcredit Initiatives

Troubled by the trend of growing social inequalities and unevenness of regional development and the persistence of various forms of discrimination against women, the United

Table 2: Customers by Region, Gender and Poverty Level

Regions	*No. of Micro-Credit Financial Institutions*	*No. of Total Clients*	*No. of Women Clients*	*No. of Poorest Clients*	*No. Poorest Women Clients*	*% of Poorest Women Clients*
Sub-Saharan Africa	1,045	1,59,45,279	85,81,990	87,27,527	58,75,258	67.31
Asia Pacific	1,119	16,69,08,164	———	10,14,27,062	8,55,22,494	84.31
Latin America & Caribbean	672	1,74,07,431	1,07,25,886	27,51,885	20,08,379	72.98
Middle East & North Africa	99	52,79,706	27,85,940	12,50,061	9,08,991	72.71
A. Developing World Totals	2,935	20,55,40,580	———	11,41,56,535	9,43,15,122	82.61
North America & Western Europe	87	1,68,815	57,000	42,101	23,631	56.12
Eastern Europe & Central Asia	76	54,10,152	2,82,821	1,12,950	50,218	44.46
B. Industrialized World Totals	163	55,78,967	3,39,821	1,55,051	73,579	47.45
Grand Total (A+B)	3,098	21,11,19,547	———	11,43,11,586	9,83,88,701	86.07

Source: Table 7: Regional Breakdown of Microfinance Data
https://stateofthecampaign.files.wordpress.com/2015/12/tf_table-7_regional-breakdown-of-microfinance-data_en_socr-2015.png
(Accessed on 30 August 2017)

Nations declared in 2000, its Millennium Development Goals (MDGs) by 2015 where the goals to end poverty and women's disempowerment figured prominently. These goals were incorporated, with added dimensions, in the UN's Sustainable Development Goals (SDGs) for realization during 2015-2030. Since microfinance was seen as having the potential to alleviate poverty and help women's development, the UN declared 2005 as "the year of microcredit." Incidentally, in common usage, the distinction between microcredit and microfinance is not strictly maintained. However, strictly speaking, microfinance as a broader term includes microcredit and other small financial services for purposes such as health and education. Some of these forms of support are also called 'micro-services' whose scope has continued to grow. For all these activities by participating in the microfinance system, women are encouraged to save small amounts of money for emergencies as well as for other purposes. When the microfinance institutions appeared as dominant agencies on the scene, microfinance acquired greater meaning aiming at providing many kinds of services to women and poor people. After 2015, the SDGs also defined poverty in a more inclusive way adding the lack of access to healthcare, education and shelter and other deprivations that some MFIs tried to address. Interestingly, much of this was anticipated by the pioneer microfinance initiative the Grameen Bank model in Bangladesh in 1983 through the 16 Decisions that self-help groups (SHGs) were obliged to adopt (See Appendix). The phenomenon of microcredit and microfinance gained currency because it facilitated the provision of small amounts of loans to poor women who, lacking financial collateral, were considered "unbankable."

Thus the UN initiative gave an impetus to the microfinance phenomenon all over the world.

But, by the time the UN took note of microcredit's potential in 2005, the concept had already taken root in some form or the other in many countries in different parts of the world. In Bangladesh, besides the Grameen Bank there was another important initiative, namely, Bangladesh Rural Advance

Committee (BRAC), which began as Bangladesh Rehabilitation Committee in 1972 after the country's formation and currently renamed as Building Resources Across Communities. One of the largest NGOs in the world, BRAC has taken the lead role in providing credit to the poor, particularly to indigent women, since 1974. In India, the Self Employed Women's Association (SEWA), a trade union of women in the informal economy started the SEWA Cooperative Bank in 1974 to provide loans to low-income self-employed women. In the last three decades numerous NGOs, such as Professional Assistance for Development Action (PRADAN), Centre for Youth and Social Development (CYSD) and Sadhan, alongwith the National Bank for Agriculture Rural Development (NABARD), a semi-governmental bank, have been major players. In 2001, the Government of India initiated the Swayamsiddha programme to empower women's SHGs to avail themselves of both credit and other social sector benefits at village level. In Indonesia, microcredit was pioneered by the Bank Rakyat Indonesia (BRI) or 'people's bank', the country's oldest bank which has been largely state-owned during its 130-year history, while in Vietnam the Vietnam Bank for the Poor, or Vietnam Bank for Social Policy modelled on Indonesia's BRI, its Bank for Agriculture and Rural Development (VBARD) and other state agencies have provided microfinance and small credit to individuals, small enterprises and SHGs (see Chapter 4).

In developed countries too such initiatives were not rare. For example, a US NGO, the Women's Economic Ventures (WEV) has been active since 1991 giving credit to help single and disadvantaged women to develop microenterprises. We take up some of these cases in this volume.

Microfinance in Practice

In regions far beyond its birthplace in Bangladesh and India, women microcredit clients have demonstrated their enthusiasm in procuring loans for productive purposes. Even farmers having small pieces of land avail themselves microcredit alongside high interest rate loans from seed companies or traditional moneylenders. Yet despite gaining popularity at both grassroots and UN levels, experts were still divided on the relevance of microfinance and whether it actually played any positive role in the lives of the poor in eradicating poverty. A related question that has also been fiercely debated is whether women have been empowered in transforming the patriarchal structure of their societies or not, particularly in the South Asian context. An exercise to assess its impact was important because four decades had passed since microcredit became part of public policy as well as a major focus of international donors with some $ 25 billion credit in circulation under this scheme.[2] As of 2009, microcredit had reached 190 million people globally, of which the absolute poor constituted 63 per cent. Among these, 81 per cent are women.[3]

Needless to say, the UN figure is only one of the various available estimates, cited here to give a broad picture of the magnitude and pervasiveness as well as the popularity of microcredit all over the world. Each country, each national organization involved in microcredit has generated its own estimates; these may include groups that might now be defunct[4]. Despite the problems of accuracy, we can get some idea about its practice.

Recent statistics inform us about the reduction of the extreme poor worldwide to the extent of 13 million within one year, that is 2010 and 2011 due to microcredit.[5] The total number of beneficiaries, living on less than $ 1.25 per day, for example, is 124 million. However, the number would be more if one includes the number of beneficiaries living at a level slightly above the international poverty line.[6] Around 2010 many MFIs faced a serious crisis of transaction breakdown in India. Perhaps the absolute number of microcredit clients would have declined because of the severe crises affecting both MFIs and beneficiaries leading to much distress among the borrowers and a large number of suicides in various parts of South Asia, especially in Andhra Pradesh in 2010 and 2011.[7] As the table shows that the total number of clients all over the world reached the apex in 2010 after which it declined. That year happened to be the crisis year in India where people committed suicide. In 2013 again, it began to increase but the previous confidence has not returned yet.

Assessment of microcredit experience in various parts of the world has centred around certain specific issues such as rate of interest.

In so far as interest rates are concerned, there is very scanty information about the different rates charged by MFIs, and by women who borrow from the various MFIs and lend in turn to other needy women in their villages. But it can be safely pointed out that the rate charged by the MFIs and women lenders would be higher than the commercial banks but lower than the rates charged by the traditional moneylenders. All over the world interest rates vary. In one case, for instance, a particular bank in Mexico charges 150 per cent, the reason being the enormous handling charges for small loans.[8] In addition, MFIs need a large number of staff to travel to borrowers in dispersed places. Secondly, the above source points out that sometimes the women who want to expand their small enterprises do not mind paying the high interest rate though in general it does hurt to pay. In the case of Bangladesh, both BRAC and Grameen Bank became alert to this issue and tried to be flexible in terms of rates and mode of payment in as early as 2003. The first thing they did was to abolish the need for collateral. Nobody is made responsible for the payment unlike the earlier model where the members of the group used to remain as collateral. Beneficiaries wait till loan collectors come to collect the amount.[9] Clients now take microcredit as one of the sources of financing. Secondly, some of them borrow from multiple sources and make cross payments 'apparently' quite judiciously. Perhaps these resourceful entrepreneurs know exactly how much they are going to gain and when and accordingly arrange their portfolio. But others are not that resourceful and their nature of venture is such that a certain amount of risk always exists.

In India, three types of rates exist: one fixed by the Reserve Bank, the other by the MFIs for lendees, and the third by lendees themselves who in turn lend to other people. After the microfinance crisis of 2010 abated, the Reserve Bank removed the cap of the rates for registered MFIs. The MFIs can charge more than 26 per cent if the cost of borrowing is higher from the banks.[10] The MFIs in turn charge 36 per cent per year to women. But if women lend the money to other women, they charge 60 per cent per year since the risk is very high. In certain cases, it led to suicide of small tribal farmers whose crops failed in backward states like Odisha even after the crisis.[11]

Issues in Debate

Scholars continue to have divergent views on whether microfinance has played a positive role in addressing the problems of the poor in general, and women in particular.

In other words, the crux of the matter was whether micro-credit as a policy instrument has liberated women structurally by empowering them financially and socially, or whether it touched the problem of financial subordination of women only cosmetically. Did it indicate that the state had abdicated its welfare role in alleviating poverty and gender injustice in favour of NGOs or does the state still play an important role in ameliorating the life of the poor? Could it be argued that microcredit opens up some limited but concrete opportunities for poor women to maximize their hidden potential?

Critics have observed that microcredit had at best benefited lower middle class women and done very little for poor women. They have cited evidence to show that while launching microcredit programmes the state had cut down allocations for welfare schemes. Because in this case, NGOs and MFIs, not state agencies, played the dominant role in providing credit for the poor and for women's groups, the state-run financial institutions did not play a major role in this process. The MFIs took on the major role in managing microcredit and it was well known that many of them became more interested in maximizing profits rather than helping the poor, this point could not be glossed over. These MFIs generally looked for profitability and often used coercive tactics to recover loans.[12] Reports showed that many individual 'lendees' complained of shameful treatment and humiliation by the intermediary borrowing groups.[13]

Moreover, the campaign for microcredit spread so rapidly that there was stiff competition among NGOs to fulfil lending targets set by national and international donor agencies. In this situation, many women were encouraged to accept loans from the institutions and NGOs without a careful assessment of their ability to repay. Along with the stiff competition and many MFIs working simultaneously, the market got overheated and crashed.

Hence, the critics concluded that microfinance as a policy instrument did not serve its stated purpose of eradicating poverty or empowering women—poor women remained poor and traditional as well as modern patriarchal values were perpetuated.

The advocates of microcredit, too, had persuasive arguments. They pointed out that microfinance had the potential to improve the financial conditions of poor women and thereby improve their bargaining strength. That was why it should be supported as a policy instrument. Many proponents regarded it as an important liberating force, particularly in traditional societies where poor women struggled against oppressive social and economic structures. It was important to recognize the principle underlying the introduction of microcredit programmes. Women in traditional societies had an enormous range of skills starting from weaving and handicrafts to tasks relating to agriculture, seed preservation and food processing and even entrepreneurial capacities which needed enabling conditions and a little capital to flourish. Secondly, women of a locality had social cohesiveness as well. Microcredit provided that support, some capital, however small, to cope with the difficult situation of contemporary times. This could ignite those talents, creating a ripple effect in social, political and economic life.

One conclusion is fairly balanced: "while microfinance does make an important contribution to poverty reduction, generalized claims about its transformative effects do not always hold up in practice. Microfinance can not automatically empower women."[14] It is pointed out that like political representation, access to wages, and any other form of government intervention, it was *just one of the entry points to social change*. Like many other initiatives, microfinance too required organizational commitment and the capacity to utilize its full potential.[15]

Besides, it is not true that national governments had abdicated their welfare roles in this sector. The famous example of the Kerala model of microfinance for women known as Kudumbashree,[16] among many others, showed the continuation of active governmental role in social development programmes. In fact, recently the government has converted the programme of Kudumbashree to a mission. Moreover, there were examples of women's movements having adopted the microcredit programmes as a part of their larger agenda of women's empowerment. Further, the critics did not seem to take into consideration the non-economic consequences accruing from microcredit processes such as the creation of group solidarity among women borrowers who collectively took up development needs and human rights issues in the public sphere, using their microcredit experience to leverage a larger political role in village level institutions such as the panchayats in India. In the latter case, the successful microcredit workers contest elections to posts of members and chiefs of local government institutions and with the help of microcredit federations, take a lead role in engendering the development of their villages.[17]

Here, we introduce the principles underlying the microcredit process and show that it is not a substitute for structural measures, but has a significant role to play in the economy and polity to open up opportunities for women's collective role in social development.

Why Microcredit?

Let us start with the basics. Poor men and women need money, first of all, to meet their daily consumption needs. Then there are other requirements as a part of their life cycle that includes both normal and crisis times, regular livelihood as well as securing some safety net. They involve:

a. Lifecycle needs related to such events as weddings, funerals, childbirth, education, home building, widowhood, and old age.

b. Personal emergency needs related to sickness, injury, unemployment, theft, harassment, and the untimely death of breadwinners.
c. Disaster needs for dealing with fires, floods, earthquakes, cyclones and tsunamis, and human-caused events like war or the destruction of homes in displacement by development projects.
d. Investment opportunities for expanding or starting a business, buying equipment, raw materials or land, and housing.

To meet all such needs people without assets formerly relied on their wages or income from whatever profession they pursued with their physical labour or skill. Often that fell far short of meeting their needs. For personal needs they could approach their better-off family members but for agricultural and entrepreneurial needs they traditionally went to the moneylender or some private source which became yet another cause of their miseries. The horrendous accounts of exploitation by moneylenders by their usury practices have been widely documented. Paying exorbitant interest rates, mortgaging the homestead land, working on the lender's land as bonded labour or even working on one's own land mortgaged to the lender were some of the practices. This type of condition of the poor in the developing countries was too well known to need any elabouration. In many countries banks were called upon to move in and support the poor by advancing loans. But in all cases they asked for collaterals which the poor were unable to provide. It is to address such situations of dire poverty and helpless sense of the poor, especially women, that an institutional initiative such as microcredit was conceived.

As has been pointed out in a succinct way by Prahalad (2004),[18] this initiative can be considered to be an "opportunity" to tap the "fortune" at the "bottom of the pyramid." Microcredit may be regarded as an effective channel to potentially fulfil a range of unmet needs of the poor, not least the need to save for contingencies. If a microenterprise is well designed and successful, it has the potential to meet and exceed the cost of capital. Donor agencies try to target their efforts at generating savings through the investment in microenterprises, and spreading it to other activities.[19]

Principles on which Microcredit Works

Effective microcredit works when based on a set of principles. These include capacity building of a homogeneous group having intimate bonding known as social capital,[20] the inculcation of saving habits, trust building, ensuring the availability of raw materials, markets, and skills, and generating employment through funded microenterprises. It also involves the availability of some funding to cover risks related to unforeseen failure. The rules and the framework which Muhammad Yunus enunciated for Bangladeshi women before they join a microcredit group are articulated mostly from the beneficiary's point of view (See Appendix). In addition, our field level findings show that democratic relations within the family, support from male family members contributes to the success of the system. We find that in many places and especially when there is a pressure to fulfil the assigned targets the functionaries employed by the MFIs fail to respect the rules and ignore family and social dynamics thus causing hardships to the beneficiaries and bringing the system to discredit.

Aside from this, the success of microcredit, especially in the context of Third World countries always required a high degree of mutual trust. In other words, success requires the formation of social capital, which Putnam has emphatically stressed for the effective management of common property.[21] As many scholars have lamented, the MFIs worked under the notion of pure profitability forgetting their social objective. They not only gave huge salaries and other incentives to their functionaries to expand the microcredit groups, compromising the basic principles, but also instructed them "to recover the entire loan under any circumstances." However, we get evidence of some successful cases from India . It is worthwhile to mention them.

The first one, known as the "Kerala model" of microcredit programme, fully funded by the government had been in operation since the 1980s which, in 1998, was streamlined under the name of Kudumbashree.[22] In this model, women of any rural or urban administrative ward could get organized and form groups to avail themselves of credit to start small businesses collectively. Some of the groups had become so powerful that they had been given the role of running the government-owned canteens all over the state or manufacturing school uniforms for all government schools. In other Indian states that adopted the Kudumbashree model, the groups were given charge of conducting social audit for the money spent under many government-sponsored schemes such as the rural employment guarantee scheme. Extensive evaluations had concluded that these women groups had proved in practice that they were important agents of social change achieving economic as well as social objectives.[23]

A 2013 study compared the performance of two types of microfinance organizations, public and private fund-givers.[24]

One was Self Help Groups (SHGs), or joint liability groups backed by the government or public banks like the National Agricultural Bank and Rural Development (NABARD), and the other was private, profit-oriented microfinance institutions (MFIs) which make lending to the poor a lucrative business. These cases showed how the latter type, the MFIs made a profit causing severe distress among small borrowers. The study conclusively showed that the state-linked initiatives were more successful than the private ones. Incidentally, the study area was the Indian state of Andhra Pradesh, where, as mentioned earlier the microfinance organizations faced a severe crisis in 2010.[25] However, it is also to be noted that the government played a double role in that it not only supported the SHGs along with the MFIs but also gave subsidies to those who failed miserably. Because of electoral politics the government sometimes waived off the total loan amount.[26] In addition, some social activists persuaded the women not to repay the loans.

State-backed microcredit, gradually, became a widespread phenomenon in India. According to one estimate, in 2011 there were about 67 million SHGs in India backed by the state-led banks, and most of their members were from poorer families.[27]

There are some other organizations such as PRADAN, CYSD and Society for Helping Awakening Rural Poor Through Education (SHARE) which are NGOs who also provide loans to the SHGs but, as I have gathered from my visits to their areas of work, are known for looking after the interests of the poor. These NGOs represent one model that follows the bottom up principle. Some other examples are: Mysore Resettlement and Development Agency(MYRADA) or Development of Humane Action Foundation (DHAN). They are conspicuous for the fact that they did not succumb to the market crisis of 2007. They showed "...the importance of the power of communities in resolving issues that can not be solved by market and state institutions."[28] But actually both MYRADA and DHAN were also backed by the NABARD, thus the community action after all got support from a state institution.

Therefore, it would be wrong to dismiss the microfinance experience as a failure. It is relevant to note that since the crisis period in Andhra Pradesh in 2010, the Indian government has been trying to regulate microfinance institutions.[29] It is also trying to expand the scope of microfinance into urban areas under many new schemes and enlarging the sphere of support by renaming the NABARD as National Rural Livelihood Mission (NRLM). In addition, the 2013 national budget funded a new all-women's bank, called Bharatiya Mahila Bank.[30] Simultaneously, MFIs branded as bankruptcies were also trying to rework their corporate social responsibility image.[31]

A related question raised above was to what extent the poor had achieved financial viability and women had become socially empowered? These questions are context-specific. In order to answer them, we will now turn to our contributors to the volume.

Agencies Involved in Financial Transactions

The nature of the agencies working in the microcredit sector, matters a lot in determining their social outcomes and financial viability. To what extent their focus is on the social objectives rather than making profit for their organization and mechanically complying the donors' rules and procedures is consequential for the poor. It is noted in our volume that with the exception of Vietnam where the government is the direct agency for providing microcredit, in all the other Asian and Latin American countries (Pakistan, Bangladesh, India, and Iran and Peru) not only the government but also the NGOs and international agencies have equal involvement in the microfinance sector. International agencies try to route their capital mainly through NGOs with the consent of the government. In Bangladesh, the big NGOs like the Grameen Bank and BRAC are the major sources of lending (Karim). In the USA the NGOs seem to be the major players in the field (Bailey). There is much evidence presented in these studies that show that the success of a microcredit project very much depends on the nature of the organization from which a women's group borrows money. In case of USA, the WEV for example helped the women entrepreneurs to become successful in their effort. On the other hand, Weddle (Peru) pointed out that the lenders discriminate against the women borrowers but for their own initiative to overcome the same. While some agencies try to recover loans from poor women using arm-twisting measures (Karim), there are NGOs that work with poor widows and give loans with a view to allowing them to live in dignity (Pandey, India). Similarly, a Maharashtra-based social movement initiative called Swayam Shikshan Prayog (SSP) has encouraged the formation of women's collectives called *sakhi* or a friend (Menon). In many cases in India, the panchayats and the SHGs work together to secure loans using the channels of NGOs and banks under government-initiated programmes for purposes of meeting a wide range of their essential needs. (Mohanty). On the other hand, the lending organization in Iran discriminated against old and illiterate women in favour of young and educated women thereby leading to the failure of the microcredit enterprise.

It is also important to note that the amount of microcredit loans varies from country to country. In developing countries like Bangladesh, India, or Pakistan, the loan amount is often fairly small—even below one hundred dollars—but in countries like Peru or the USA the loan amounts tend to be in thousands of dollars. But in both kinds of situations, the social purpose seems to guide the endeavour.

Who are the Beneficiaries?

This work also sheds light on the nature of microloan beneficiaries. In developing countries, women form groups and are supposed to act as united teams to make their project a success. In India, our case studies show that women have not only created new streams of income but they have also been acting as networks of pressure groups lobbying in the gram sabha (village assembly) for expanding access to basic services (Mohanty). The experience is not uniform everywhere either in India or elsewhere. Similarly, Pandey's study showed that a group of widows seized the opportunity and tried to improve their luck with success. Menon's study showed that the members of the group coming from poor families reinterpreted the loan not in terms of profit or loss in the neoliberal sense but treated it as a strategy of survival and nobody got penalized if she could not pay on time. According to the results of the Bangladesh study, on the other hand group dynamics faltered due to conflict and lack of trust at some point. In the case of Iran, again the group could not hold together because of age and education disparities among its members. On the other hand, the Vietnam study shows the capacity of the poor women's self-help group achieving notable success in fulfilling many community needs. In other words, SHGs in the developing countries considerably depended for their success on group dynamics and the support structure.[32] In the USA and Peru, group formation was absent as a factor of analysis: The women acted as individual borrowers.

Several common threads emerge from the contributions collected here. First, the majority of beneficiaries of microcredit are from the very low income groups, particularly in India, Bangladesh, Pakistan, Iran and Vietnam, while beneficiaries in Latin America and the USA are comparatively less poor. Second, as regards issues of the broader cultural setting of beneficiaries, women's groups in the Asian context are shown to be working under the influence of traditional patriarchal values. In some cases, this has led to hardship and suffering, while in others there were positive outcomes despite social constraints. For example, we see the case in which widows, though neglected by patriarchal institutions, have tried to come together to live in dignity. In the Bangladesh study, we notice that the social practices often frustrate the objectives of the microcredit initiative. This happens elsewhere too. In the case of Iran, interestingly, conflict between young women having education but lacking skills in bee-keeping and older illiterate women having the required skills, led to bitter inter-group distrust and failure of the enterprise (Alirezanejad). In the USA and Peru where traditional forms of patriarchy are relatively less pronounced, women in these countries, like their Asian sisters, also face discrimination in acquiring capital for their enterprises, compared to males. Had the women borrowers in Peru got access to the same amount of capital as men, the total welfare of society would have been considerably improved. To circumvent discrimination they join male colleagues to pursue their enterprise (Weddle).

Microfinance and Women's Empowerment

It should be stressed that microfinance cannot be treated as a "magic bullet" leading to economic vitality and social well-being of the poor, especially women.[33] As for women's real empowerment, much more needed to be done than financial intervention alone. Besides microcredit, fulfilment of educational and health needs as well as political representation in decision-making, through reservations or quotas, are essential requirements for women's empowerment. It is true that since their inception, MFIs have been striving to attain the twin lofty goals of securing financial sustainability and fulfilling a social mission, particularly meant for poor women. These are termed as the Double Bottom Line (DBL). It should be pointed out that while financial sustainability is relatively easy to assess, the indices of "social mission" remain difficult to define and hence measure in concrete terms. Yet both these dimensions need to be broken down in a specific context for making policy and designing social action. For example, financial inclusion would take into account the amount of loan, choice of specific economic activities, organizational mechanism that brings sustainability in a changing market situation and so on. Social mission may involve increasing women's autonomy in the family and assertion of various rights by women individually and collectively, exercising control over assets including cash flow, expanding choices in social, cultural and economic matters. Above all, whether they add up to 'political' empowerment—expanding the realm of freedom of women—would be even more complex in practice. However, this whole process can be examined from various vantage points. In our context, it is the specific window of microcredit and self-help groups and the extent of their capacity to pursue the goal of women's empowerment.

Many studies conducted in different parts of the world, qualitative as well as quantitative, including randomized-controlled-trial and non-randomized studies show that microcredit initiatives have often achieved concrete gains for women's empowerment while revealing serious limitations in many cases. There are many instances where microcredit contributed to women gaining control over finances and raising their social status. A number of cases pointed out the inability of the women's groups to exercise financial power and thus unable to withstand patriarchal pressures and fail to improve their level of education, health and welfare. That these studies have a range of findings has been pointed out by many experts such as Katheleen Odell, 2010.[34] A study to gauge the financial impact of microfinance worldwide reported that in so far as the developed world goes it has helped to reduce poverty but with regard to the developing countries it is not certain.[35]

Over the years, commercialization of MFIs or the stress on the effort to access funding from commercial sources has led some of them to drift away from their social goals. As a result, MFIs increasingly gave priority to profit at the cost of their avowed social mission. Needless to say, commercialized MFIs have been under increased scrutiny for harassing women borrowers. They are accused of charging high interest rates, over-lending, lack of transparency, and use of coercion to collect debt service from "delinquent borrowers." These defaulters largely happen to be the vulnerable, poor women, often living under the severe control of family patriarchy.

At the same time, as for financial sustainability of women borrowers, many studies show that the microcredit has led to an increase in income of the entire villagers. Rajasthan provides some evidence for this.[36] We also have a report that narrates the successful story of a woman in Tamil Nadu who not only helped her husband to become de-addicted of liquor but also started selling flowers and became a successful entrepreneur.[37] The Institute of Social Sciences' study in tribal areas of Odisha conducted in 2012-13 revealed that some of the tribal women had undertaken the rearing of goats and hens which were easy to raise and quick to yield income. In order to facilitate their efforts, the panchayat constructed sheds for goats and hens separately along with the low cost shelter to families.[38] Similarly the Dalit SHG members had been given the charge to collect local tax from the villagers for the maintenance of drainage, supply and use of electricity and other petty block level works including the management of midday meals for school children. Thereby they had attained some financial sustainability.

As indicated earlier, case studies presented in this volume also provide a mixed picture. In the case of the beekeepers of Iran neither did the group achieve financial stability nor social respectability. On the other hand, even though the women in (Punjab), Pakistan did not succeed much either in financial sustainability or in social esteem, their daughters acquired education in this process which was itself a positive gain for them. The Peru case shows a level of success; however the women borrowers could not scale up operations to the level of male borrowers without the support of men. In USA on the other hand, there were different constraints which were largely overcome by intensive training courses in business management. As a result, they achieved financial viability. As we noted the Vietnam story was a positive one both in terms of poverty alleviation and women's development. In the Bangladesh study, on the other hand, though there are many positive stories that are widely known, the author cites the case of the mobile-phone-owning ladies who instead of helping the group as a whole were more interested in cornering the benefits for themselves by dominating over poorer women. Moreover, it did not lead to enduring or long lasting financial security for the ladies since mobile phone use became quite common. The author also mentions how some middle class women borrowed microcredit and in turn, as intermediary, lent to the poorer women at much higher rates. These intermediaries also used strong-arm tactics, even invoking cultural norms and family honour to recover loans. Thus, according to the author, these women defeated the entire purpose of the microfinance, limiting the economic as well as the social effect of the initiative. Actually, I too found similar instances happening in India in case of the tribal marginal farmers who committed suicide during 2015-16. Their family members cited similar situations. They had taken loans under microcredit schemes from SHGs run by their somewhat better off relatives, who were after them to make repayment. This was a factor driving them to bankruptcy and commit suicide.[39]

Thus as for the impact on alleviation of poverty, the picture is mixed. Given the multidimensional nature of poverty in the context of the Sustainable Development Goals (SDGs)-2015 it is evident that one has to go beyond the financial impact of the microcredit to fight poverty. Along with the small amount of finance, one also must fulfil the need for other basic services as well, namely, shelter, health, education, sanitation and access to safe drinking water.[40]

The microfinance sector has also seen some significant initiatives. Many MFIs around the world work towards their social mission by reaching out to the poor and the extremely poor by making them eligible to access microcredit and make them economically active. In order to do this, these organizations not only seek funding from governmental and other donor sources, but use their own resources, such as a portion of their profit, to pursue their social mission goals. As an example, BRAC in Bangladesh, has been reaching out to the extremely poor through their "Targeting the Ultra Poor," (TUP) programme, which is funded by grants from a variety of sources including its own. The Grameen Bank started the Grameen-2 programme in 2003 and had introduced mobile telephones and many other new modern instruments for rural women to operate, but with varying consequences. Before the 2010 crisis in Andhra Pradesh, the Grameen too faced a severe crisis in 1996 when the Islamic fundamentalist forces opposed the idea of both credit and women's empowerment. Under the pressure of the fundamentalist leaders the borrowers refused to repay their loans and many of the members left the programme without any repayment. In 1998 Bangladesh also experienced severe floods. Beset by several crises the Grameen remodelled its style of functioning and adopted a degree of flexibility in modes of payment. Grameen also started micro pensions, making it an obligation for everybody to save, in order to be entitled to an equal contribution from the Grameen organization[41]. It is claimed by some that the recovery rate of Grameen loans is as high as 97 per cent and the process is generally smooth. It is also believed that many social changes have taken place after the introduction of microfinance in Bangladesh. Women could go to the bank alone without veils. The fact that literacy as well as life expectancy of females has increased, and the infant mortality rate and maternal mortality rate have declined may be partly connected with women's participation in the microcredit programme. On top of all this, in spite of having a lower per capita income than in India, the rank of Bangladesh is much above India in HDI as well as GDI. Amartya Sen has frequently highlighted this.[42] He attributed this achievement largely to the imaginative initiative of Grameen Bank and BRAC along with many welfare-oriented government policies (ibid).

In India, there are also some positive cases though their impact has not been as conspicuous. The microcredit scheme initiated by the CYSD, Odisha, operating mostly in the tribal area is supported both by government as well as international donor agencies. Among the beneficiaries 67 per cent are from the Scheduled Tribes (ST) and 7 per cent from Scheduled Castes (SC). The CYSD has started a micro insurance policy in which families get medical benefits at a low cost. In addition, a federation of the SHGs has been formed to coordinate among the women's groups and make better use of their collective funds. The federation gets contracts from the panchayats for development work in the local area and implements them using the services of local youth, women and men.[43] Similarly, an end line survey conducted by an independent feminist in 2012-15 showed that the women belonging to SHGs in PRADAN's operation areas, have gained a limited agency in terms of mobility, bargaining power and decision-making power in the family. In addition, it has increased their to access to knowledge about the many programmes and opportunities and more importantly, about their potential political participation in the village panchayat system. Although largely uneducated themselves, SHG members' attitude towards educating their girl children has changed considerably as a result of this cumulative process.[44]

In recent years, several surveys on microcredit impact assessments point to the fact that the benefits of microcredit could be modest compared to the exaggerated claims made earlier by the microfinance industry as well as campaigners, that it could alleviate poverty on a large scale. Slowly but surely, what has emerged during the last forty years is that, microcredit is a necessary but not sufficient agent of social and economic change. In this regard, one needs to point out that the microfinance initiative has expanded its scope and dimensions providing many new services such as micro-savings in new forms, micro-insurance—as seen in the CYSD example, and micro-leasing as evident in the Kudumbashree's many experiences in Kerala. All such groups have been increasingly interested in securing essential services such as literacy, health care and skill-acquiring programmes. They include concrete training programmes in financial literacy, livelihood development, hygiene, nutrition and sanitation, which can be accessed by the poor in their fight against poverty and attain better life conditions.[45]

Have Women Been Empowered?

Now the moot question is whether microcredit has led to women's empowerment. It is clear that reports are not unanimous. A major study of the well known case of

Kudumbshree in Kerala as the most successful microfinance model for trying to eradicate poverty concludes that as for raising feminist consciousness it has failed miserably. The authors point out that while adding an additional income to the family or working as agents of Social Audit for MGNREGS, the women have indeed accrued some self-confidence and financial literacy, but in the family it has not led to deconstructing their mindset. Patriarchal norms in the family persist despite social reform movements in Kerala. Hence the authors conclude that though microcredit has had a certain limited impact for women's empowerment, it did not do much for their 'liberation'.[46] In a similar vein another important study in Bangladesh has summarized the findings of an *Imp Act* study (Improving the impact of microfinance on poverty) which involved a few MFIs in South Asia in 2005 examining the economic and social consequences of microfinance.[47] These organizations were BRAC in Bangladesh, and PRADAN, CYSD and SHARE in India. According to this study, microfinance is just like any other entry point such as education, political participation, etc., contributing to the process of structural transformation.

It should be noted that the authors of this volume are not unanimous on the issue of the contribution of microfinance to women's empowerment. It is well known that one of the indicators of empowerment is the increase in women's collective bargaining power. Neither the US nor the Peru cases indicated how such an increase in collective bargaining power occurred even though there were other gains. The Vietnam case is a positive example of women collectively engaged in community welfare programmes. Menon's findings in Maharashtra as well as Pandey's account of the poor widows' initiative and Mohanty's study of the elected women representatives backed by women's SHG collectives show one common minimum outcome of the process. Microcredit experience, through its zigzag process produces a kind of social bonding among women to work in united fashion to champion the cause of women. As indicated in Mohanty's chapter, it is often manifested in trying to influence the panchayat decision through their intervention in the gram sabha. But the women beneficiaries in Bangladesh, as analysed by Karim, do not demonstrate united collective functioning. Hence the group dynamics fails to overcome the constraints though there may be exceptions.[48] Similarly, in case of the beekeepers association of Iran, women members did not gain uniformly from the collective. Nor did the members of SHGs of Punjab, Pakistan achieve their objectives.

It is to be stressed that a modern state cannot eradicate poverty or empower women through the microcredit programmes alone. Along with microcredit, relevant macroeconomic policies and social policies should also be adopted in order to create employment opportunities and provide facilities for good education and health care targeting marginalized segments of the population, especially women. Finally, in defence of microcredit/microfinance, it can be said from a social welfare point of view that, considering the neglect of women among traditional moneylending institutions, microcredit has started to erode that exclusion. To many economists microcredit may actually have created a new unexplored market segment.[49] If one takes the yardstick of full economic independence then, it may not be the answer to the problems of the poor women. Much more is needed in the form of structural intervention particularly in education and healthcare to make women economically independent. Having said that, we have to recognize the fact that the microcredit programme had generated enough multiplier effects to prove its relative worth. Undoubtedly, it had brought some social benefits to women, forged women's collective identity, uplifted them to undertake social tasks for the welfare of society, and above all, built up the confidence of many women to fight for leadership roles at the local level. What cannot be contested is that besides the direct economic benefits, however small, microcredit experience brought women into the local public and political arena with focus on issues of children's welfare, sanitation, education, health and drinking water with far more vigour than ever before. Hence, keeping all these considerations in mind, the initiative to promote microcredit has to be seen in a positive light. Keeping in mind the recent South Asia experience, particularly the fact that women are today armed with two potentially strong instruments, namely, political representation through reservation of seats in local government, and microcredit through self-help groups thus combining political and economic initiatives, we see a new momentum. Not only in South Asia, women all over the world are gradually marching forward to a new world of 'new women' more empowered and confident about their capabilities, struggling against powerful obstacles, old and new. In that historical context, microcredit may give us, 'our money' to shape 'our lives'.

ENDNOTES

1. Desai, S. 'Like Flowers and Chocolates.' *The Indian Express*. March 11, 2013 (Delhi Edition).
2. Deutsche Bank. 'Microfinance: An Emerging Investment Opportunity.' *Deutsche Bank Research*. December 19, 2007. http://www.dbresearch.com/PROD/DBR_INTERNET_EN-PROD/PROD0000000000219174.pdf.
3. Reed, L. *The State of the Microcredit Summit Campaign Report 2011*. (Washington, DC, Microcredit Summit Campaign, 2011).
4. For example, while doing an intensive interview in order to collate case studies for Voluntary Overseas Services (VSO) on behalf of the Institute of Social Sciences, New Delhi in the year 2013-15 it became evident that most of the Self Help Groups (SHGs) comprising primitive tribe have become defunct though on paper they seem to be working. Rinjha Jakesika, the first woman chief of the Bonda tribe lamented that even though some of the Dalit SHGs have been working well and helping in collection of the local tax on behalf of the government, the tribal groups are almost dead. She belongs to the Kurli panchayat in Rayagada District, Odisha, India. Similarly the organization the chairperson of the organization called Aamar Biswas that was studied by Pandey informed me that the number of microcredit groups can not be ascertained since many of those are inactive.
5. At the same time, it should be noted that microcredit could be one of the important factors among other factors. For example, there are other right-based welfare acts such as Mahatma Gandhi Rural Employment Guarantee Act, 2005 onwards and National Food Security Act, 2013 (earlier it was a scheme) along with microcredit all operating simultaneously in rural India. All these

benefit women. As it has been noted later (Chapter 7), some of the poor Dalit women avail themselves of all three and strengthen their bargaining power *vis a vis* the landlords to increase the daily wage rates.

6. UN-Non Governmental Liaison Services (UN_NGLS) "The Microfinance Illusion: The post 2015 development agenda should rethink its development approach for local financing" https://unngls.org/index.php/un-ngls_news_archives/2013/503-the-microfinance-illusion-the-post-2015-development-agenda-should-rethink-its-development-approach-for-local-financing.
7. Kaur, Prabhjot and Soma Dey. 'Andhra Pradesh Microfinance Crisis and its Repercussions on Microfinancing Activities in India.' *Global Journal of Management and Business Studies,*Vol. 3, Number 7, 2013, pp. 695-702. http://www.ripublication.com/gjmbs_spl/gjmbsv3n7_02.pdf.
8. "Banks Making Big Profits from small Loans" http://www.nytimes.com/2010/04/14/world/14microfinance.html?pagewanted=all&_r=0.
9. Focus note, 'A Microcredit Crisis Got Averted: The Case of Bangladesh' http://www.cgap.org/publications/microcredit-crisis-averted-case-bangladesh.
10. http://articles.economictimes.indiatimes.com/2014-02-08/news/47127322_1_margin-cap-lending-rate-interest-rate.
11. Ganatrantik Adhikar Sangathan Surakhya (GASS) (2014). The GASS organized public hearings among the family members of the farmers of Odisha who committed suicide since they could not repay the loan on time. Secondly they had borrowed from different sources.
12. Fernando, J. 'Introduction.' *Microfinance, Perils and Prospects* (New York, Routledge, 2005), pp. 1-37.
13. Many poor women committed suicide in Andhra Pradesh because of wrong handlings of the agents to recover the loans. https://www.washingtonpost.com/world/indian_micro_credit_crisis_puts_poor_women_in_a_bind/2011/04/21/AFpckbsE_story.html
14. Kabeer, N. *Microfinance, the MDGs and Beyond: What Difference Can Financial Services to Low-Income Women Make?* (New Delhi: IFAD and UNIFEM Gender Mainstreaming Programme in Asia, 2006). 28.
15. Ibid.
16. We will discuss the model a little later.
17. http://www.thehindu.com/opinion/columns/sainath/

kudumbashree-dominates-kerala-local-polls/article841001.ece

18. Prahalad, C.K. *The Fortune at Bottom of the Pyramid, Eradication of Poverty Through Profit* (Wharton School Publishing, 2004).
19. Robinson, M. *The Microfinance: Sustainable Finance for the Poor.* (Washington DC, The World Bank, 2001).
20. In India the MFIs to begin with, used to form groups taking the wives and sisters together so that the bonding is there. While we visited Mayurbhanj district, Odisha in the first decade of the 21st century, it was noticed that the Other Backward Castes (OBC) groups were formed taking the members of the lane. It was the working area of the centre for Youth and Social Development (CYSD).
21. Putnam, R., R. Leonard and R.Y. Nonetti. *Making Democracy Work: Civic Traditions in Modern Italy* (Princeton, Princeton University Press, 1994).
22. The meaning of the word is: Prosperity of the family.
23. Oommen, M.A. "Have the State Finance Commissions Fulfilled Their Constitutional Mandates?" *Economic & Political Weekly* 45.30 (2010): 39.
24. Reddy, D.N. "Financial Inclusion of the Poor and Marginalized: Why State Supported Bank-Linked SHGs Emerged as Clear Choice over MFIs." Working Paper 6 January 2013. Organized by the National Institute of Rural Development, Government of India.
25. Saxena, Shruti. 'The 2010 Microfinance in Andhra Pradesh, India and Its Implications for Microfinance in India'. http://reconsideringdevelopment.org/issues/volume-iii-issue-i/microfinancecrisis/Even after the legislations and the crisis the small MFIs are still charging very high rates of interest and are using arm-twisting measures to repay weekly as per the rule. As a result even the tribal farmers with one or two acres of land could not pay due to scanty rain. They committed suicide which was rare. This was revealed to us last year during the *jansunani,* the public hearing conducted by a NGO, Odisha. Also, in 2010 alone around 200 men and women committed suicide because they could not repay loans borrowed from microfinance organizations. http://www.businessinsider.com/hundreds-of-suicides-in-india-linked-to-microfinance-organizations-2012-2
26. Nair Tara and Tankha Ajay *Microfinance, India http://www.accessdev.org/downloads/SOS_Report_2013.pdf*
27. Reed, 2011, op. cit.
28. Sharma, K. "Small Loans Big Dreams: Women and Microcredit in a Globalized Economy", *Economic and Political Weekly* 46.43. (2011):

60.

29. Puhazhendhi, V. *Microfinance in India: State of the Sector Report* (New Delhi, An Access Publication and Sage, 2013).
30. Desai, Sonalde. "Like Flowers and Chocolates." *The Indian Express*. March 11, 2013.
31. Puhazhendhi, V. *Microfinance in India: State of the Sector Report* (New Delhi, An Access Publication and Sage, 2013).
32. Ghosh, Budhdev Bidyut Mohanty and Nitya Jacob. *Local Governance. Search of for New Path* (New Delhi, Concept, 2011). In Mayurbhanj District, Odisha it was noticed that the CYSD had encouraged them to form the group taking each lane separately. All those women were not only recruited from one caste but were related to each other intimately.
33. Kabeer, Naila 'Is Microfinance a Magic Bullet? For Women's Empowerment : Analysis of Findings from South Asia', *Economic and Political Weekly*, October 29, 2005, pp. 4709-4718.
34. Odell, Katheleen. *Measuring the Impact of Microfinance,* (Bangladesh, Grameen Foundation, 2010).
    Three studies of Random Control Trials have been conducted in different parts of the world. The results are not uniform. For example, Abhijit Datta et al., 2009 taking the case of Andhra Pradesh noticed that the microcredit supports household borrowing and investment expands the scope of small business. Similarly, Dupas and Robinson, 2009 taking Kenya as a test case noticed that the microcredit increased the business investment and expenditure for women but the third study on Manila by Karlan and Zinman (2010b) noticed that the microcredit in fact helped the males of the household. But in so far as the social impact goes it did not have any impact on women's empowerment, increase in school enrolment or overall health.
35. UN-NGLAS 'The Microfinance Illusion: The Post Development of 2015.https://www.unngls.org/index.php/un-ngls_news_archives/2013/503-the-microfinance-illusion-the-post-2015-development-agenda-should-rethink-its-development-approach-for-local-financing.
36. Annual Report of Women and Child Development, Ministry of Women and Child Development, Government of India-2014-15. http://wcd.nic.in/sites/default/files/AR2014-15.pdf.
37. Ibid.
38. It is indeed a useful development since in tribal areas the family members sleep along with their cattle. In the process they catch many animal-related diseases. The panchayat sees to it that the

persons in charge build the goat sheds as well by using the MGNERGS' money. In many places we saw the physical existence of those sheds. VSO Report as mentioned earlier.

39. We have already cited the event in Odisha. It is interesting to note for the first time a number of tribal farmers of tribal areas have been committing suicides. One can explain the reasons such as borrowing from microcredit groups as well as from cooperative banks, traditional moneylenders to raise cash crops. This was happening for a couple of years until last year when there were some irregularities in the distribution of rainfall, particularly during the month of October. At the same time, the microcredit group members tried to recover their weekly dues and they were unable to pay and hence committed suicide. Incidentally, in one case one of the members happened to be his young sister. Even though it shows one positive fact that the tribal peasants having a couple of acres, want to raise their standard of living, the government is yet to wake up to this fact and has not facilitated either minor irrigation nor the credit from the tribal funds. On the other hand, the government of Odisha never accepted those as the cases of suicides for loss of crops.
40. In fact taking into consideration the needs of poor women the SDG's goals have been formulated accordingly. http://www.copenhagenconsensus.com/post-2015-consensus?gclid=CM_45-LGsc8CFU9xvAodR_ANgg.
41. Kalra, Aparita and Qiulin Zhang, 'Grameen Taking the Capitalism to the Poor,' *The Citizen Journal of International Business Strategy* (Spring, 2004) pp.1-28. www.gsb.edu/chanenjournal.
42. Sen, Amartya. 'Quality of Life: India and China'. *The New York Review of Books* (May,12, 2011).
43. CYSD *The Annual Report, 2015-16.*
44. Revised Final Report of PRADAN 2015.
45. Focus note, 'A Microcredit Crisis Got Averted: The Case of Bangladesh' http://www.cgap.org/publications/microcredit-crisis-averted-case-bangladesh
46. Devika, J. et al., op. cit.
47. Kabeer, Naila, op. cit. She has discussed the research findings of group of scholars from different foreign universities regarding the economic and social impact of the microfinance in South Asia as well as other parts of the world.
48. Sen, op. cit.
49. Sriram, M.S. "Macro View on Microfinance," *Economic and Political Weekly* XL.11. (2012): 29-31.

1

Interrogating the Promise of Microcredit

Gayatri A. Menon

In the past few decades microcredit has gained increasing international currency as a tool to alleviate poverty, for, unlike subsidies and calls for land reform, this tool appears to align itself with, rather than against, the logic of market liberalization. Microcredit, a survival strategy of the poor, has largely been interpreted as a demonstration of poor people's desire for efficiently delivered credit and their willingness to pay the market price for it. It has often served as an indictment of the wasteful, moribund subsidy culture that captured the policy imaginations of many developing countries thus far and a celebration of neoliberal ideology.

In this chapter, I examine the production of the subject of microcredit, looking at the ways in which the discourse of microcredit has been employed to specify the ideal citizen-subject of neoliberal India—a subject position that is distinguished by the notion of creditworthiness. The examination is located in a particular historical moment, in the decade following the 1991 balance-of-payment crisis in India, a crisis whose resolution is widely acknowledged as heralding a slew of reforms aiming to liberalize the economy, the financial sector in particular. Drawing on fieldwork conducted in 2000 with microcredit practitioners in western India, I examine how microcredit's promise of good repayment rates and low transaction costs dovetailed with the Indian state's financial sector reform agenda.[1] Microcredit advocates sought to provide a financially sustainable method of providing credit to the poor by projecting poor women's savings and credit groups as community-based financial institutions whose norms, rationales and procedures mirrored that of established banking institutions. I also look at the way in which these practitioners have appropriated the spaces opened up by the discourse of microcredit and invested the practices with meanings that are derived out of their experience of marginality and struggles for survival. As we consider the transformatory promise of microcredit, I argue that their experiences provide a critical perspective; one that runs counter both to the narrative of those who celebrate the poverty alleviation potential of microcredit, as well as to the narrative offered by those who critique it as a practice that implicates the poor in the policies of neoliberalism, policies where individuals are made responsible for their own welfare. Microcredit is a relationship that while overdetermined, has a latent potential for disarticulating the citizenship subjectivity that neoliberalism invests into the practice.

Multivalency of Money

Through an examination of the social relationships by which money is transacted and the particular people are involved in the act of monetary exchange, Reddy (1987) illuminates the different use values they confer on the money and commodities being exchanged, He consequently critiques the tendency to see monetary exchanges as uniform, as "impersonal and anonymous" (p. xi), revealing through his analysis the heterogeneity and multi-valence of monetary exchange relationships. Drawing on Reddy's insight into the multivalency of money, I investigate the use of microcredit by the NGO, Swayam Shikshan Prayog (SSP) and the numerous community-based women's savings and credit groups (SCGs) associated with it. Reddy's insight, derived out of his analysis of the differences in use values of money that exist among the rich and the poor, alerts us to the possibility of differences in the meaning of money, in the use of credit by the state to constitute ideal citizen-subjects out of the poor, and the use of credit by the poor.[2] Consequently, the similarity that the survival credit practices of the poor bear to the logic of market liberalism, cannot lead to an automatic transposition of that logic on the practices of the poor, because the practice and the logic emerge from vastly different, complex and historically derived subject positions. While acknowledging credit's long history in attempting to fashion colonial and subsequently citizen-subjects out of the rural poor through the tremendous disciplinary power it wields, I argue that the production of 'governable subjects' through the credit relationship is not guaranteed because monetary transactions are multivalent, which while circumscribing the negotiated performance of subjectivity, do not determine it. Through my examination of the meanings that emerge out of the usage of credit by these different actors, I suggest that microcredit constitutes a site of a cultural politics of citizenship.

Attending to the structural relationships within which, and through which, meaning and subjectivity are produced, and money is transacted, is critical to understanding the particularity and potency of SSP's engagement with the practice of microcredit. When microcredit practitioners from the SCGs associated with SSP use credit to meet household consumption expenses or organize their credit practice in such a way as to not penalize their peers' inability to make regular repayments on their loans, they are engaging in cultural politics. For their usage of credit articulates a meaning that contests rather than consents to the meaning of microcredit as an endorsement of the poor to the neoliberal valorization of efficiency and creditworthiness. Through their use and organization of credit around the exigencies of survival, as opposed to the ideal of creditworthiness, these practitioners are subverting the neoliberal notion of citizenship as a subjectivity that articulates into the national project of establishing the creditworthiness of the Indian state in the eyes of global creditors. For SSP, now a well-established NGO with a thriving microcredit and livelihoods strengthening practice, ensuring that their initiative was founded on a robust principle of financial inclusion whereby the poverty of the SCG members was not penalized but constituted the very condition around which the norms and values of their rendition for microcredit was structured was critical. The financial sustainability of its practice was embedded within a broad understanding of social sustainability and inclusion.

The meanings and subjectivities that infuse and animate SSP and their SCG partners' performances of microcredit significantly diverges from the hegemonic understanding of microcredit, and are thus constitutive of a cultural politics waged on the overlapping ideological terrains of citizenship and gender. The neoliberal claim that the poor's engagement in microcredit is indicative of the poor's rejection of subsidized credit in favour of 'efficient' credit, and the criticism that microcredit amounts to a 'technology of self' do not take into account the varied nature of the social relationships within which the practice of microcredit is located. Different kinds of social relationships differently circumscribe the negotiation of subjectivity within the circuits of credit, an aspect that speaks of the need to avoid positing microcredit as if it were a singular phenomenon. Through my account of the contestatory nature of the meanings and subjectivities emergent in microcredit what is revealed is the instability of hegemonic discourses and structural processes, which while wielding considerable structuring power also contain the potential for disarticulations.

The Promise of Microcredit

In India, microcredit has largely manifested itself in terms of savings and credit groups (SCGs). By common consensus, savings and credit groups are community-based voluntary groups that commit to contribute an agreed-upon sum of money on a regular basis to a group-managed fund from which loans are disbursed to members. The emergence of these groups has usually been attributed to the failure of the formal financial sector to cater to the needs of poor women and to the harsh conditions these women face in the informal credit market. As this mechanism spread across India through peer and NGO channels, NGOs began to explore ways in which they could increase the amount of credit available to group members. The group members, being largely drawn from among the poor, could only make small 'savings' contributions to the group loan fund, and thus the loans too were small amounts, falling far below members' credit needs. One way of capitalizing savings and credit groups has been for NGOs to set up their own revolving credit funds, through donor-funded projects, that would supplement individual groups' funds. The other way has been to tap into the existing formal credit system.[3] However, while SCGs emerged as a response to the failure of the formal sector to service poor women's need for credit to meet consumption expenses, what we find is that recognition from the formal financial sector has lead to the formal sector wresting away from poor women the right to define what constitutes a savings and credit group.

Given this context, at least two stories about credit and the poor can be discerned: one about discipline and the other about transacting social change, or to use that overburdened word, about 'empowerment.' They are both about the promise of microcredit but they are not the same story. As we debate the worth and efficacy of microcredit, it is critical to tease out the tensions between the two stories, particularly at a moment such as this—that is marked by a severe crisis of social reproduction, mounting personal and public debt, and a dramatic amplification of the trend that Harvey (2003) describes as "accumulation by dispossession." In this context of deteriorating material conditions, where does the promise of microcredit lie?

The Creditworthiness of the Poor

The first story is a familiar one. It concerns microcredit's celebrated ability to package the impoverished as creditworthy and market this population as 'bankable' to the formal credit market. Their creditworthiness derives from their ability to discipline each other and ensure that loans are repaid on time. It makes the struggle for survival a narrative of entrepreneurial endeavour. With the disappearance and destruction of employment opportunities it is perhaps not surprising that the future of poverty alleviation is said to hinge on the entrepreneurial drive of individuals instead of wage-labour prospects. It is the corollary of the neoliberal policy thrust to make social welfare an individual responsibility. In India the story of microcredit is implicated in the indictment of the subsidy-based welfare schemes, including credit programmes, of the developmentalist project. Microcredit is perceived to illustrate the poor's preference for the efficiency of the market and willingness to pay market rates for services. It is a perception that articulates seamlessly with the national project, in the wake of the 1991 balance of payments crisis, of establishing the creditworthiness of the Indian state in the eyes of global creditors.

In the discussions surrounding the reform of the Indian financial sector, which constituted one of the core components of the Indian state's liberalization programme, the moneylender's methods—which had assumed the status of national evil during the development project (cf. Bose 1997 and Hardiman 1996)— were no longer uniformly disparaged. Instead we see a growing consensus of opinions that speak to the value of learning from the moneylender whose methods are seen to be superior, particularly in terms of efficiency and financial sustainability, to those of the state's banking behemoth (Mahajan and Ramola 1996 and Fischer et al., 1997). Informing these opinions is the understanding that the poor would rather pay market determined rates of interest in order to get timely access to credit, than navigate the bureaucratic labyrinth of the nationalized banking system, even though the latter offers subsidized credit. Furthermore, microcredit's promise of good repayment rates and low transaction costs dovetailed with the Indian state's financial sector reform agenda. By projecting poor women's savings and credit groups as community-based financial institutions, microcredit advocates sought to provide a financially sustainable method of providing credit to the poor.

The second story about credit and the poor offers a different notion of the promise of microcredit. Here I draw on the microcredit practices of a group of savings and credit collectives working in the Marathwada region of the western India state of Maharashtra—groups comprising primarily of agricultural labourers and marginal farmers—and on the perspectives of Swayam Shikshan Prayog or SSP, the NGO with whom these collectives are allied.

Transforming Transactions

Marathwada is a rural, drought-prone, debt-ridden region of western India where large-scale inequality of income and land distribution exists. While a significant proportion of the population is landless, the majority of the landholders own between one and five acres of land, which being rain-fed rather than irrigated, is barely enough to eke out a subsistence, leave aside enough to produce a surplus to be sold on the market. For the landless, the primary source of work is agricultural labour, for which they get paid in kind during the harvest and sowing seasons, and in cash during the weeding period. The women constituting the savings and credit groups SSP worked with largely come from either landless or marginal landholding families. For both groups, the income derived from agricultural labour constitutes their primary source of income. Subsistence needs for most of the year are met through credit. Regular credit needs are met by moneylenders, shopkeepers, *bisis*[4], and SCGs, rarely banks. For large credit needs, such as the marriage of a daughter, the poor often resort to the practice of *saalgirah,* a form of bonded labour. Men from these families take a contract with a rich landlord who pays them a lump sum of money at the end of the year in lieu of regular wages. Many members have lost their land to local moneylenders, and others have had to leave the village.

My focus here is on the women's savings and credit collectives that I encountered in Marathwada during the course of my fieldwork—specifically, the nature of their credit transactions and savings practices—for they offer an alternative way of conceiving of the promise of microcredit. Like many of the savings and credit groups elsewhere in India, in these groups members agree to make monthly contributions to a group managed fund, from which small loans are provided to members, through a collective decision-making process where need is the principal criterion by which loan requests are evaluated. While within a group, each member puts in the same amount of money, monthly savings across groups differ, ranging from Rs. 20 to Rs. 50.

It is important to note that the term 'savings' that is

attributed to the monthly contributions of SCG members is a misnomer. The Rs. 20 and Rs. 50 that women bring every month to the monthly meetings is not money that is left over after all the subsistence needs of the household have been met, which is the usual connotation of the term. Rather they constitute the accumulation of little bits of change over a month-long period. They are products of thriftiness on the part of poor women for whom making ends meet in terms of household expenditure is already an exercise in thriftiness. The meagre savings contributions, while limiting the group's ability to meet all the credit demands of its members, serve to dissuade women from wealthier households from participating in and taking control of the group. For, as was pointed out to me, "they do not think much of Rs. 25, Rs. 50 savings." The process of creating groups where every member contributes an equal amount and the amount itself is decided by the group according to their members' income level establishes a relatively level playing field in terms of the social relationships governing the practice of credit.

What is distinctive about these women's collectives is that their use and organization of credit centres around the exigencies of survival. Their records revealed that the majority of credit is used to meet consumption needs and that penalties are minimal and rarely levied if members are unable to keep up with their repayment schedule. In some of the groups I visited in Osmanabad district their savings ledgers revealed that for a few months in the year none of the members could make even the monthly savings contribution. Post-harvest they would put in savings for the previous months. Or as in the case of Sunita Gaikwad, some women put in savings contributions for future months, at the rate of Rs. 20 per month, when they have the money in hand. When Sunita's husband returned after a year of serving an indentured labour contract with a rich landlord, she drew on his wages which were paid in a lump sum at the end of the contract to make savings payments for the next five months, because she knew the money would evaporate quickly and she did not know if she could make those payments in the coming months. While most of the groups claimed to fine members who did not make their savings contributions regularly, the records show that few actually did so. The loan ledgers of these groups tell a similar story. Irregular repayments of loans were the norm, reflecting the irregular income flows of the debtors. While groups claimed to impose a fine on those who were late in repaying their loans, their records showed otherwise.

Much to the consternation of visiting bankers and other representatives of financial institutions, loan defaulters are not penalized or 'exiled.' Their peers do not treat their inability to repay a loan on time as a symptom of moral bankruptcy or profligacy, but of attenuated circumstances. It is a practice that recognizes the fluctuating circumstances of the majority of the poor, and whose practitioners know all too well, what would happen if one of their neighbours were deprived of the opportunity to borrow money that they needed, for each of their bodies bear the memory of such deprivation. It is an understanding of relationships among peers that does not translate into peer pressure but into mobilizing collective resources, meagre as they are, so that members do not have to succumb to the exploitative terms of the local moneylender. This reluctance to weaponize the relationship between neighbours through the credit relationships that bound them, stood in marked contrast to the financial discipline that many microcredit interventions have sought to establish, where peers worked to pressure a borrower into paying back a loan on schedule (cf. Elyachar 2002 and Karim 2008).

From the perspective of Swayam Shikshan Prayog, since the precariousness of the poor's economic situation is something that is outside their control, it did not make sense to develop norms that would criminalize it in the course of their credit operations. Instead what was seen to be important was the need to develop mechanisms that allowed the collectives to deal with this always-present contingency in a socially sustainable manner. For they saw the credit intervention as not just a way by which women learnt to collectively manage money according to some pre-set rules to ensure the financial sustainability of their effort, but a space where they could develop new ways of thinking about credit, and people. It is because of SCGs' attempts to set their own rules and regulations, that do not conform to traditional banking procedures, that the savings and credit group is not just an alternative mode of credit delivery, but a 'space of insurgency'.[5] Consequently, the thrust of the NGOs' mediation of the relationship between the savings and credit groups and formal credit institutions is to compel the state and financial institutions to recognize a process in which poor women, rather than professionals, determine how credit should be used and under what terms. Given the power and legitimacy that the conventional image wields this is no easy struggle, for at every step of the way they are challenged by donors, policy makers, bankers and other NGOs. Here Miraftab and Willis' (2005) elabouration of Holston's (1998) discussion of insurgent spaces of citizenship and subsequent distinction between invented and invited spaces of citizenship participation is useful. Invented spaces are those that marginalized populations create in order to assert their rights, a space of insurgency where innovative forms of problem-solving are devised and rehearsed, much like the SCG in its early days before the form was seized by mainstream financial institutions. Subsequently though, the practice of the SCG has become increasingly scripted by the formal financial sector, making it more akin to what Miraftab and Willis, drawing on Cornwall (2002), describe as invited spaces of citizen participation, those channels created from above, whereby the state seeks to engage marginalized citizens under largely predetermined terms.

Consuming Credit

Let us now consider what these loans were used for. The need for credit by group members is not so much about requiring seed capital to start some kind of income-generating enterprise, as it is about being able to finance daily subsistence in the face of uncertain and irregular income flows. The distinction between credit to meet consumption needs and credit to meet production needs plays a critical role in building up the image of microcredit's success in alleviating poverty. The underlying assumption is that in time the need for credit to meet consumption needs will wither away and investment in economically productive activities will be the financial engine that will enable the poor to rise above the poverty line. However, as Selvarajan, a development professional affiliated with SSP, pointed out to me, "Even when women take Rs. 1000 for livelihood activities—what can you do with Rs. 1000 subsistence." Having blurred the boundaries between production and consumption, he went on to make the argument that the consumption needs of the poor do not decrease over time, i.e. they are not a 'stage' in the life of a savings and credit group (SCG). For the poor, he argued, given their levels of deprivation, the marginal propensity to consume increases rather than decreases with any increase in income.

This observation was corroborated by others like SPARC, an NGO working in urban India, who explained that their savings and credit experience proved that the need for consumption credit never goes away. SPARC's director likened the distribution of credit to a triangle where in terms of the proportion of the total credit managed by Mahila Milan, the least amount is used to service consumption and crisis needs, while the biggest proportion of funds is used to finance the housing credit needs of the urban poor. However, she indicated that in terms of the number of loans, the largest number of loans go to meet crisis and consumption credit needs, while the fewest go to finance housing and infrastructural credit needs.

The consumption credit needs of the poor persist because for many the SCG is a financial safety net that prevents further impoverishment rather than a springboard for enterprise that will launch the poor out of poverty. The neoliberal contention that the savings and credit groups of the poor demonstrate a rejection of state-controlled subsidized credit and a subscription to the neoliberal ideal of efficient credit is an insidious romanticization of the poor. It takes the phenomenon of poor people mobilizing resources and creating institutional arrangements to meet their credit needs out of the context of the daily survival strategies of the poor—to make 'heroes' of neoliberalism out of them (cf. Hyatt 1997). Indeed it is only when we situate savings and credit groups within the context of the worsening subsistence conditions, i.e. the politics of survival, and investigate what group members are taking loans for that we can begin to understand that microcredit is an indictment rather than a celebration of the neoliberal policies that the Indian state has pursued since the early 1990s.

Changing the Rules of the Game

For many microcredit practitioners, the creation of institutional arrangements to make credit available to the poor has meant playing by the existing rules of the game. That is, the formation of SCGs or women's banks have usually entailed emulating the techniques used by the formal banking system with regard to the repayment of loans and the treatment of defaulters. Indeed their creditworthiness in the eyes of the formal banking system, and thus their ability to leverage funds to supplement group funds, depends mainly on their ability to post high repayment rates and show that defaulters will be penalized. Microcredit therefore has largely meant creating credit delivery solutions that exemplify existing mainstream banking rationality.

Yet, the extension of mainstream banking rationality is not the only possible outcome of microcredit interventions. SSP's perspective on and practice of microcredit has developed out of a critical understanding of the disciplinary potential of credit. The de-criminalization of default is a central tenet of their credit intervention. It is a principle that the NGO's staff identify as what distinguishes them from other microcredit interventions wherein techniques of the formal banking system with regard to repayment, default, etc. are reproduced.

The poor's experience of credit relations bear testimony to the tremendous exclusionary potential of credit, people who are not able to play by the rules are criminalized and marginalized as 'defaulters' and 'delinquents'. Developing institutional arrangements in which people are not penalized or marginalized when, because of particular circumstances, they cannot repay a loan on time is a way of imbuing a different meaning and significance to the practice of credit and to community mobilization. Mainstream rules are not made with poor people living in extremely precarious economic circumstances in mind. Therefore when poor people default on loans because of a sudden change in their economic situation, what is being penalized is not just them but poverty itself.

Yet when we see the microcredit transactions of groups such as those affiliated with Swayam Shikshan Prayog, we see that money, the very medium by which the poor are devalued and alienated, acquires a different valency as the transactions are informed by and accommodate the exigent circumstances of the poor. Given the neoliberal valorization of microcredit, it is difficult to immediately discern the ways in which the poor have been able to appropriate the spaces opened up by the discourse of microcredit and inflect them with their own meanings. It is only close inspection of the form of savings and credit in circulation that reveals that they do not make a virtue of disciplining defaulters or increasing the corpus through raising interest rates, practices of exclusion that arguably increase rather than decrease the vulnerability of the poor. Rather, the focus is on social inclusion, i.e. on the collection of daily savings of small, even minuscule amounts of money that represent very little in material terms (even to the urban poor) but convey much symbolic and organizational value that is communicated and replenished regularly. Their practice offers a timely reminder that social inclusion and financial inclusion cannot be used interchangeably. Rather, it prompts a scrutiny of the terms of financial inclusion measures to assess whether or not they foster social inclusion, whether or not they can accommodate the precarious material conditions that shape the lives of the impoverished.[6] As Gibson-Graham (2006, p. xxxv) indicates with reference to savings and credit collectives of the urban poor, "To join such a group is to engage in new practice of the self—setting aside savings from what is already too little to live on .... In the process, new senses of self are instituted—through self-development as citizens, house designers, investors, or entrepreneurs, through self-recognition of their survival capacities as poor women and migrants, through daily recommitment to the cultivation of solidarity." For what is exchanged in these visits is not just small change, but information, people, and trust, the sinews of their political formation. This, I contend, is the promise of microcredit, a promise that is worth pursuing in today's world of accelerating economic and political insecurity.

ENDNOTES

1. This chapter draws on fieldwork conducted in Tuljapur block in Osmanabad district, Maharashtra in 2000, almost a decade after government agencies had decided to focus on self-help groups as a promising way of channelling credit to the poor, one that appeared to avoid the pitfalls, repayment of loans in particular, of previous methods. Financial support for fieldwork was provided by Cornell University's Einaudi Centre for International Studies.
2. Reddy (1987) critiques the liberal presumption of the universal univalency of money, which is premised on the universality of the desire for gain. He argues that such a presumption camouflages not only "the great diversity of motives for engaging in money exchange" but also "the great diversity of effects of such exchange" (p. 63).
3. In 1992 a pilot project was launched that linked SCGs to the banking system. SCGs could take a loan from the bank, and then on-lend it to its members. A win-win solution had apparently been achieved through this linkage project, meeting the needs of banks who wanted to cut down transaction costs of delivering credit to the poor, and those of the poor who needed credit, and for whom the developmentalist subsidy-based credit delivery system was not working. Spurred by the success of the pilot project in devising an effective system of credit delivery to the poor that met the efficiency and profitability norms instituted by financial sector reforms, in 1996 the Reserve Bank of India directed nationalized banks to incorporate the linkage programme into their mainstream lending operations (Nair 2000).
4. *Bisis* are time-bound rotating savings and credit associations. Individuals agree to contribute an agreed upon sum of money at regular intervals for a stipulated time period. The understanding usually being that each "savings" contributor will get an opportunity to take home the entire fund created by these individual contributions in any given cycle, much like a lottery.
5. Holston (1998).
6. The concept 'social inclusion,' must be subject to some scrutiny.

For as Angus Cameron (2006) argues, the problem with most analyses of 'social exclusion,' is that they often "represent a narrative of poverty: one originating elsewhere" (p. 401) instead of one that is situated in relation to the terms of social inclusion. "As such, he continues, "the social exclusion/inclusion debate is an exercise in normative boundary setting" (p. 401), where crossing the boundary is a matter of pulling oneself up by the boot-straps and acquiring the properties of the 'socially included'.

REFERENCES

Bose, Sugata (1997). Instruments and Idioms of Colonial and National Development: India's Historical Experience in Comparative Perspective. In Frederick Cooper and Randall Packard (Eds.), *International Development and the Social Sciences: Essays on the History and Politics of Knowledge* (pp. 45-63). Berkeley: University of California Press.

Cameron, Angus (2006). Geographies of Welfare and Exclusion: Social Inclusion and Exception. *Progress in Human Geography*, 30(3), 396-404.

Cornwall, Andrea (2002). Locating Citizen Participation. *IDS Bulletin*. 33 (2): 49-58.

Elyachar, Julia (2006). *Markets of Dispossession: NGOs, Economic Development and the State in Cairo*. Durham: Duke University Press.

Fisher, Thomas, Mahajan, Vijay and Singha, Ashok (1997). *The Forgotten Sector: Non-Farm Employment and Enterprises in Rural India*. London: Intermediate Technology.

Hardiman, David (1996). *Feeding the Baniya: Peasants and Usurers in Western India*. Delhi: Oxford University Press.

Gibson-Graham, J.K. (2006). *A Postcapitalist Politics*. Minneapolis and London: University of Minnesota Press.

Harvey, David (2003). *The New Imperialism*. New York: Oxford University Press.

Hyatt, Susan Brin (1997). Poverty in a 'Post-Welfare' Landscape: Tenant Management Policies, Self-Governance, and the Democratization of Knowledge in Great Britain. In Cris Shore and Susan Wright (eds.), *Anthropology of Policy: Critical Perspectives on Governance and Power* (pp. 217-238). London: Routledge.

Holston, James (1998). Spaces of Insurgent Citizenship. In Leonie Sandcock (ed.), *Making the Invisible Visible* (pp. 37-56), Berkeley: University of California Press.

Karim. L. (2008). Demystifying Microcredit: The Grameen Bank, NGOs, and Neoliberalism in Bangladesh, *Cultural Dynamics* 20(1): 5-29.

Mahajan, Vijay and Ramola, Bharti Gupta (1996). Financial Services for the Rural Poor and Women in India: Access and Sustainability, *Journal of International Development*, 8(2), 211-224.

Miraftab, F. and S. Willis (2005). Insurgency and Spaces of Active Citizenship: The Story of Western Cape Anti-Eviction Campaign in South Africa, *Journal of Planning Education and Research*, 25: 200-217.

Nair, Tara S. (2000). Rural Financial Intermediation and Commercial Banks: Review of Recent Trends, *Economic and Political Weekly*, XXXV (5), 299-306.

Reddy, William M. (1987). *Money and Liberty in Modern Europe: A Critique of Historical Understanding*, Cambridge: Cambridge University Press.

2

Gender, Social Capital, and Microenterprise in Peru[1]

Brooke Weddle Ricalde

> Most of the people in the world are poor, so if we knew the economics of being poor we would know much of the economics that really matters.
>
> *(Theodore Schultz Nobel Prize Lecture, 1979)*

The Context

In Peru, microenterprise owners still struggle to escape poverty despite the expanded accessibility of financial capital through microfinance programmes, new laws that mandate investments in the human capital of small business owners through training programmes, and other widespread efforts by government and non-government institutions to simplify and reduce the costs of the microenterprise registration process and, more broadly, to support entrepreneurship.[2] The failure of microenterprises to become a viable source of income generation is a significant problem given that they employ 60 per cent of the Peruvian workforce.[3] In fact, Banerjee and Duflo (2007) noticed that 69 per cent of Peru's urban poor were self-employed and operating a non-agricultural business.[4] This makes the problem particularly salient in Lima, Peru's capital city, which contains approximately one-third of the country's population.

I argue that Peru's efforts to encourage business productivity and growth in the microenterprise sector are complicated by a lack understanding about the women who work there. Thus, my study investigates the role of gender in the relationships between human capital, social capital, microcredit, and net business income in the microenterprise sector of Lima, the capital of Peru. It is a comparative study that uses quantitative data to analyse gender differences with respect to the marginal returns of each capital. There is a growing literature on the positive returns to microcredit. Governments and multilateral institutions around the world have invested in microcredit programmes as a strategy to help the self-employed climb out of poverty. Women are often featured as the "heroines" of these programmes. The Grameen Bank, Foundation for International Community Assistance (FINCA), and Americans for Community Cooperation in Other Nations (Acción International), three of the world's largest microfinance institutions, have all highlighted women's high loan repayment rates. From a lender's perspective, it is important to understand these "rates" because they largely determine the return on an investment. Nevertheless, by focusing entirely on loan repayment rates, important welfare questions are overlooked. Are women receiving microcredit actually growing their businesses at a rate faster than women who are not receiving microcredit? Are they making productive investments with their microcredit? Research has only begun to address these questions in a rigorous fashion.

Some studies show that women receiving microcredit do indeed increase their incomes at a faster rate than women not receiving microcredit.[5] Likewise, the data I analyse in this article indicate that there is a significant, positive correlation between net business income and receiving microcredit for female microenterprise owners in Lima. Moreover, the data further suggest that women are able to realize a higher return on their financial capital compared to men. One of the main questions arises then is how! I also investigate why, given women's higher returns, men are more likely to receive microcredit and to obtain greater amounts of microcredit. There are clearly important welfare losses that would result from a scenario in which microcredit is not extended to those who would realize the greatest return on investment.

Turning to the "how" question, it is important to note that

women are over-represented in the microenterprise sector, but they are far less likely to own a business (rather, they are employed by them). Female microenterprise owners must contend with disproportionately less access to microcredit and formal schooling, greater household labour burdens, and, in many cases, discrimination. They are more likely than men to engage in production characterized by low capital requirements, crowding in traditional industries, and informal labour arrangements.[6] All this means that although Peruvian women have been able to realize greater than before economic security and independence, their work in the microenterprise sector is primarily survival-based.

These gender differences are investigated by examining how (1) human capital and (2) social capital, a term I use to refer to advantages derived from social networks (including informal and formal group membership), impact the probability a microenterprise owner will access microcredit. Given that some women do access microcredit, I investigate if their access might be more closely correlated with social capital, rather than human capital. I also analyse the mechanisms through which social capital, human capital, and microcredit have differing impacts on the level of net business income that women and men entrepreneurs derive from their businesses. My analysis of the mechanisms through which these effects manifest takes into account the gender-specific barriers that women face. These barriers stem from current and historical norms[7] associated with Peruvian society and, more broadly, with the developing country context.

Research from Peru indicates that microenterprise growth depends critically on schooling and training, participation in skill-based industries, and access to financial capital.[8] Men are better positioned in all these factors of production than women. However, these findings do not take into account how entrepreneurs' social capital might be correlated with economic outcomes such as net business income, with the magnitude of the effect possibly being greater for women. Likewise, these findings do not investigate social capital's role in access to microcredit despite the rise in popularity of microcredit in the last half-decade—and concurrent evidence that women use it more effectively. *The question is whether the difference in income that men and women realize from their microenterprises would be even larger were it not for women's marginally more effective use of social capital and microcredit. What would such a finding imply for microenterprise policy in Peru and other developing countries?*

My conceptual framework draws directly on feminist economic theory[9] and outlines how social capital and microcredit might serve to "level the playing field" with respect to economic outcomes.[10] The result is a revision of the traditional human capital model,[11] which is normally defined as follows:

$$\log Y_i = \beta_0 + \beta_1 S_i + \beta_2 E_i + \varepsilon$$

In this model, S is a vector of schooling completed; E represents accumulated business experience and ε is an error term. My model, on which I elabourate in the methodology section, is different for including a vector of social capital variables.[12] The result, in its basic form, is as follows:

$$\log Y_i = \beta_0 + \beta_1 S_i + \beta_2 E_i + \beta_3 SC_i + \varepsilon$$

Here, SC represents a vector of social capital variables. I also interact the vector of human capital and social capital variables with being female in order to test for structural differences in the slope coefficients. The final model is:

$$\log Y_i = \beta_0 + \beta_1 S_i + \beta_2 E_i + \beta_3 SC_i + \beta_4 S_i * F_i + \beta_5 E_i * F_i + \beta_6 SC_i * F_i + \varepsilon$$

I consider social capital as a "resource for action" through an application of a definition used by Coleman[13]. More specifically, I agree with Coleman that "[l]ike other forms of capital, social capital is productive, making possible the achievement of certain ends that in its absence would not be possible."[14] Furthermore, I conceptualize social capital in terms of social networks. In this way, I also draw on Putnam's definition: "social capital refers to connections among individuals—social networks and the norms of reciprocity and trustworthiness that arise from them."[15] In the context of my data, I examine several specific measures of social capital: associational membership, time lived in Lima (whether or not a business owner has lived in the city for a generation or more—which is important given the high proportion of migrants), whether or not the microenterprise owner employs his or her spouse, and the strength of a microenterprise owner's kin-based networks in the capital. I argue that each of these measures offers different types of resources for action: informal and non-formal education, opportunities to generate trust and build one's reputation, and the creation of network-specific (or, in this case, market-specific) norms. Many of these resources overlap with the three forms of social capital on which Coleman[16] focuses: obligations and expectations, information and channels, and social norms. In contrast to Coleman, however, I analyse how the returns to each form of social capital will be different for men and women.

Here, I analyse a data set collected by the International Labour Organization (ILO) in 2003 that includes information on 1,137 microenterprise owners in Lima, Peru. The data represent a census of the first commercial centre for microenterprise owners in Peru, "Polvos Azules." The history of Polvos Azlues is of some note, as the market is quite well-known among residents in Lima.[17] While the original Polvos Azules market was a rather informal amalgamation of microenterprises, the *Polvos Azules* of today is a covered market with restrooms, ATM machines, security guards, an underground parking garage, and website. The current Polvos Azules market opened in May, 2001, after the original Polvos Azules burned down in a fire. It is governed by an elected committee, and has a full-time staff of approximately ten people. To operate in Polvos Azules, microenterprise owners must pay to have a stand.

Today, Peruvians typically shop at Polvos Azules for discounted international brands, particularly shoes and clothing, but also for electronics[18]. Typical Peruvian artifacts and food stuffs are also popular, as are service-focused enterprises such as restaurants, Internet cafes, and repair shops. More recently, there has been a slight rise in the number of tourists visiting Polvos Azules—which might be attributed to a general rise in tourism in Peru since the end of the internal terrorism that marked the 1980s and early 90s, increased efforts by the municipality and federal government to gentrify the downtown area of Lima where Polvos Azules is located, or the growth in the range and quality of products offered at the market.

The data I have on the microenterprise owners in Polvos Azules are cross-sectional, from the year 2003. Using these data, I study the marginal effect of human capital, social capital, and microcredit on female-headed and male-headed microenterprises.[19] Not only do I analyse the marginal effect of social capital and human capital for men and women on access to microcredit, I also examine the marginal effect of social capital and human capital on the amount of microcredit obtained. I then model the relationship between social capital, microcredit, and human capital on net business income. Additionally, I analyse data that I collected in 2006—exactly three years following the original data collection. For this wave, I surveyed a random sample (n=120) of the original ILO census using the same survey instrument.[20] However, given the small sample size collected, I use these data in the context of a feasibility study for future work. They are useful for identifying trends in the market from 2003-06.

Contributions

Microenterprises represent a crucial source of employment for the poor in developing countries. The Peruvian microenterprise sector, and the proportion of women who work there, is growing. It is not an overstatement to say that understanding this sector will be crucial to the long run economic survival of millions of people.

My study was the first to examine the differences in the way women and men create and use social networks in a developing country context. This investigation was also the first to relate social capital differences to human capital, and explore the ways that the former can be used as a substitute for skills and knowledge that are normally accumulated in the formal schooling system. Finally, my study contributes to the literature on microfinance and capital markets in developing countries by outlining—and quantifying—the "capital trail" of microenterprise owners. I will relate initial capital levels to access to microcredit, amount of microcredit obtained, current capital levels, and net business income. Moreover, I show how this trail is gendered—with resulting welfare losses that could be potentially ameliorated with more effective policies. Indeed, the end goal of this exercise is to make a series of policy recommendations that will help women and men in the Peruvian microenterprise sector develop more sustainable businesses and increase their net business income.

This study sought to examine the role of gender in the relationships between human capital, social capital, microcredit, and net business income in the Peruvian microenterprise sector. In terms of access to microcredit and the amount of microcredit obtained, I have concentrated on the differing effects of a vector of human capital inputs, including different levels of formal schooling and experience, and a range of social capital inputs. I modelled net business income by including the same human capital and social capital inputs, in addition to microcredit. My study is the first to examine the different ways women and men create and use social networks in the developing country context.

Findings of the Study

For each of the three models, namely human capital, social capital and microcredit, I have tested for structural differences in the slope coefficients for men and women by examining the interactions between female, human capital, and social capital. For the model of net business income, I also considered the interaction between female and microcredit. My results, while preliminary, lend support to my core hypothesis that gender is a valid moderator. They suggest that, for men and women, there are several important differences between and within groups with respect to human capital, social capital, and microcredit. These differences help us to better understand the microenterprise sector in Lima and, more specifically, the role of gender in the country's first commercial centre for microenterprise.

The Capital Trail

Given that this work is about different forms of capital, it makes sense to start at the beginning of "the capital trail." I have examined univariate statistics of the data that show that men and women—not controlling for other factors such as occupational category—have roughly equal levels of human capital and social capital. However, in terms of financial capital, women are at a serious disadvantage.

According to the data, both women and men microenterprise owners are likely to obtain their initial capital from family members, friends, or personal savings.[21] However, women have initial capital levels of $2,788, whereas men have initial levels of $3,533. Perhaps because of their lower levels of initial capital, women are slightly less likely to receive credit: 44 per cent of women receive microcredit, whereas 46 per cent of men do. While two percentage points is not a particularly large gap, it is the difference between 225 and 235 women receiving microcredit, which translates into approximately $48,900 less capital invested in women microenterprise owners. Taking into account the greater returns to investment in women-owned enterprises, which I discuss below, this implies a significant welfare loss.

Furthermore, an even more serious discrepancy emerges when I consider the amount of microcredit women and men receive. Women receive considerably less credit than men: the average for women is $4,890, whereas for men it is $6,432. I believe that this, more than anything else, is responsible for stifling the potential economic success of women. Women have lower levels of current capital ($10,749 for women versus $14,578 for men)[22] and lower yearly business income ($2,861 for women versus $3,506 for men). In fact, the capital trail I outline here might hide some very important market failures related to the gendered returns of microcredit.

Men receiving microcredit have lower net business incomes than their male peers not receiving microcredit in all occupational sectors except one: technology intensive retail. On the other hand, women who receive microcredit have higher net business incomes than women who do not receive microcredit in all occupational sectors except the non-technology intensive sector—where men receiving microcredit also have lower net business incomes than men who do not receive microcredit. Why, then, would men receive 10 per cent more microcredit than women in the non-technology retail sector and 4 per cent more microcredit than women in the non-technology service sector? Women and men receive microcredit at the same rate in the technology intensive retail sector, but men receive an average of $2,589 more. In the technology intensive service sector, I find that 40 per cent of women receive credit, versus 18 per cent of men, but there are only five women in this sector and 45 men. Moreover, while men receive an average of $20,344, women receive an average of only $5,750.

The policy implications of this capital trail are important. Why are men more likely to receive microcredit if this is associated with lower net business incomes? Perhaps even more crucial, why do men obtain consistently higher amounts of microcredit when women prove they are better able to convert microcredit into higher net business incomes? What is more, there is sometimes even a negative relationship between a man receiving microcredit and current capital levels. This stands in contrast to other studies which have suggested that men are more likely to invest their microcredit in their business, and women are more likely to take it "home" to their family. My results show that in the technology intensive and non-technology intensive service sectors, men receiving microcredit have lower current capital levels in addition to lower net business incomes. In contrast, women receiving microcredit have higher current capital levels in every sector.

Overall, the welfare losses from the capital trail are significant. Consider microcredit's effect on net business income. Women receiving microcredit have net business incomes that are $1,235 higher than women not receiving microcredit. That is almost exactly 25 per cent of the average amount of microcredit women receive. Alternatively, men receiving microcredit have net business incomes that are $408 higher. That is six per cent of the average amount of microcredit men receive. In terms of microcredit's effect on current capital, I find that women receiving microcredit have current capital levels that are $6,575 higher than women who are not receiving microcredit. That increase represents 134 per cent of women's average amount of microcredit obtained. For men receiving microcredit, the average increase in current capital levels is $5,712, which represents just 89 per cent of men's average amount of microcredit obtained. It seems rather obvious that women make a better investment.

Assuming these same returns, I have calculated women's microcredit effect if they received as much microcredit as men (Table 1). Women would have net business incomes that are $1,608 higher and current capital levels that are $8,648 higher. For net business income, this translates into a welfare gain of $83,925 (225 women receiving microcredit multiplied by the difference between $1,608 and $1,235). Moreover, if women had the same access to microcredit as men (46 per cent versus the current 44 per cent) this would translate into ten more women receiving microcredit, contributing an additional $3,730 in welfare gains. In terms of the welfare gains resulting from microcredit's effect on current capital, these would be $466,425 (225 women multiplied by the difference between $8,648 and $6,575). Assuming gender parity with respect to access, the gains increase to $487,155. Overall, the Polvos Azules market has total yearly welfare losses of $574,810—losses that likely stem from sex discrimination in capital markets.

Table 1: Potential Welfare Gains Resulting From Gender Parity in Microcredit

	Microcredit Effect: Business Income (Individual)	*Microcredit Effect: Current Capital (Individual)*	N	*Total Welfare Gain from Microcredit (Market)*
Men	$408	$5,712	288	$1,762,560
Women	$1,235	$6,575	225	$1,757,250
Gender Parity Gains	+ $373	+ $2,073	+ 10	+ $574,810
TOTAL GAINS	$2,016	$14,360	523	$ 4,094,620

Principal Findings

Principal Finding 1

"Imputing only desirable outcomes to social capital, or equating them with it, ignores the possibility that these outcomes may be attained at another group's expense, that given outcomes may be suboptimal, or that desirable outcomes attained today come at the price of significant costs tomorrow."[23]

The capital trail leads me to my first principal finding: social capital can serve as a complement or a substitute for formal schooling, but it is not a panacea for economic development. According to my analysis, social capital is a gendered double-edged sword. While some forms of social capital have an effect that holds up regardless of gender, such as the positive correlation between being a migrant who has lived 20 years or more in Lima and amount of microcredit obtained, often there are observable, gendered trends.

In Model 1, kin-based networks are a form of social capital that works to men's advantage, but that is detrimental to women's access to microcredit. And, in Model 2, I find that associational membership and having lived in Lima for 20 years or more are both associated with higher levels of microcredit obtained. In contrast, no social capital variable is significant for women. Might we interpret this to mean that men are using social capital to siphon off resources from women? If so, this result would be similar to that which Ibarra found when she studied male Fortune 500 managers.[24]

Women do benefit from social capital, however, as I had hypothesized, they profit more from diverse, extra-group networks. More specifically, women who employ their husbands and who had lived in Lima for 20 years or more increase their access to microcredit. But the costs and benefits of social capital shift, depending on the model, as well as on the microenterprise owner's level of formal schooling. While having kin-based networks may help men to access microcredit, it hurts them in terms of the amount of microcredit obtained. We might imagine that men are very good at using their intra-group ties to find out how to apply for credit and meet the prerequisites, but that these kinds of ties do not serve men at the hour of getting a large loan. My findings suggest that diverse network ties are more important to women when accessing microcredit, but they are more important to men for obtaining greater amounts of microcredit.

Other results, such as employing a spouse, further suggest that certain forms of social capital can be helpful to one sex and unhelpful to another. Employing a husband helps women to gain access to microcredit, but employing a wife seems to make no difference for men in this model. Nevertheless, to say that women should always employ their husbands is clearly over-simplistic. My results show that having a husband employed helps women gain access to microcredit, but they also show that women who receive microcredit and employ their husbands have lower net business incomes than women who receive microcredit and do not employ their husbands.

These findings, combined with those that show significant social capital effects to be concentrated among those with lower levels of formal schooling, may provide initial evidence that the impact of social capital changes over time as a microenterprise owner makes different contacts, acquires new skills, invests more capital, etc. It suggests that the "optimal calculus of costs and benefits associated with particular combinations of bonds and bridges"[25] changes with the needs of the microenterprise owner—and is necessarily gendered.

Principal Finding 2

The Microcredit Summit of 2007 declared: "Experience shows that women are a good credit risk, and that women invest their income towards the well-being of their families. At the same time, women themselves benefit from the higher social status they achieve within the home when they are able to provide income." If microcredit is going to live up to its international reputation as a solution to world poverty, then policymakers should view its impact in a broader context. More specifically, we need to start taking into account what is likely to be gendered discrimination and its very significant economic (and social) costs. While it seems clear that microcredit is a major constraint facing microenterprise owners, especially women, and that having access to microcredit generally leads to increased net business income, it is not the only constraint. Thus, policies that aim only to increase women's access to microcredit will not do enough to improve women's status. Women not only need increased access, they also need to receive microcredit at the levels their male colleagues do. And policy makers and banks alike need to consider them to be more than just a good "credit risk."

Along these lines, there need to be more studies that analyse the gendered effect of microcredit taking into consideration its impact on net business income, but also its effect on the financial health of a microenterprise and the socio-economic role of the microenterprise owner. For example, as mentioned previously, women who receive microcredit and employ their husbands have lower net business incomes. But men who receive microcredit and employ their spouses have higher net business incomes. This signals the unequal role of women as income earners in the household and requires further investigation.

Human capital, especially post-secondary schooling, might act as an important "equalizer" among women and men microenterprise owners. Whereas experience is a significant source of human capital for many women microenterprise owners, those who manage to achieve institute or technical/vocational levels of schooling have a higher probability of accessing microcredit, obtaining more microcredit, and achieving higher net business incomes. In fact, for women, the effect of formal schooling and experience may work through microcredit—and current capital investment—to impact net business income. Although the effect of formal schooling is small and not significant in the model for net business income, it has a positive and significant effect on a woman's access to microcredit. Experience is also positively correlated with a woman's access to microcredit, but the effect is non-significant after controlling for social capital. Finally, human capital is significantly and positively correlated with current capital investment—with the magnitude of the effect being quite large.

Overall, these results challenge us to think about policies that would help women access human capital, especially post-secondary schooling. While women may accumulate skills and knowledge through experience and social capital, the credentialling of a post-secondary institution might be a significant deterrent to gender discrimination in markets for microcredit. Investments in microcredit programmes must be made in conjunction with increased investments in human capital if microcredit is to offer a long-term solution to women's poverty.

Principal Finding 3

According to an expert, "Microfinance should be seen as the provisioning of small-scale financial services to businesses and households traditionally kept outside the financial system rather than the more narrow view of microfinance as services for poor microenterprise owners."[26]

Microenterprise owners in Polvos Azules and, more broadly, all those who work in the microenterprise sector in Lima (as well as in other Latin American urban centres) represent a group that has been neglected by policy makers. While many governmental and non-governmental policy makers have made tremendous strides in serving the poorest (or those who are poorer than the microenterprise owners in Polvos Azules), the fact of the matter is that the majority of microenterprise owners are not "the poorest." Moreover, what is the evidence that microenterprise owners in developing countries who have a secondary education, receive microcredit from commercial banks, and work in a fixed stand require less attention? Perhaps they are considered to have reached a level of financial success that makes them invulnerable to poverty and its many manifestations. However, this is likely not the case, especially when we take gender into account. Inefficiencies in the capital trail starting with the disproportionately lower levels of initial capital investment for women, as well as the declining proportion of women microenterprise owners in the market (as evidenced in the 2006 data) have led me to conclude that while microcredit may be effective at relieving financial constraints, it is unclear if it leads to women's long run socio-economic progress.

Thus, there need to be more policies aimed at these more "advanced" borrowers that would address the gender-specific constraints that women face. My results show that women microenterprise owners are relying more on family-based forms of social capital—such as employing a spouse—or very diffuse forms of social capital—such as having lived in Lima for a generation. Unfortunately, especially in the case of having a spouse employed, these networks might simply serve to perpetuate many sex-based stereotypes. (The analysis I did of daughters' and sons' wages suggests that future generations are inheriting the unequal treatment of women and men.) Additionally, relying on these forms of social capital presents three additional problems: one, they do not apply to everyone (such as female-headed households); two, they produce other externalities with respect to the health of the business (evidence the contradictory impact of employing a husband); and three, they take a long time to accumulate (one cannot hasten the process of living in Lima for a generation).

Policy Recommendations

1. Access to Credit: (If it is true that time in Lima helps to increase a woman's access to microcredit because it helps them to gain familiarity of institutions, it is in the best interest of women microenterprise owners to systematize and increase the speed of this learning process. This will not be easy. Data from 2006 and 2003 indicate that women still face discrimination in the microenterprise sector. Thus, the state and other non-governmental organizations should have a role in this effort, finding ways to help women microenterprise owners learn about the many different resources offered in the capital and how to access them. At a minimum, a more formal system needs to be in place to increase the rate at which businesses and other properties are formalized. Currently, there are many different entities that deal with such issues, such as the Programme for Self-Employment and Microenterprise (PRODAME), the National Council for the Development of Small and Microenterprises (CODEMYPE), and the Organism for Formalization of Informal Property (COFOPRI), but it is still difficult for microenterprise owners working "on the ground" to navigate the bureaucratic process.

Beyond this, there needs to be greater recognition of women such as those working in Polvos Azules, who need guidance in getting to the next level of entrepreneurial success. For example, there are important policy implications resulting from my analysis of women, microcredit, and the role of spouses. In short, it is hard to know if women are better or worse off: although their business income is lower, they are paying their husbands more, and that supposedly contributes to household income.

The 2006 data, which probe into the household responsibilities of women, also reveal that they devote far many more hours to the household. Many of the findings in my dissertation raise new questions about unequal gender roles and the impact of this on a women's economic independence.

Commercial banks need to be aware of this issue. If women plan to "share" their microcredit with their husbands, then the husband should also be legally obliged to repay the loan. This could be accomplished by agencies offering "husband-wife" loan products and publicizing them by offering a slightly lower interest rate. The requirement for receiving the loan would be having the husband/wife co-sign for it.

2. Amount of Credit Obtained: The findings from this model underline the importance of increasing a woman's access to "inputs" such as human capital and social capital. Peru has already made tremendous strides in narrowing the gap between men and women in terms of schooling. While efforts to improve a woman's social capital may be more difficult, or at least less intuitive, it is important to consider two important tactics. First, it is important to develop the diverse social capital of women by recruiting them to associations that are relevant to their needs. As stated before, non-governmental organizations focused on first time microfinance customers are largely irrelevant.

Furthermore, it is important for women to network with microenterprise owners—men and women—working in different industries. Microfinance institutions focused on the poorest frequently expose women only to other women and, furthermore, only to women that work in very similar lines of work. While it is a valiant and important effort to include the poorest in the microcredit process, the women microenterprise owners working in Polvos Azules (and similar markets) simply need different resources. If it is true that the small, closed networks designed to serve very poor women are effective, there must be ways to "graduate" women by encouraging them to seek new skills through increased formal training or joining new associations that have a greater diversity of members, such as trade associations.

On the other hand, commercial banks could consider unconventional ways to help women in the microenterprise sector. This may involve strategies for "forgiving" women's lower levels of formal schooling and/or physical capital. Alternatively, banks could require women to take training classes before receiving microcredit or by requiring that a proportion of the loan be directed to a savings account.[27]In fact, they could partner with local institutes and technical/vocational education schooling programmes to provide new training services, offering graduates of the programme lower interest rates.

3. Net Business Income: Results from Model 3 also suggest that the kinds of association to which microenterprise owners belong may not serve them as well as their businesses grow. Similar to the policy implications suggested in the previous section, microenterprise owners such as those in Polvos Azules need more relevant resources. Associations that concentrate on the very poorest will simply not meet the needs of a growing group of microenterprise owners who need information about how to break into the next tier, the small business tier. While microfinance institutions have increasingly begun to offer microcredit in conjuncture with a range of ancillary programmes, such as healthcare services, empowerment and leadership courses, and disaster relief packages, there is a dearth of programmes that concentrate on transitioning microfinance clients. These programmes could potentially focus on new products and services—for example, insurance, savings accounts and CDs, and even online banking—for microenterprise owners. It is essential that microfinance institutions, and the government, look for ways to keep microenterprise owners' profits growing years after the initial microcredit loan.

Second, results from Model 3 also suggest that we need to

do more work on understanding how microenterprise owners use microcredit. While there is a substantial literature on investment spending versus consumption spending, there is less work done on how microenterprise owners actually go about raising profits. For example, while I have found that women are more likely to increase their net business incomes as a result of receiving microcredit, I do not have very good data on the process by which that occurred. Profits are clearly a function of revenues and expenses—but a microenterprise owner's decision-making process often remains a black box. While some recent studies have used game theory to begin work on these questions, there are still few studies that evaluate improvements in clients' financial management—despite the fact that it is one of "the main justifications of microfinance."[28]

Needless to say, microenterprise owners are not a homogeneous group. Indeed, "poor people demand a wide range of financial, business development, and social services for different business and household purposes."[29] Different types of resources will be required at different levels of growth, and more research needs to be devoted to longitudinal studies that can address these questions. Moreover, this research must be disseminated among microenterprise owners. As research on microcredit becomes more sophisticated, it becomes increasingly important to share the results with those whom they will benefit most: the microenterprise owners.

To foster the growth of a growing and dynamic population of microenterprise owners, Polvos Azules will need to be a leader in promoting an efficient capital trail. In doing so, it will be important for Peru's first commercial centre to pay very close attention to the role of gender.

Limitations

To be sure, there are serious limitations to my study. First, the problem of measurement error is almost certainly affecting the results. Having conducted subsequent investigations of the microenterprise owners in this sample, I know that few microenterprise owners have very accurate estimates of their income. This is, in part, because very few of them have received training—neither as formal schooling nor as "on the job training"—in accounting and record keeping. Compounding this problem is the fact that incomes vary greatly due to frequent fluctuations in inventory, personal issues that cause the microenterprise owner to miss work, and other problems typically associated with microenterprise owners operating in the often precarious microenterprise sector.

Yet another factor creating measurement error is the informal aspect of many microenterprises in the sample. The 2003 data indicate that 15 per cent of the microenterprises report not having a taxpayer identification number and in 2006, this number increases to 28 per cent. There is certainly a knee-jerk reaction on the part of microenterprise owners to deny any informality. The market has, in the past, been raided by the government during anti-piracy campaigns, and those incidents create enormously high levels of anxiety. While my study does not focus exclusively on informality, having an informal business might induce microenterprise operators to provide inaccurate information about other variables, such as initial or current capital investment.

The problem of omitted variable bias is also, most probably, affecting the results. Most importantly, my measures of social capital might be suffering from inaccuracies. For example, my results show very low levels of associational membership—despite evidence from the literature and personal investigation that microenterprise owners do participate actively in clubs and associations. (Of course, this could be an artifact of the literature, which tends to focus on the poorest or, alternatively, small and medium sized enterprises.) Future work would benefit from more detailed network data.

A final shortcoming of the present study is the non-stochastic nature of the models. The 2003 data are cross-sectional and obviously cannot provide a dynamic view of the microenterprise sector. While I do report on data from 2006, the size of the random sample is very small. Furthermore, the data used in the present study do not take into account a particular microenterprise owner's access to institutions. Given that "local contexts shape and interact with conditions related to community institutions that are expected to enhance effectiveness"[30] it would be important to know more about microenterprise owners' networks of institutional support, which include access to healthcare, formal housing, and other community-based social services.

9.5 Concluding Remarks

I began this chapter with a quotation from Theodore Schultz's Nobel Lecture, "The Economics of Being Poor." Schultz denotes the major part of this lecture to discussing the economics of being poor with respect to agriculture and farmers, challenging economists to understand the rational decisions, indeed the efficiency, of the poor. The "central thrust" of his lecture, as he put it, was that "population quality and knowledge do matter"—especially for entrepreneurs that use knowledge to make decisions.[31] While I have chosen to concentrate on the urban poor and, more specifically, microenterprise owners, I believe Schultz's argument is still relevant. Moreover, I would argue that gender is an essential element of the economics of the poor, and understanding how to help women-owned microenterprises—through different channels such as social capital and microcredit—is a very effective way to improve socio-economic outcomes in developing countries such as Peru.

NOTES

1. This chapter has been carved out of the PhD Dissertation, entitled "The Role of Gender in Returns to Human Capital, Social Capital and Microcredit Enterprise Sector, Lima, Peru" submitted to the University of Virginia, Charlottesville, VA in 2007.
2. Following the classification system of the Peruvian government, in this study a microenterprise consists of ten employed workers or less and a small business, 11-49 employed workers.
3. Chacaltana, J. *Public Policy and Employment in Micro and Small Enterprises in Peru*. (International Labour Organization, 2003).
4. Banerjee, A. and E. Duflo. "The Economic Lives of the Poor." *The Journal of Economic Perspectives: A Journal of the American Economic Association* 21.1. (2007): 141.
5. Khandker, S. "Microfinance and Poverty: Evidence Using Panel Data from Bangladesh." *The World Bank Economic Review* 19.2.

(2005): 263-286. Pitt, M. and S. Khandker. "The Impact of Group-Based Credit Programmes on Poor Households in Bangladesh: Does the Gender of Participants Matter?" *Journal of Political Economy* 106.5. (1998): 958-996. Todd, H. "Women at the Centre: Grameen Bank Borrowers After One Decade." (1996).

6. Honig, B. "What Determines Success? Examining the Human, Financial, and Social Capital of Jamaican Microentrepreneurs." *Journal of Business Venturing* 13.5. (1998): 371-394.
7. The traditional norms of Peruvian society has been that males take the role of bread earner and women take care of domestic work. In the process, sons are preferred. http://www.everyculture.com/No-Sa/Peru.html
8. Honig, B. "What Determines Success? Examining the Human, Financial, and Social Capital of Jamaican Microentrepreneurs." *Journal of Business Venturing* 13.5. (1998): 371-394. De Soto, H. *The Mystery of Capital: Why Capitalism Triumphs in the West and fails Everywhere Else.* (Basic Books, 2000).
9. Indeed, the study of gendered processes in the paid labour market is one of the main areas of investigation in "feminist economics."
10. Never do I intend to imply that women are inherently better at using social networks. Instead, I adopt Meyerson and Kolb's notion of gender differences as "an active, ongoing social construction" (p. 563). Using this "gender lens," I argue that it is possible for women to become more adept at using social capital and microcredit because of disadvantages they face in the microenterprise sector. However, this would be a consequence of gendered social constraints and not of an advantage women possess a priori.
11. Schultz, T. "Investment in Human Capital." *The American Economic Review* 51.1. (1961): 1-17. Cook, R. and P. Belliveau. "The Influence of Human Capital Attributes in Microenterprise Training." *Journal of Small Business and Enterprise Development* 11.4. (2004): 467-473.
12. Honig employed this model in his research, but operationalized social capital with marital status and frequency of church attendance. Honig, B. "What Determines Success? Examining the Human, Financial, and Social Capital of Jamaican Microentrepreneurs." *Journal of Business Venturing* 13.5. (1998): 371-394.
13. Coleman, J.S. "Social Capital in the Creation of Human Capital." *American Journal of Sociology* (1988): S95-S120.

14. Coleman, J.S. "Social Capital in the Creation of Human Capital." *American Journal of Sociology* (1988): S95-S120.
15. Putnam, R. "Social Capital: Measurement and Consequences." *Canadian Journal of Policy Research* 2.1. (2001): 41-51.
16. Coleman, J.S. "Social Capital in the Creation of Human Capital." *American Journal of Sociology* (1988): S95-S120.
17. The Polvos Azules website is http://ccPolvos Azules.com/
18. Some of these goods are false reproductions (i.e. pirated), others are not. I discuss the issue of informality at length in various sections of my study.
19. Although the data are cross-sectional, I refer cautiously to marginal effects (implying causality) rather than correlations. The details of the explanation have been discussed in various chapters of the dissertation.
20. As I will explain later, I made some small changes to the survey to give me additional information on variables pertinent to my study.
21. Over 50 per cent of women and men microenterprise owners report that their initial capital came from personal savings.
22. It is worth noting that women have 21 per cent less initial capital than men, but they have 26 per cent less current capital than men.
23. Woolcock, M. and Narayan, D. (2000). Social Capital: Implications for Development Theory, Research, and Policy. *The World Bank Observer*, *15*, *2*, 225-49.
24. Ibarra, H. 1997 . Paving an Alternative Route: Gender Differences in Managerial Networks. *Social Psychology Quarterly*, *60*(1), 91-102.
25. Woolcock and Narayan, 2000, p. 231.
26. Gulli, H. (1998). *Microfinance and Poverty*. Washington, DC: IADB, p. 15.
27. I am not the first to suggest that banks take into consideration other factors when women cannot provide typical forms of collateral, such as physical capital. Muhammad Yunus, founder of the Grameen Bank in Bangladesh, recognized that the poor—particularly poor women—did not have collateral to back the microcredit they needed to grow their businesses. This was the impetus for "group-based lending" where small groups were held responsible for every group member's loan repayment. When a group member defaulted, the other group members were all held responsible for the loan's repayment. This kind of "peer pressure" constituted a different form of collateral. Instead of

human capital or physical capital, this was social capital as collateral.

28. Gulli, H. op. cit., p. 58.
29. Gulli, 1998, p. viii.
30. Scheerens, J. (2000). Improving School Effectiveness. *UNESCO and IIEP Fundamentals of Educational Planning* Series, No. 68, p. 2.
31. Theodore Schulz (1980). Nobel Prize Lecture reprinted in *The Journal of Political Economy*, Vol. 88, Issue 4, p. 649.

3

Women Beekeepers in Iran: Challenges and Prospects of a Microcredit Project

Soheila Alirezanejad

Introduction[1]

The experience of the Grameen Bank has inspired many people around the world, including Iranians, to formally implement the micro-financing approach.[2] In Iran, as a component of development projects, microcredit loans are given directly to poor people[3] and while there are numerous similarities among developing countries, different social, cultural, and economic factors may lead to different outcomes.[4] Microcredit has been called "one of the most significant innovations in development policy over the past twenty-five years" and has been recognized as a "trickle up" approach, which has a long history in Iran.[5]

Microcredit loans for Iranian women officially started in 2000. The Land and Water project focusing on the watershed of the Hableh Rood River in three provinces of central Iran was launched at about the same time in three provinces of central Iran including Semnan province where the site of this study is located. The project's facilitators decided to apply the idea of microfinancing in Rameh,[6] a satellite village of the city of Garmsar. For the project investigated in this paper, fifty-three rural women formed an association to raise honey bees. Based on their meagre savings and a loan from the Land and Water project, the members of the association received four beehives each and initial training in beekeeping. As the group started to earn money, their success attracted the financial cooperation of two more organizations, one national and one international, in 2002-03: the Agricultural Bank of Iran, and the UNDP-affiliated Small Grants Programme (SGP).[7] The women's association operated for nearly ten years, but by 2010 its members had decided to split into five smaller groups. Their journey from success to dissolution and restating again raises at least three important questions: Why did the association break up after 10 years?

In 2002, as a member of the team that was reviewing SGP's projects in Iran, I met members of an association called the "Women Beekeepers of Rameh" which had started its activities about two years before I met them. I observed the group for about three months and reviewed documents about its activities. The women seemed to be accomplishing their tasks successfully, a positive evaluation that was supported by other consultants and facilitators. I became interested in the association, wishing to learn how these women had achieved their success. In particular, I was interested in their community because:

1. They earned and saved money.
2. The association was able to give small loans (about $100-$150) in turn to some members. The loans were collateral-free.
3. The women seemed conscientious about repaying their loans.
4. The women accepted responsibility.
5. The women seemed to be self-confident.
6. No individual seemed to be the centre of power in the group, not even the group's representatives.
7. There was a feeling of camaraderie and friendship among the group of women and they spoke freely and easily about each other, particularly their representatives.
8. The women seemed to have clear ideas about their future.

These features are important characteristics in any development project, so this team seemed to present a worthwhile object for investigation. The fact that more than fifty women could work together and interact harmoniously was remarkable. One was able to imagine that they could continue their activities for years. To find out more about the women I became involved in their activities for more than eight years. Moreover, this Rameh Women's Association displayed some features that made it a suitable case study of Iranian microfinance. Most key stakeholders engaging in financial activities, including microfinance, in rural areas of Iran were already involved with this community; international donors, the local and national government, the Agricultural Bank of Iran, and even interest-free microcredit funds played a role in the association's story.[8]

Methodology

Having worked in different parts of Iran, I have learned the importance of employing a mixed methodology (including qualitative and quantitative methods) when conducting research on the social and economic situation of Iranian women.

Thus the research modality pursued here was mainly qualitative, grounded in my close, long-term relationship with the beekeepers association. To support my observations, I included in the research approach a quick survey and prepared a questionnaire to gather quantitative data on the women's experiences.[9] The questionnaire worked well with the young women in and out of the group, but most of the older women did not wish to answer the questionnaire. So in this case I conducted semi-structured interviews to implement the questionnaire.

I interviewed about 30 members in total. Some also took part in focus group discussions.[10] During some of our interactions, certain members of the association exhorted us not to remain as passive observers, but to cooperate with them in solving their problems, both in the public, social domain and in the private sphere of their homes. Gradually we became aware of their unhappiness with some of the project's outcomes and the reasons for the underachievement of their beekeeping activities.

The women we observed became sufficiently comfortable with us to feel safe criticizing the donors. Nevertheless, they repeatedly reminded us that outsiders, including myself, did not really understand their situation, and they seemed bent on changing this outsiders' perspective, at least as they conceived of it. The women openly shared their life stories, and such uninhibited interaction with us we took as an indication of their trust in us. We conducted semi-structured interviews but most of the time our interactions were open-ended.[11] The members were not just a target group for collecting data, but also active partners in the data collection process.

The Story-Forming the Association

In 2000, some UN agencies cooperated with the Iranian national and local government to start a water resources management project in three different provinces: Tehran, Semnan, and Mazandaran. The aim of the project was to manage the watershed of the Hableh Rood River.

The funding agencies intended to improve women's participation in public life by implementing microcredit. Rameh village fell within the scope of this project. A group of facilitators from the University of Tehran and the Ministry of Jihad and Agriculture went to Rameh to introduce themselves to the villagers.[12] The facilitators visited the villagers regularly, holding meetings in the local mosque. The villagers and facilitators told us subsequently that it was mainly men and only a few women who attended the first meeting. However, these women informed other family members and neighbours about the meeting and encouraged them to take part in subsequent sessions. At first the women sat behind the men, but gradually moved to the front of the men's section. Increasingly, women began to express their concerns about the village, and the men learned to listen to the women.

Meanwhile, the facilitators invited the women to take part in workshops held in Garmsar, providing a van to transfer them back and forth. Some rural women were escorted by a few elderly men who took part in the workshops.[13] The women came up with some interesting proposals amongst which the idea of gathering indigenous herbal medicine and keeping bees were the two most popular. Both these activities had a historical precedent in that area. In the end the women chose to be beekeepers. The women of Rameh were certain that they could successfully keep the bees and earn good money by selling this popular and widely consumed traditional food.

Introducing Microcredit Fund to the Association

After attending a few donor workshops the women of Rameh decided to establish their own association, and thus met in informal gatherings with the facilitators. The women expected to receive money from the Land and Water project directly to buy beehives. In connection with the establishment of their association, the Rameh women contributed a small amount of money (about $2) every month to a collective fund. Thus when the association decided to buy beehives it could draw from two resources: Its own small monthly savings that had grown to about $500, and the money contributed by the Land and Water project, which totalled approximately $2,000.

About fifty members of the association held a meeting with some of the facilitators and government officials to formalize their decision. Subsequently, three association representatives, one official of the local government, one elderly gentleman from the village who was an expert in keeping bees, and a driver travelled to northern Iran to buy bees. The representatives returned feeling satisfied that they had accomplished their job well. Each member of the association received four beehives, but for a variety of reasons that I will elabourate on later, the women of the association did not keep all the beehives in one place. This issue notwithstanding, soon enough the women began to generate income from the harvested honey. They proved successful and soon attracted the interest of new donors.

Basic features of the Association

The association's basic features were as follows. Members were all married,[14] and some had been married more than once. The youngest member of the group was 27 years old while the oldest one was 68. The mean age was 41.2 years. Of the 50 members of the association, four of them had no children, while one had 10 children.

Table 1: Distribution of Age Category and Education Among the Members of the Association in 2009[15]

Age Group *Level of Education*	*Unanswered*	*25-30*	*31-35*	*36-40*	*41-45*	*46-50*	*51-55*	*56-60*	*Total*
Illiterate	1	0	0	0	0	1	6	1	9
Elementary School	3	0	2	2	0	11	3	0	21
Intermediate School	0	2	5	1	1	0	0	0	9
High School Diploma and BA	0	4	6	3	1	0	0	0	14
Total	4	6	13	6	2	12	9	1	53

Table 1 shows the distribution of the two variables, "level of education" and "age" of the association's members. Many members specified that when they became involved with development programmes, they began to think about the significance of education. Some of the younger members of the association even decided to go back to school to gain higher degrees. This resulted in a number of women becoming literate and some women achieving a high school diploma. A statistical analysis (Pearson chi-square) showed a significant covariance between "age" and "level of education" of the association's members, and that the higher the age of the women, the lower their level of education. This shows that the association is polarized when it comes to "age" and "education."

No other variables were found to show such impact across the group as those of "age" and "level of education" had greatly affected the performance of the members of the association. Therefore the two variables "age" and "education" appeared to be key attributes of association members. While the younger women enjoyed higher levels of education, the older women possessed more abilities and skills in handicrafts and in traditional forms of knowledge such as herbal medicine and keeping bees. Summarizing the distribution of the variables education and age, two identifiable categories of association members were distinguished:[16]

1. Older women:[17] Women over 40. These women tended to be more skilled in traditional handicrafts and indigenous knowledge about plants and agriculture. They were mostly uneducated.

2. Younger women: Age below 40. These women were literate; some even had a high school diploma, but often had few skills in traditional crafts and little knowledge of indigenous herbs and vegetation.

The two categories of members had different abilities, knowledge, and awareness. Although, fundamentally, these different capabilities could be considered as complementary and positive, in fact the members of the association were polarized on the basis of these differences. This polarization affected all activities of the group in both negative and positive ways.

Opportunities and challenges for the two categories of women members corresponded to both the number of beehives they could obtain and the number they could manage to keep. While some members were losing their bees, a few variables intensified this situation.

Age Categorization Among the Representatives

The members of the association elected five representatives when they formed the community. Both old and young women were elected as representatives. Interestingly, the two oldest representatives gained the most votes. For some reason there was never a second vote. One of the young and well-educated representatives quit the association very soon after being elected, soon followed by another. These two representatives were replaced by women who had gained fewer votes in the original election and both of them were among the younger members. One of these two new representatives had a high school diploma while the other completed hers while serving as an association representative. These two shouldered most of the administrative activities for the following seven years. The five elected representatives of the association kept their positions with no rotation, a lack of turnover that eventually led to dissatisfaction among some members, especially those with less formal education who did not think that information was being properly disseminated among the members. Older representatives also complained about a lack of new information and felt that they had less access to donors.

New Stakeholders, New Opportunities

The beekeeper association had been working successfully for about two years. This success gave the facilitators the opportunity to negotiate with two new donors, including governmental and international donors that supported microcredit associations in Iran. There are several stakeholders that work in rural areas of Iran. Among them, the Agricultural Bank of Iran is a very important actor in addressing villagers' financial concerns. Based on negotiations with the project facilitators, the Agricultural Bank of Iran agreed to provide interest-free small loans to some of the younger members of the association. The facilitators had argued that any loans should be directed to all members of the association, but the bank decided only to give them to members who were under 40 and jobless. At the same time, the programme also approved a grant to the association, and thus two new stakeholders provided new opportunities for association members to improve and upgrade their business. In sum, the facilitators attracted three different financial resources to the association: 1) a developmental loan without repayment from the Land and Water project, 2) interest free loans from the Agricultural Bank of Iran, and 3) a grant from the international programme. A brief explanation of the latter two follows.

The Agricultural Bank of Iran

As part of the development policy of Iranian national and local governments, the Agricultural Bank of Iran provided 33 individual members of the association with small interest-free loans of approximately $1000 each. The loans were also collateral-free and the members to whom they were offered agreed to repay them within four years at a monthly rate of about $21 per month. The total amount of the loan package was about US $33,000.[18] Despite the facilitators' request that all members of the association receive the Agricultural Bank's loans, only 33 women—all of them association members under the age of 40—qualified for loans. Loan conditions stipulated keeping about $300 to cover personal and family expenses, while the rest of the money was to be used by recipients to buy more beehives. Consequently, recipients were able to purchase about 10 more beehives each. The facilitators asked the younger member recipients to share their new resources with the rest of the members, but the 33 women did not wish to share with those who had not received loans because they believed that they could not do so given that every recipient was personally responsible for paying back their loan. Unsurprisingly, members who did not obtain loans were very disappointed, and it gradually became clear that they neither forgot their disqualification nor forgave loan recipients for their perceived selfishness. The older women thought that their representatives and facilitators should not have accepted the loan package unless it was provided to all members of the association. On the other hand, the younger members never regretted this unequal situation. Because of these circumstances some of the older members who did not receive the Agricultural Bank's loans decided not to repay the instalments of an internal loan arrangement provided for them by the association.[19] For the first time, the age difference among association members became a divisive issue.

The International Programme

The UNDP-affiliated Small Grants Programme was the third stakeholder to contribute to the association. This international programme gave the association a grant of $17,500 to implement the project "Integrated sustainable conservation of Rameh village rangelands," whose goal it was to improve the village pastures and natural environment.[20] The agreement between the programme and three representatives of the association specified certain tasks that the association became responsible for performing and stipulated guidelines on how to spend the grant. Thus the association could not spend the money in any way it wanted. Association members of both main categories cooperated to accomplish the goals of the project, and members also collectively visited different projects' sites, took part in workshops, and met successful and entrepreneurial women. This gave the women of the association new opportunities to go out of their homes and work together. During this process the women got closer to one another and the financial, social, and emotional distance between them diminished. However, the story ended on a less harmonious note. Because the younger and more educated representatives of the association had signed the project's contract, they had to take charge of the project. The donors preferred to work with the younger representatives because they were literate, but in this way the older and less educated women again lost their customary position of honour. In fact, the older women of the association were admired by the locals, the facilitators, and the donors, and it is only natural that these women expected to have more control of the association and closer relationships with the donors. But as we have seen this expectation was frustrated twice—the first time when the Bank only granted loans to individual younger members and now again when the older women lost control to the younger educated members with the project.

Emerging Problems and Their Roots

For the first two years of the project everything went more or less well. Some women lost their bees in the first year, and a few more women lost theirs in the second. But in the third year most of the remaining women lost their bees and only a small group managed to keep their hives. The official reports showed that most of the women lost their bees because of drought. However, some not only maintained, but actually even increased, the number of their hives under the same environmental conditions. In any case, the women who lost their bees did not restart their businesses as beekeepers; very few ever started another business jointly.[21] Then, members of the association began searching for a charity loan like the one they had received from the Land and Water project, but unfortunately no such charity was forthcoming this time. They also tried to take out a low-interest loan from the Agricultural Bank, but fewer of these kinds of loans were available. Finally, having considered several options, the association elected to break into five smaller groups after 10 years in existence. It is clear that a variety of internal and external variables influenced this situation, but it appears that two internal components ultimately account for the group's demise: first, the association was polarized on the basis of age and education; second, the women members did not have the association as their first priority, and thus primarily followed individual agendas.

Interaction Between the Two Categories within the Association

There is a significant covariance between association members' education level and age and the administrative staffing of the group (younger women were more educated and were actual representatives of the association). The distribution of the administrative positions (representatives, treasurer, and inspectors) among members was unequal. This is a very important detail because actually the association's relationships with different organizations, donors, and stakeholders were facilitated and carried out through these positions. Members who occupied administrative roles could extend their relationships and reach out to powerful resources in the public domain.

Even though members of the older and less educated segment were the highest vote getters in the original election, future events pushed them to the sidelines, thus concentrating power in the hands of a few younger and more educated representatives. As discussed previously, the Bank's decisions first to deal with the women as individuals rather than as a collective, and then to extend the loans only to the younger more educated members, further divided the association into two unequal groupings. Later circumstances exacerbated the divide, compounding a problem that could not be satisfactorily resolved.

The international programme, despite its intention to work with the association as a whole, chose two younger and more educated representatives to be their main points of contact. The international programme's project contractual mandate empowered these two women but antagonized many others.

Another factor contributing to the divide was lack of training in financial and administrative work within the association. Some of the older and less educated women were willing and able to participate and capable of leadership, but feared that their lack of education and training[22] made them less competent and thus did not take any actual lead. Many members felt unable to grasp or to manage the association's financial and administrative responsibilities. In 2009, some members brought their husbands to the association to help them try to evaluate its financial reports.

Over time, the key positions of the association were occupied by younger, educated women, such that older and less educated women felt they had no chance to assume these roles. Given the situation, skilful older women were disappointed by not being able to reach the donors, while nevertheless believing that they were sufficiently qualified to lead the association. As one of them kept telling us: "I am illiterate, but I can negotiate very well. The younger representatives should let me accompany them to different meetings with the donors. If I were there the donor might not waste our money," which in this context meant forcing the association to spend the money according to the narrow mandate of the specific stakeholder.

The opportunity offered to certain members of the association turned into a hazard for the group as a whole, and tensions rose as the financial gap between the younger members who received the Bank's loan and older members who did not increased.

Association Members – or Individual Members of the Association

The main problem may have begun, early on, when the majority of women decided to keep their bees individually.[23]

Drawing on the Grameen Bank's experience, when women organize themselves as a group it seems that their situation both in the association and individually may be similar to what Yunus describes when he notes that women who want to be involved with the Grameen Bank's loan programme have to actively participate in forming their groups.[24] In this process a level of trust and cooperation is built. Each woman realizes that being a member of a group will help her increase her chances of securing a loan. But the experience of the Association of Women

Beekeepers was quite different because, ultimately, the members focused individually on the financial help from donors rather than on one another. This was exacerbated by basic demographic features of the association hitherto discussed, as well as the particular conditions for the intervention of stakeholders. In retrospect, it seems that when the women decided to save money, they did not think of it as a form of communal savings but as individual bank accounts to be drawn from at will. Furthermore, because of the relatively large size of the group (53 members) it was hard to build trust among the entire membership. Consequently each woman kept her four beehives individually, with all the difficulties that this would entail. As beekeepers actually live in Garmsar they had to transport the bees among different places and keep them in the urban environment of Garmsar, which further added to their difficulties.

Another significant cultural belief contributed to the women's decision to keep their beehives individually. Some association members told me that they kept their hives separately because they feared the evil eye.[25] They were afraid that friends, family, and neighbours who might be envious of their success would give them the evil eye and thus ruin their business. Most of the members never told others the exact amount of honey they produced or sold, not even their closest family members like sisters and parents.

Each member therefore took her beehives and kept them near her home. Many problems ensued. Some neighbours, husbands, and children did not like to live near the buzzing and stinging bees. Some of the neighbours complained to the municipality in an attempt to force the beekeepers to remove their hives. Some irate people even removed the beehives themselves. Also, because moving the hives to different areas in search of the right flowers was very expensive, and because the women in the meantime still had to take care of their traditional duties as wives and mothers, the situation for many of them became unsustainable.[26] Thus, as the situation got worse some members decided to sell their hives.

Diminishing trust and unravelling group solidarity could

be seen in some other phases as well. As discussed, the Agricultural Bank's loans were given to younger members who did not share their loans with the older members despite the facilitators' advice to do so, choosing to act as individual beekeepers rather than as a group. So despite our initial observations about group camaraderie, in this crucial case the women chose not to support one another.

The case of the project credit is another important manifestation of the decreasing trust. Some members, especially the older women, could not understand why the international programme paid out the grant money[27] but imposed all kinds of restrictions on its disbursement. These women believed that once they were given the money it belonged to them, and they should be free to decide how to spend it. In their frustration they criticized their own representatives for the way they disbursed the money, yet the representatives had to spend the money based on the contract they had signed with the international programme, an arrangement that did not make much sense to the older members. The two young representatives kept holding meetings to provide all members with information in order to convince them of their honesty and win the older members' trust. But they were not successful; the representatives never managed to get the group beyond the stage of members talking past each other to actually negotiating to reach agreements.

Separation—The End of the Story

Given the situation described in this chapter, most of the members of the association wanted to start a new and easier venture, involving fewer women. They wished to once more take out loans individually or as a community-based organization (CBO). However, fewer loans were available due to changes in external circumstances. The women looked for a donor to support them without a requirement to repay the funds. No such donor emerged. Applying for a new grant from the international programme did not appeal to the women both because they had misunderstood the stipulations of such a grant and because of their low trust in fellow members who were in direct contact with the international programme.

The representatives of the association saw the growing lack of trust among some members as the expression of an increasing desire among the members to break up. In the opinion of some, they could work better in a smaller group. At the same time, the members were deeply disappointed by the improbability of receiving another financial loan from the donors. This situation ultimately led the members of the association to split into five smaller groups after more than nine years together as one body. The new groups' members were closer to each other geographically and seemed to have many similar approaches towards the venture they wished to undertake, but now the five groups had become one another's competitors, rather than collabourators. One of the representatives told me that we need to compete together to reach a better situation.

After a period of passiveness one group, under leadership of one of the representatives, began to prepare some new projects in 2011. They prepared some dried fruits, herbal medicines, etc. for sale in local and national exhibitions but maintained the old name. They also accepted some new members and tried to be in touch with some new donors. They have negotiated with some national and international donors and have begun some new small projects. Some of them, including a couple of older and young women, have kept their beehives and sold honey. They are continually seeking for new opportunities of earning money but the older and more experienced women are not in this group..

Conclusion

This chapter has examined achievements and failures of the Association of Women Beekeepers of Rameh in rural Iran. Initially the members of the association included two categories: younger and educated women, on the one hand, and older, mostly uneducated women but skilled in traditional crafts and local herbal medicine, on the other. Initially, association representation was drawn from both categories but later only the educated and younger members represented the association. The loans given to young members on an individual basis intensified the divide between these two categories. Step by step, different stakeholders' interventions deepened the gap, finally leading to the break up of the earlier association. The tension between the older and the younger members intensified partly because of the unintended consequences of the actions of the national and institutional donors. The Land and Water parent project created expectations that could not be met again later, despite requests from the women who wanted further assistance. The Bank preferred one category of women over the other, and the international programme support had to live up to UN-mandated standards which some women of the association neither understood nor wished to abide by.

The two categories of association members possessed different kinds of awareness and knowledge. Some women, mainly the older ones, could not distinguish among the types of financial support that the association had received and the rules governing the distribution of the support. This led to older members believing that the money was being wasted, for which they held their young project representatives accountable. Suspicions increased inside and outside of the association because of this. A few of the members' husbands exacerbated the problem by attending the meetings unexpectedly or provoking their wives against some association representatives, resulting in gossip and rumours spreading both inside and outside the association. Gradually, a majority of the members stopped taking part in the group meetings. The association representatives felt frustrated interacting with fifty disgruntled members. In sum, the unintended consequences of the actions of different stakeholders intensified the diminishing trust among members of the association.

The results of this study reinforce the oft-repeated conclusion that a microcredit project, as a modality of development, cannot be implemented as an abstract project. It needs to be tailored to the social needs and cultural contexts of the people involved. Different stakeholders might become interested in taking part in development-focused projects like the one involving the Association of Women Beekeepers in Rameh. However, careful stakeholder analysis should precede such involvement, as it can help facilitators prevent, mitigate, and more effectively deal with the unintended consequences of developmental interventions such as the ones discussed in this chapter. Stakeholder analysis needs to be done by individuals who are intimately familiar with the social and cultural circumstances of the people whose lives will be impacted by these projects.

By the time our story ended, many members of the Rameh Beekeepers' Association did not have practical plans for their future. While microcredit loans helped the women gain self-confidence and familiarity with non-traditional[28] activities, the economic and social infrastructure could not support and sustain the objectives of the association in the long run. Thankfully, a few of them were empowered enough to find a way in this foggy sphere of developmental interventions to make money and become socially active. Fortunately these few women came together in one of the smaller groups. Some new members joined them (they are more than 20 nowadays) and they could attract some governmental donors to continue their story in a new atmosphere.

NOTES

1. I would like to express my gratitude to Professor Shahla Haeri, former director of the Women's Studies Programme at Boston University, for her continuous support during my tenure as a visiting scholar there and a key advisor for this study. I would also like to thank Dr. Mohammad Behnam Shadmehr for reading the study carefully and giving me valuable advice for improving it. Finally, I owe thanks to Seyyed Babak Mousavi for his reading of various drafts of this study and his helpful comments.
2. Some UN agencies and a number of governmental and non-governmental organizations help implementing microfinance projects in Iran.
3. The office of Rural Women's Affairs in the Ministry of Jihad and Agriculture have been involved with microcredit financing since 2000. On the other hand, it is true that some Muslim communities have problems with microfinance but the community of women beekeepers was a community of Shiite people which has no problem with the idea of microfinance. Women and also men in Iran have been actively involved with traditional microfinance

funds called Gharzolhasaneh. The author conducted extensive research on the traditional microfinance funds.

4. Karim, R. and Osada, M. "Dropping Out: An Emerging Factor in the Success of Microcredit-Based Poverty Alleviation Programmes." *The Developing Economics.* 36.3 (1998): 257. Reevers, H. and Baden, S. "Gender and Development Concepts and Definitions" prepared for the Department of International Development (DFID) for its gender mainstreaming intranet resources—Report 55. (Institute of Development Studies, University of Sussex: BRIDGE: UK, 2000).
5. Ahlin, C. and Jiang, N. "Can microcredit Bring Development?" 31/82. (2007): 1.
6. Rameh is a satellite village of Garmsar, which is located about 55 kilometres to the northeast of Garmsar which in turn is about 100 kilometres east of Tehran. Garmsar and all its satellite villages including Rameh are irrigated by the Hableh Rood, the most important waterway in Semanan province. The 2006 census showed that Rameh had about 70 households and about 350 villagers, most of whom migrate back and forth to Garmsar and who leave Rameh deserted in the fall and winter. Rameh villagers engage mostly in farming and animal husbandry. The villagers plant wheat, barley, potatoes, tomatoes, and a variety of beans in a land of about 205 hectares. There are also numerous orchards in both Upper and Lower Rameh and about 50 hectares are dedicated to gardens with cherries, apricots, mulberries, walnuts, and apples.
7. The Small Grants Programme (SGP) comprises part of Global Environmental Facilities (GEF) which in Iran is related to the UNDP. It works with civil organizations such as NGOs and community-based organizations. The SGP is trying to raise public awareness and involvement to protect and preserve the natural environment.
8. Results of an assessment conducted using Participatory Rural Appraisal showed that there are different kinds of financial institutions in rural areas of Iran. The comparative matrix showed that the Agricultural Bank of Iran, traditional usurers, unofficial interest-free funds, and microcredit associations are the resources which are available for villagers. Women, however, are not used to borrowing money from the banks and the usurers individually. Microcredit associations are the most available resource of loan for Iranian rural women. Based on the Arab Mazar's report, Agricultural Bank of Iran is the most important

donor in rural areas of Iran. He believed that interest-free loan funds provide 5 per cent of credits in rural areas. The local shopkeepers, future commodity contracts, and acquaintances are the other available resources for villagers. The Acquaintances offered about 15 per cent of credits. Mafy, F. *Microcredits, Characteristics, Experiences, Concerns and Strategies* (2008). The Agricultural Bank of Iran has provided a loan programme similar to microcredit loans since 1994, named Hazrate Zeinabe, whose target group is poor rural women who are breadwinners of their households. These women are supposed to own no land or business. The Agricultural Bank of Iran had another facility for rural women named Iran. But a consultant of the Agricultural Bank of Iran believes that Iranian women prefer not to work with banks. According to the aforementioned Participatory Rural Appraisal, unofficial and official microcredit institutions are as effective as traditional usurers but the banking system is not a resource for Iranian rural women. Balaly, L."The Report of the Microcredit Funds of Iranian Rural Women, Phase 2." Office of Rural Women's Affair, Empowerment and improvement of Rural Women's Organizations Department (2007). The UN agencies are also supporting microcredit institutions.

9. Creswell, J.W. *Research Design: Qualitative and Quantitative Approaches.* (California: Sage Publications, 1994). 175-178.
10. In 2008-2009, Dr. Shahla Haeri former Director of Women's Studies Programme, Boston University accompanied me to Garmsar on several occasions, where we further observed and interviewed yet other members of the association.
11. Reinharz, S. *Feminist Methods in Social Research.* (New York: Oxford University Press, 1992), 18-21.
12. For more information see: Shaditalab, J. *Development and the Challenges of Iranian Women*. (Tehran: Nashre Ghatre, 2002).
13. I asked one elderly gentleman if men were worried about women being transported. He replied there was nothing to be worried about because "I was there to monitor the situation."
14. Most of the spouses of association members were not in a good enough financial situation to adequately support their spouses and families, so this attribute was fairly uniform across the membership.
15. Some members got their diploma and used the adult education system to promote their education level, so the situation at the beginning of the cooperation was different.
16. If we add the number of children to the basic features of the

association, the categorization will not change.

17. We used the age of 40 because historically women of Rameh first had access to a local school about forty years ago. The elderly people told us that before the Islamic revolution in Iran, there was an elementary school in the village in which boys and girls could study but soon the school was closed for lack of sufficient number of students. At that time parents who wanted their children to continue their education migrated to Garmsar. Some women and their parents told us that the girls had to live in Garmsar or closer satellite villages while their parents stayed in Rameh.
18. This information was gathered via interviews with facilitators, especially Mr. Mohseny and some members of the association.
19. The association managed members' savings, which amounted to a meagre sum. They used to pay some collateral-free loans to the members of about $100-$150. A few older members had received this loan from the association before.
20. GEF Small Grants Programme. "Community Action Global Impact." UNDP. 2012. http://sgp.undp.org/.
21. One of them could start a new business and another one wanted to promote her business as a beekeeper individually.
22. There were certain sorts of training offered to the members. These were typically about preparing dried fruits and keeping bees.
23. It does not mean that they did not want to keep working with the association. They mostly said that they wanted to keep the association.
24. Yunus, M. *Banker of the Poor: Micro-lending and the Battle Against World Poverty.* (Public Affairs, US, 2007). 63.
25. For more information see: Spooner, B. "The Evil Eye in the Middle East." *The Evil Eye* (1976): 76-84.
26. Despite all the problems women approached the local government to give them a piece of land where they could keep their bees. The government suggested that they keep their bees in the national park, quite close to Garmsar, which the government agreed to lease to them for 99 years. But the women did not accept this plan. Then the government asked them to find a piece of suitable land which belonged to the government but the women could not find it. When their problems became unmanageable, they thought about keeping bees collectively but unfortunately it was too late. Only one group of about five members of the same extended family reported that they kept their bees together in one place.

27. This characteristic was very important, and we plan to write an article to clarify the socio-cultural meaning of money.
28. Although beekeeping was a traditional knowledge in Raṃeh but mostly some older men earlier had this knowledge as well as a few older women. Then actually younger women seek modern training about beekeeping. Some younger women asked me to negotiate with my colleagues in veterinary school to train them.

4

Microcredit: A Way of Poverty Alleviation and Empowerment of Women in Vietnam

Le Thi My Hien

The Poverty Situation in Vietnam

In the last three decades Vietnam has transitioned from a poor, war-ravaged, under-developed country to lower middle income status with rapid economic growth and increasing integration in the global economy. Until ten years after the country's reunification in 1975, a majority of its population was deemed to be living in poverty, the national economy remained attenuated and Vietnam was completely dependent on foreign aid.[1] Till the early 1990s, about 70 per cent of the population was categorized as poor with a significant proportion living in extreme poverty. A series of political, economic and financial reforms launched in 1986 under the Doi Moi (Renewal) initiative for reconstruction and economic growth, and affirmative action aimed at poverty alleviation by government programmes and state-owned banks enabled Vietnam to halve the number of people living below the poverty line in less than two decades. The official poverty rate was estimated to be less than 10 per cent in 2010.[2]

The Government of Vietnam's Hunger Eradication and Poverty Reduction Programme (HEPR), was first implemented in Ho Chi Minh City in 1992 and expanded to the rest of the country in 1998.[3] Together with high levels of economic growth from the mid-90s on and overseas development assistance, the

HEPR has helped to dramatically reduce poverty levels.[4] The proportion of people living on less than US$ 1.25 a day adjusted for purchasing power parity dropped from 58 per cent in 1993 to 16 per cent by 2006.[5] Between 1993 and 2008 the proportion of people living on less than US$ 2 per day fell from 85.7 per cent to 43.4 per cent.[6] However, the rate of poverty reduction varies across different geographical regions and ethnic groups. Among Vietnam's 54 ethnic groups the Kinh, who represent 86 per cent of the total population, have largely been able to raise their economic status and rise above poverty. The 53 ethnic minorities who constitute only15 per cent of the population accounted for almost 44 per cent of the total poor households in the country and above 50 per cent of the poorest in 2006, at a time when only 10 per cent of the majority Kinh population were deemed to be poor. Concentrated in remote, mountainous areas and the Mekong Delta, these groups are also extremely vulnerable to the adverse impact of climate change and environmental degradation.[7]

The P135 programme for Socio-Economic Development of the Most Vulnerable Communes in Ethnic Minority and Mountainous Areas in Vietnam is the largest poverty reduction programme targeting the ethnic minorities of the Northern and Central Highlands and the Mekong River Delta. It is administered by the Committee for Ethnic Minority Affairs (CEMA), under Vietnam's Comprehensive Poverty Reduction and Growth Strategy (CPRGS).

In addition to lower levels of poverty reduction in ethnic minority and other disadvantaged areas, rural-urban poverty levels show increasing disparity. Rapid urbanization and migration has aggravated the urban poverty situation.[8] Due to a national economic slowdown and the effects of the global financial crisis of 2008, Vietnam's GDP growth that reached 7 per cent by 2007 has slowed down. Urban residents and migrant workers in the new industrial economy face increasingly higher costs of living including the rising costs of urban utilities such as water and electricity tariffs as well as unemployment levels that have forced migrants to return to their rural homes.

Already in the 2000s, there were signs that as a result of

rapid economic growth and GDP growth averaging 6.4 per cent in the 2000s and over 7 per cent in 2001-2010, inequality between different sections of society had risen in both urban and rural areas. Transition to a market economy has led to income disparities between regions and different population groups, including between better off and chronically poor households in rural areas.[9] The relapse rate or return-to-poverty dynamics are still a difficult issue for all segments of society, and permanent alleviation is a far more intractable problem.

Measuring Poverty Levels in Vietnam

Vietnam has used two different methods to measure poverty, both devised in the early 1990s and modified at intervals since then. The first approach was developed by the Ministry of Labour, Invalids and Social Affairs (MOLISA) the official agency responsible for proposing official urban and rural poverty lines and budget allocations for sectoral programmes at the beginning of each five-year Socio-Economic Development Plan (SEDP). MOLISA lines were earlier formulated by assessing rice sufficiency at household level based on measuring per capita incomes required to fulfil caloric intake norms. Since 2005, with technical support from the General Statistics Office (GSO), they have used a Cost-of-Basic-Needs (CBN) methodology similar to the second approached by GSO. MOLISA updates its list of target households annually using a mix of local surveys, and consultations at commune and district levels to determine the number of poor households. Figures are then aggregated to calculate provincial and national poverty rates.[10]

The GSO measures poverty and monitors progress on the basis of nationally representative household surveys, such as the Vietnam Household Living Standards Surveys (VHLSS) conducted bi-annually. GSO uses two methods, one based on official poverty lines adjusted for inflation and applied to per capita incomes and one developed by a joint GSO-World Bank team for the 2000 Poverty Assessment. The GSO-WB poverty line is constructed using the CBN methodology, "based on a reference food basket for poor households anchored in caloric norms (through 2008, 21,00 kilocalories per person per day) plus an additional allocation for essential non-food needs based on consumption patterns of the poor."[11]

This second methodology has kept lines roughly constant with real purchasing power indicated by per capita expenditure measured in successive rounds of the VHLSS. According to the GSO-WB's estimates, the country's poverty headcount fell from nearly 60 per cent in the early 1990s to 20.7 per cent in 2010. For the same period, MOLISA's official poverty rate showed the incidence of poverty falling from 58 per cent to 14.2 per cent in 2010.[12]

In 2000 the Government of Vietnam signed the UN Millennium Statement, thereby committing itself to achieving the eight Millennium Development Goals. Goal number one is the eradication of extreme poverty and hunger, and according to several sources, this has been considered a major success in Vietnam. Since then, the poverty rate has decreased from 63.85 per cent in 1993 to 16.85 per cent in 2005. Acute hunger has been eliminated for all regions and population groups. The poverty rate has continued to decrease, reaching 13 per cent by 2009.[13] However, the standard of living of Vietnam's poor is rather low, particularly in the highlands. So while many people have technically been raised out of poverty, the standard of living has improved only slightly for them and the relapse rate is still at 50-60 per cent, especially in remote areas and communes where ethnic minorities are concentrated. There are signs that as a result of rapid economic growth, inequality is rising. The problem of increasing income disparities in a market economy has become a new challenge.[14]

New methods of assessing poverty can throw up new challenges. In 2009, the Vietnamese government decided to raise the poverty level income cutoff from 200,000 Vietnamese Dong (VND) to 300,000 VND per person per month in rural areas, and from 260,000 to 380,000 VND per person per month in the urban areas (1 USD = 21,000 VND) by a Decision of the Prime Minister, No. 170/2005/QĐ-TTg.[15] With this new poverty rate in place, the percentage of poor families increased to 22 per cent, especially in Ho Chi Minh City, Vietnam's largest urban concentration of more than 6.6 million people according to 2008 statistics.

Poverty Lines are revised continuously; the Poverty Line applied for 2011-2015 by the Decision of the Prime Minister No. 9/2011QD-TTg was VND 400,000 per capita per month or VND 48,00,000 per capita per year (roughly US$ 19 per capita per month) for rural areas and VND 500,000 per capita per month or VND 60,00,000 per capita per year (US$ 24 per capita per month) for urban areas.[16] The poverty rate was revised and estimated at 12 per cent in 2011.

Besides the HEPR, now the National Targeted Programme for Poverty Reduction in its second phase, several other targeted programmes have been implemented which have without question helped to reduce the poverty rate. Microfinance/microcredit programmes are among the various programmes initiated to both reduce poverty, increase employment, and raise agricultural productivity for the rural poor. In the next section we will take up the details of the microlending programme to assess the extent to which it has been able to help in reducing the poverty ratio. Incidentally, microcredit/microfinance was one of the most important pro-poor measures that benefited many poor families along with measures on health and education. More importantly, special microcredit schemes and projects run by both government banks and non-governmental organizations including United Nations agencies have targeted women. Women constituted a little over half of Vietnam's total population of 92 million in 2011. Not having sufficient incomes, business capital or valuable assets, particularly in the form of land or houses to mortgage for bank loans, women account for the majority of the poor, as in most developing countries. "Mass organizations" like the Vietnam Women's Union (WU, Vietnam's first women's organization, set up in 1930) and Farmers' Union (FU) and many Vietnamese and international NGOs or CSOs carry out microcredit programmes to help poor women approach banks for credit and manage the financial resource so that they can change their families' lives and living standards for the better. This chapter highlights the role of microfinance/microcredit agencies in Vietnam showing that this intervention for poverty reduction and equitable economic growth plays a crucial role in supporting the poor and poor women. Cases presented here show the various approaches of agencies providing microfinance/microcredit facilities, from state-owned banks to large social organizations like the WU and voluntary agencies carrying out their microcredit programmes in different parts of the country—the TYM operating mainly in Northern Vietnam, CDF in Northern, Central and South Vietnam and the CEP in South Vietnam.

Forms of Microfinance and Microcredit Organizations and Definition of Microcredit

In 2005 the government of Vietnam passed a decree on the organization and operation of small-sized financial institutions in the country, as one of the measures of the government to implement the HEPR initiative.[17] The decree related to the following activities:

1. ***Small-Sized Finance/Microfinance***: Activities providing small and simple financial and banking services to low-income households and individuals; and

2. ***Small-Sized Credits/Microcredit***: Loans of a small amount, with or without security assets, provided for low-income households or individuals for use in income-generating activities and improvement of living conditions.

The concept of "small-sized credit" was propagated through a circular in support of the decree regarding the organization and activity of small size financial organizations. Loans of less than 30 million VND are defined as small-sized credit, a level that can be adapted by the governor of the State Bank of Vietnam as needed.[18]

Forms of Microfinance in Vietnam

Microfinance activity in Vietnam is rather different from that in other countries of the world. Such activity is carried out largely as "projects," or as a part of government programmes targeting poor households or communes, as there are only a few independent microfinance institutions solely providing microfinancial services. There are not enough structures to enable microfinance institutions to use commercial capital, and furthermore, in many projects, and with many local partners, the microfinancial activity is only a secondary component.[19]

At present there are three kinds of microfinancial services providers in Vietnam: (i) formal organizations, which include the People's Credit Fund System, the Vietnam Bank for Social Policies (VBSP), and the Bank for Agriculture and Rural Development (VBARD); (ii) semi-formal organizations, including national and international non-governmental organizations, social organizations and programmes, development aid centres, and groups affiliated with the Women's Association; and (iii) non-formal organizations, in which the activity of loans takes the form of 'Tontine'—that is, spontaneous credit associations, which give high interest loans, among other characteristics. The government urges the poor to use the credit services of formal and semi-formal organizations to achieve safer and more effective results, rather than the non-formal financial services with higher risks and interest rates.[20]

The Vietnam Bank for the Poor (VBP)

Among the earliest government owned banks which gave loans to the poor were the Vietnam Bank for the Poor (VBP) and the Vietnam Bank for Agriculture and Rural Development (VBARD). VBP, in fact, emerged out of a "Fund for the Poor" operated by the VBARD. The VBP was set up in 1996 by the Government of Vietnam with the specific aim of eliminating hunger and alleviating poverty. During its lifetime, its schemes of non-profit savings and loans brought help to more than one million households across the country. VBP set up a network of branches at provincial, municipal and district levels and boards of poverty reduction at commune level which identified those entitled for receiving collatter-free loans and set up Savings and Credit Groups among the poor households.

GSO's data on access of the poor to credit offered by different agencies showed that VBP with 58 per cent of market share was the main microfinance/microcredit provider in 2002, while VBARD at 23.25 per cent was the second most important provider. PCFs at 2.83 per cent, social organizations and NGOs at about 8 per cent and relatives and friends at 6.64 per cent were other sources of credit for the poor. Despite a variety of credit providers, the percentage of poor households with access

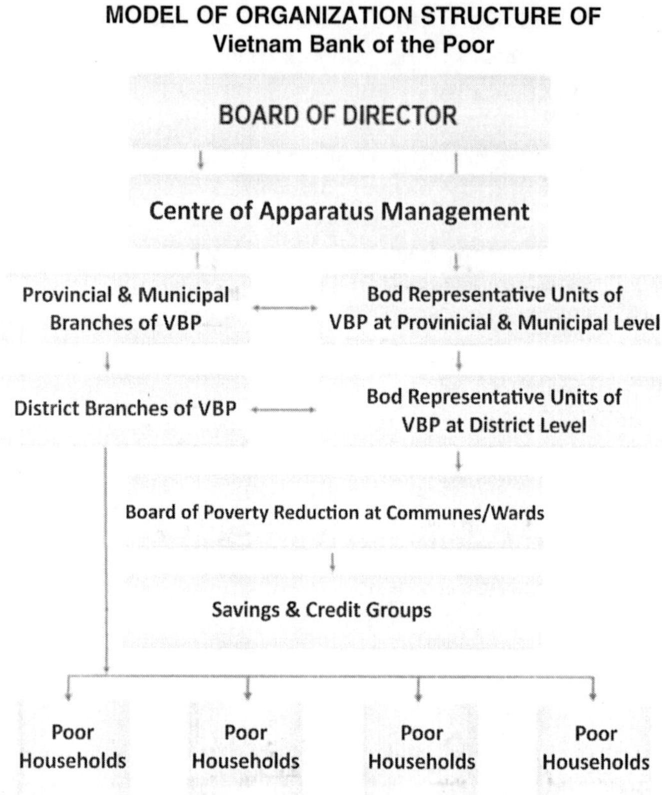

Source: VBSP website: http://www.vbsp.org.vn/evbsp/view_detail.php?mtt=117&mamm=10. Retrieved 2008

to credit was only 32.46 per cent. About 25 per cent of such credit went to female-headed households.[21]

The Vietnam Bank for Agriculture and Rural Development (VBARD)

The VBARD, begun even earlier, in 1990, seems to have tried to replicate the Indonesian model of a microfinance network known as Bank Rakyat Indonesia (BRI—the 'People's Bank'), the largest profitable network for microfinance. The BRI, a bank that has been mostly government-owned over the course of its over 120-year history, had adopted a commercial approach to microfinance issues, including such features as no subsidies, sustainable interest rates, efficient management, and efforts to mobilize savings. VBARD not only serves farmers and the rural areas but has a diverse array of customers: officials, employees, students, sales people, entrepreneurs and manufacturing facilities. It caters to the needs of customers who can afford to pay collateral and those who can't. For those who can't afford collateral, the bank has adopted a policy of lending to an entire group. In 2001, the bank had already served fifty per cent of the poor and was catering to the needs of forty per cent of the formal and semi-formal credit requirements of rural markets. [22] With support from the World Bank's Rural Finance Project, VBARD had expanded its rural outreach through mobile banking units delivering credit and deposit services to people in remote areas. An innovation in banking practice, the visits of VBARD's mobile banks are announced in advance and coincide with weekly market days when people from distant villages gather in one place for their marketing needs.[23]

The Vietnam Bank for Social Policies

The Vietnam Bank for Social Policies (VBSP) was established in 2003 under a law reorganizing the Vietnam Bank for the Poor.[24] Also owned by the government of Vietnam, VBSP caters to households with permanent residence near the bank's headquarters. Earlier, government banks providing preferential lending required borrowers to fulfil certain criteria—that is, they should have contributed to the Vietnamese revolution as soldiers or be relatives of deceased soldiers. Borrowers repay loans monthly or yearly. At present VBSP is mandated to cover 100 per cent of households designated as poor. All households have access to this bank if they have an official residence with mortgaged property.[25]

In 2011, the active members of the beneficiaries numbered eight million of which five million were women. The main objective of the bank's loans is to give credit for productive purposes and to create employment opportunities for everyone.[26]

Semi-Formal Organizations

Vietnam has more than 36 microfinance institutions (MFIs). A few of them were established between 1990 and 1994, while most were established in the period 2000-06. The majority of the MFIs have their activities registered under Decree 148; very few organizations are established under the structure of unions, international non-governmental organizations, or provincial or cooperative models. In most of the microfinancial organizations, information management is still carried out through manual methods. However, a few large organizations such as Capital Aid Fund for Employment of the Poor (CEP) have professional information management systems.

It is noteworthy that the rate of capital balance of risk in Vietnam remains one of the lowest in Asia. This shows credit discipline on the part of borrowers and close cooperation between customers and staff. Among the surveyed microfinance institutions, CEP has the largest number of customers, namely 193,238 in 2011 followed by the Cooperation Fund of Ho Chi Minh City with over 44,000 and the Tao Yeo May (TYM) or "People Loving People" Fund (see below) with over 40,000. [27] The TYM's ratio of credit officers to customers is about 10 to 2,606, which is much higher than international standards.

The loan products of microfinance institutions include two common loan types and emergency capital. The time limit for loans ranges from three to twenty-four months, with loan amounts typically between 500,000 and 30 million VND, though the average loan amounts are about 3 million VND, with interest rates between one and 1.5 per cent per month.[28]

The TYM Fund

Established in 1993, the TYM Fund is managed by the Vietnam Women's Union. Initially, it was modelled after the Grameen Bank and was later adapted to the conditions specific to Vietnamese microfinance. Members are poor women in good health between the ages of 18 and 55 who have permanent residence in the locality and who are the main wage earners in the family. Per capita monthly income is below 100,000 VND/ USD $6.5.[29] The standard TYM model involves groups of five members, in clusters of 30-40 members, using the structure as a mechanism to generate capital. The loans are from 500,000 to over 15 million VND with repayment of principal and interest on a weekly basis. A mortgage is not required as collateral.

The CEP – Capital Aid Fund for Employment of the Poor

The Capital Aid Fund for Employment of the Poor (CEP) is a poverty-focused Vietnamese microfinance institution that was set up by the Labour Federation of Ho Chi Minh City (HCMC) in November 1991. The CEP soon converted to the Grameen Bank model. Borrowers were organized in groups of five members and met monthly in the group leaders' houses to repay loans. In December 2005, CEP had 59,868 active loan clients, making it the largest non-government microfinance institution in Vietnam. Some key findings from the CEP Annual Report 2009 are given below:[30]

- CEP had 134,141 active loan clients with an average loan size of $374. For a first-time client the average loan size was $288.
- 78 per cent of CEP clients repay their loans in equal weekly instalments over a 40-week period, 5 per cent of clients repay on a daily basis and 17 per cent on a monthly basis.
- 64 per cent of all loans were used for working capital to fund trading activities, and 10 per cent of all loans were used to make housing and sanitation improvements.
- CEP had 140,886 savings clients with an average savings balance of $66.
- 76 per cent of CEP clients were women.
- 90 per cent of CEP's first-time clients were defined as either "poor" or "poorest" with respect to the CEP poverty classification. The basis for this classification is the income-based poverty line defined by the Hunger Eradication and Poverty Reduction Programme for HCMC, augmented by a measure of assets, housing quality, and dependency.
- Clients were prioritized for loans on the basis of their poverty status with the poorer client given the higher priority for inclusion within the programme.

Other Microfinance Institutions

A number of other microfinance institutions perform activities in addition to financial ones, such as consultancy, training, project development and research, support in economic development, and so on. One example is the Microfinance and Community Development Institute (MACDI), which is a non-governmental financial and social scientific organization established in 2007 that has been awarded an operating license from the Ministry of Science and Technology.

In addition, some non-governmental organizations have rekindled the idea of forming microfinancial institutions for the poor through a process of implementing community development projects in the provinces. For example, the group Environment and Development in Action (ENDA) began associating credit institutions at project sites in different cities with the aim of forming the National Community Development Fund (CDF). By coordinating ENDA with the Vietnam Association of Municipalities, over fifteen cities have been linked to deploy the model.

More than eighty per cent of the members of CDF are women, many representing groups and credit institutions involved in community development projects. Currently, apart from meeting the demand for business and production loans, credit groups and organizations in the city have moved towards multi-purpose products including credit to make improvements in infrastructure and housing.

Unofficial Types of Borrower Groups

Various kinds of informal credit groups have traditionally been formed by people in the community—called "hεi," "hÍ," or "phýÝng" in Vietnamese, who are moneylenders who charge very high usury interest rates of 20-60 per cent per month. It is often poor families, especially women, who access this resource because they do not have the mortgage required by the official credit institutions. There is a very high risk connected to this kind of loan since it is not regulated by either national or local governmental associations.

The Role of Microcredit in Poverty Reduction and the Empowerment of Women

For assistance in the form of microcredit and small loans with short-term repayment, poor women usually seek out semi-formal or informal microfinance institutions rather than the formal ones. Microcredit gives women the opportunity to access more formal loans and reduce usury while helping them manage their family expenses, using the loans for appropriate purposes to improve the income and living conditions of their families. Women can also accumulate earnings as their own source of capital, or purchase needed assets. Access to credit at low interest rates is considered the main purpose of engaging in microfinancial activity.

Microcredit also has a social dimension for women. Through the methods applied by several credit organizations, members have the opportunity to participate in group activities such as self-organization and workflow management. Training sessions allow participants to gain knowledge and skills that help them to manage their capital. The trainings also offer a chance for the women to meet and share their experiences of work and life, and thereby become more confident in knowing how to control their own business. In addition, microcredit can facilitate a change in women's social position: for instance, gaining a voice in the family and community as women's roles become more important by being involved in the financial decision-making processes. Thus, microcredit is considered a means of enhancing women's capacities and status.

Poverty Alleviation

Microcredit and microfinancial models are key elements of poverty alleviation in Vietnam. This assertion is supported by the positive changes these models have facilitated for many people. According to a report by the TYM Fund presented at the international conference on 'Micro-Credit in Poverty Reduction: Objectives and Challenges' held in Ho Chi Minh City in 2003, within five to six years of joining the TYM Fund, 96 per cent of household members had built houses and the income level of members had increased by 176 per cent.

CEP: Client Household Poverty Movement

Client household poverty levels, as well as client poverty movement (improvement or decline) over time, are assessed by the CEP using a composite indicator made up of a client's household income, household assets, housing condition, and dependency level. Based on these factors, a client's household is classified into one of the following categories: poorest, poor, and moderately poor. The income measure is based on that of the Vietnamese government's Hunger Eradication and Poverty Reduction programme. Because each client that joins the CEP programme is assessed in this manner, it is possible to use the classification as a comparative tool for assessment of clients on the basis of different loan durations. Table 1 below summarizes some key points from each classification.

Table 1: CEP Poverty Classification Summary

Household Classification	*Dependency Ratio*	*Income (USD per day)**	*Assets*	*Housing*
Poorest	3 or more	Less than 0.65 (U) Less than 0.43 (R)	None to minimal, and of low quality	Low quality, non-permanent housing, lacking access to water and electricity
Poor	Between 2 and 3	0.65 - 0.86 (U) 0.43 - 0.65 (R)	Old and of low quality	Low quality, semi-permanent, but with access to electricity and water
Moderately Poor	Less than 2	More than 0.86 (U) More than 0.65 (R)	Low to medium quality	Permanent, owned outright with direct access to electricity and water

(U) refers to clients in urban areas and (R) to clients in rural areas. Source: Thi Hoang Van, Nguyen (2005).[31]

Table 2 provides a summary of findings on the poverty movement of clients. It shows a significant improvement in the overall well-being of households among each of the three client types, based on those who have remained with the CEP programme over a forty-three month period. Furthermore, the greatest level of improvement in the clients' poverty status was identified at the beginning of their participation in the CEP programme. Within the three client type categories, the percentage of clients that remained poorest after forty-three months fell to 2 per cent for daily clients, 8.5 per cent for weekly clients, and 0 per cent for monthly clients. This is a significant decrease in the number of clients classified as "poorest" when compared to the metrics gathered upon entry into the programme, irrespective of loan type.

Table 2: Client Household Poverty Movement – Percentage of Clients in Each Poverty Category: Daily, Weekly and Monthly Clients (Baseline = Classification on Entry into the CEP Programme)

	Overall Poverty Classification		
Client Classification	*Poorest (%)*	*Poor (%)*	*Moderately Poor (%)*
Daily			
Baseline (average May 2002)	27.5	52.9	19.6
November 2003	5.9	62.7	31.4
December 2005	2.0	52.9	45.1
Weekly			
Baseline (average May 2002)	37.1	55.4	7.5
November 2003	11.3	68.1	20.6
December 2005	8.5	54.9	36.6
Monthly			
Baseline (average May 2002)	27.6	41.4	31.0
November 2003	6.9	48.3	44.8
December 2005	0.0	31.0	69.0

Source: Table 6, CEP Impact Assessment, February, 2006, p. 16.

Client households had significantly increased their incomes after joining the CEP (43 months from May 2002 through December, 2005). The increase in income ranged from 85.7 per cent to 123.6 per cent after 43 months.

Table 3: Average Per Capita Household Income Increase (in US Dollars)

	Income Per Day Upon Entry	*Income Per Day in December 2005*
Daily clients	USD 0.94	USD 2.01
Weekly clients	USD 0.70	USD 1.53
Monthly clients	USD 0.98	USD 1.74

Source: Based on the data of the CEP Impact Assessment, 2006

Besides the increase in income, CEP's assessment also showed that households increased their assets and obtained better housing conditions, employment opportunities, and resources for educational expenses.

Empowerment of Women

As mentioned above, microcredit and microfinancial lending play an important role in the empowerment of women beyond contributing to the reduction of poverty. Data from relèvant organizations show that female members account for approximately 80-100 per cent of membership (CEP: 76 percent; TYM: 100 per cent female).

Most credit programmes have applied an organizational form involving groups with around five to ten people or more, in which the members themselves organize and manage group activities. All members, as well as the group management board, are trained to understand the purpose, operations, and management of their own groups. Through the knowledge and skills derived from participation in groups, and through the use and management of capital, women become more confident, take on all the work of production and business, have a voice in their families, and participate in community decisions. Thus, the social position of these women has improved.

CEP's Assessment of the Empowerment of Women

The empowerment of women is a significant objective of CEP's operations. CEP addresses this issue by providing loans predominantly to women and by promoting greater interaction of recipient women with their communities. The provision of credit to a largely female clientele empowers women by providing them with the capacity to generate their own income and decide on how to spend it.

As noted above, this financial empowerment may lead to greater equality and integration in other social areas, for instance, in general decision-making within the household. Supplementing those benefits are the close relationships that clients maintain with each other due to the group-based lending methodology. The formation of client groups enables a social network to develop where issues can be discussed and support can be found.

Data from CEP support these claims. Female clients were asked whether they participated to a greater extent in the decisions made within the household and community since joining the CEP programme. Table 4 depicts the findings, which imply that women who stay in the programme for the full forty-three months grow in confidence and feel that they are participating more significantly in decision-making processes within the household and community.

Table 4: Percentage of CEP Female Clients Who Participate to a Greater Extent in the Making of Community and Household Decisions, by Type of Client

	Daily Clients (%)	*Weekly Clients (%)*	*Monthly Clients (%)*
Household General Decisions	50.0	55.1	64.3
Household Financial Decisions	57.1	60.4	78.6
Community Decisions	40.5	38.0	85.7

Source: Table 15, CEP Impact Aassessment, 2006, p. 21.

In addition, clients were asked whether the group and centre meetings provided them with the opportunity to share experiences and raise issues of concern. Sixty-two per cent of daily clients, seventy-five per cent of weekly clients, and seventy-nine per cent of monthly clients indicated that this had been the case. However, only forty-three per cent of daily clients, fifty-nine per cent of weekly clients, and seventy-one per cent of monthly clients stated that they actively took part in such discussions. Thus, a significant proportion of clients did not actively take part in these forums.

Table 5 below shows that the proportion of female clients who participated to a greater extent was higher for clients in their fifth loan cycle than for clients in their second loan cycle. This suggests that the longer that clients remain with the CEP programme, the more they grow in confidence and feel that they are more significantly participating in the decisions of the household and community.

Table 5: Percentage of Female Clients Who Since Joining CEP Participate to a Greater Extent in the Making of community and Household Decisions, by Loan Cycle

	2 Loan Cycle Clients		*5 Loan Cycle Clients*	
	Urban (%)	*Rural (%)*	*Urban (%)*	*Rural (%)*
Household General Decisions	35.8	45.5	50.0	53.2
Household Financial Decisions	40.5	46.2	50.7	54.0
Community Decisions	30.4	37.1	43.5	39.6

Source: Table 34, CEP Impact Assessment, 2006, p. 32

Enhancement of Women's Status Due to Participation in Credit Groups

In a yearly group assessment, thirteen out of fourteen members (92.8 per cent) of a saving-credit group in district 8 in Ho Chi Minh City said that thanks to their participation in savings-credit activity and their acquisition of credit, they have prestige in their family. They are now being treated with respect by their husbands and children since they can contribute more to their family income and meet the needs of their children.

A group leader in Danang City, in a meeting to share experience with visitors and specialists, happily said that her hands no longer shake nor does she speak with a wavering voice like the first time when she facilitated or chaired a group meeting. Many women in the savings-credit groups have opportunities to go beyond their community and meet people from other communities and localities, even people from abroad and donors. For some women it was a moving experience to visit areas outside their own communities for the first time.

Moreover, women selected as group leaders have more

prestige in the community, and many group members have become members of the Women's Union or trade unions. These organizations give members of the savings-credit groups a chance to participate more in community activities and hence develop social relations and social assets.

Microcredit and Development in Vietnam: Challenges

Currently, microfinance institutions such as CEP and TYM are in the process of formalizing the guidelines of their banking models. However, the completion of this process requires a long-term outlook. For one thing, microfinance experts have identified challenging conditions for microfinance in Vietnam because of the limited number of members with expertise and experience in management, accounting, and banking. Another key challenge for Vietnamese microfinance institutions involves information management, which is currently handled manually making it difficult to scale up operations and expand.

International aid organizations supporting economic development programmes have observed that the provision of low interest, small-scale, collateral free loans by state-owned banks distorts the market for microfinance/microcredit institutions (MFIs) in Vietnam. Besides the government policy of subsidizing official interest rates, a 2005 directive of the State Bank of Vietnam laid down a minimum capital requirement of MFIs. According to one study, private players and several NGOs focusing on microcredit are at a critical juncture—if they fail to reach minimum capital requirements they may be forced to close their credit programmes by the government and if they fail to reach financial self-sustainability they run the risk of losing donor funding.[32] They may have to cease to be microfinance institutions that focus on poverty alleviation and switch to more commercial objectives to survive. Either of these scenarios would have an extremely negative impact on the nearly 70 per cent of poor households that still do not have access to vital credit services in Vietnam.[33]

As we have seen, in regard to microcredit, women still represent the major component of total borrowing. As loans are limited in terms of size, the development of businesses and level of production are limited, making it difficult for borrowers to get a broader vision of the potential of taking microcredit loans. Still, in the case of the cities building a network of urban Community Development Fund (CDF) efforts to form larger-scale institutions for savings-credit groups in communities, these efforts have improved the lives of group members, especially women. The Community Development Fund is bolstered by the Association of Cities of Vietnam (ACVN), a specialized technical agency, to expand operations into other provinces and cities.

By being associated with credit institutions in other localities, women group leaders and group members have increased their understanding of business principles, which has enabled them to perform activities beyond credit in such areas as housing and infrastructure. However, small credit groups at the community level experience many obstacles in terms of mechanisms, human resources, and procedures once they enter the world of microfinance.

Some cities show positive signs of understanding the nature of credit activities and their importance in contributing to improvement in the lives of poor households. However, it often remains a challenge to convince high-level actors of the relationship between planning, home improvement, financing, and microcredit. More time is needed for microcredit to be normalized in the society, and for improvement in the management skills of women leaders in microcredit institutions.

In short, although there are controversies and challenges, microcredit has without any doubt led to positive changes for poor women all over Vietnam. The institutions of microcredit and microfinance are still extremely relevant to and essential for poverty reduction and the empowerment of women in poor communities across the country. It is to be hoped that these activities will continue to empower and increase the capacity of women in a direction consistent with global economic and social change.

NOTES

1. *Vietnam 2016*. New Delhi: Embassy of the Socialist Republic of Vietnam.

2. World Bank, 2012. *Vietnam Poverty Assessment 2012. 'Well Begun, Not Yet Done: Vietnam's Remarkable Progress on Poverty Reduction and the Emerging Challenges.'* Hanoi: World Bank] HEPR was expanded to all of Vietnam by the Prime Minister's Decision No 133/QĐ-TTg dated July 23, 1998. See: The Programme Poverty Alleviation of Ho Chi Minh City—Period 2009-2015. http://datafile.chinhphu.vn/file-remote-v2/DownloadServlet?filePath=vbpq/2010/04/98579_QD22UB2.RTF.
3. UN site: https://www.un.org/esa/socdev/egms/docs/2009/Ghana/ Quan.pdf
4. World Bank, 2012, ibid.
5. World Bank, Development Research Group, 2008. "Vietnam – Poverty Headcount Ratio," *Index Mundi, 2008:*http://indexmundi.com/facts/vietnam/poverty-headcount-ratio.
6. www.un.org/esa/socdev/egms/docs/2009/Ghana/Quan.pdf
7. Valerie Kosel in World Bank, 2012, ibid.
9. Asian Development Bank 2012. Vietnam: Country Partnership Strategy (2012-2015) – Poverty Analysis (Summary) at https://www.adb.org/sites/default/files/linked-documents/cps-vie-2012-2015-pa.pdf., and World Bank, 2012, ibid.
8. World Bank, 2012. ibid.
9. World Bank, 2012. ibid.: p.13 Box 1.1 How Does Vietnam Monitor Progress at Reducing Poverty?
10. World Bank, 2012. ibid.
12. World Bank, 2012. ibid., p. 52, Table 2.5 Poverty Estimates for 2010.
13. However, according to the World Bank it is 20.7 per cent by 2010. http://www.mo.be/sites/default/files/article/attachment/Well%20Begun,%20Not%20Yet%20Done.%20Vietnam%E2%80%99s%20Remarkable%20Progress%20on%20Poverty%20Reduction.pdf
14. World Bank, 2012, ibid.
15. http:// www moj.gov.vn/vbpq/lists/vn20bn%20php%20lut/view_detail.aspx? itemid=18067.
16. World Bank, 2012. ibid., p.52, based on official MOLISA poverty lines.
17. Decree No. 28/2005/ND-CP of March 9, 2005.
18. Circular 02/2008/NĐ-CP to Implement Decree 28/2005/NĐ-CP.
19. Swain, R.B., N. Van Sanh, and V.V. Tuan. "Microfinance and Poverty Reduction in the Mekong Delta in Vietnam." *African and Asian Studies* 7.2-3. (2008): 2-3.

20. Vietnam Bank for Social Policies. "Microfinance—An Efficient Tool in Hunger Alleviation and Poverty Reduction, the news from Vietnam Bank of Social Policy," *VBSP*, August 27, 2008, May 20, 2010. http://www.vbsp.org.vn/viewarticle.php?artid= 995.
21. Hong Son Nghiem and James Lawrenceson, 2005. "The Nature of NGO Microfinance in Vietnam and Stakeholders' Perception of Effectiveness." *East Asia Economic Research Group Discussion Paper No. 3*, October 2005, Table 1, p. 6. Queensland: School of Economics, University of Queensland.
22. Banking with the Poor Network. "Vietnam Bank for Agriculture and Rural Development (VBARD) or AGRIBANK," *BWTP*, April, 2003. http://www.bwtp.org/arcm/vietnam/II_Organizations/MF_Providers/VBARD.htm.
23. BWTP - Asia Resource Centre for Microfinance, 2005. https://www.microfinancegateway.org/.../mfg-en-paper-vietnam-microfinance-country-profile-2005.pdf and
24. Government Decision No. 131/2002/QD – TTg
25. Vietnam Bank for Social Policies. "Home Page," *VBSP*, 2002. http://vbsp.org.vn/evbsp/.
26. VBSP document: http//www.vbsp.org.in/evbsp/view_detail.php?mtt=118&mamm=31
27. Kiva. "TYM Fund," *Kiva*, 2010. http://www.kiva.org/partners/67. For CEP date, see http://www.mixmarket.org/mfi/cep.
28. The State Bank of Vietnam. "MHN, Disclosure of Microfinance Institutions Financed from Reciprocal Capital Support Funds"*SBV*, May 18, 2010. http://www.sbv.gov.vn/vn/home/tinHDNH. jsp?tin=6044.
29. Tran, N. and T See Yun. "Good and Bad Practices in Micro-Insurance." *TYM's Mutual Assistance, Vietnam* 3. (2004): 1-37.
30. Capital Aid Fund for Employment of the Poor. "An Impact Assessment of the Microfinance Institution Capital Aid Fund for Employment of the Poor." *CEP Impact Assesments.* (2006): 1-82.
31. CEP Impact Assessment submitted to AusAid and Ho Chi Minh City Federation of Labour, February 2006. Capital Aid Fund for Employment of the Poor submitted to AusAid, 2006.
32. Hong Son Nghiem and James Lawrenceson, 2005. "The Nature of NGO Microfinance in in Vietnam and Stakeholders' Perception of Effectiveness," *East Asia Economic Research Group Discussion Paper No. 3*, October, 2005, p. 17. University of Queensland, School of Economics: www.uq.edu.au/economics/eaerg/dp10305.pdf.
33. Hong Son Nghiem and James Lawrenceson, 2005. ibid.

5

Making of 'Entrepreneurs': Women and Microfinance Practices in Bangladesh

Lamia Karim

Introduction

This chapter is an ethnographic study of the effects of microcredit on gender relations in rural Bangladesh. Focusing on the 2006 Nobel Peace Prize winner, the Grameen Bank of Bangladesh and three other leading non-governmental organizations (NGOs) in the country, I analyse the role of gender in the expansion of globalization and neoliberalism in Bangladesh. The Grameen Bank has become a global symbol of poor women's empowerment and is celebrated for its 98 per cent loan recovery. In this article, I examine some of the NGO tactics behind the loan recovery programmes. In particular, I examine how Bangladeshi rural women's 'honour' and 'shame' are instrumentally appropriated by Micro Finance Institutions (MFIs) in the furtherance of their capitalist interests to maximize profit at the cost of poor.

While economic globalization refers to the removal of trade barriers and open markets, its effects on communities are variable, contingent, and locally constructed. This article is an interpretation of these variables, contingent, and local expressions of grassroots globalization through an ethnographic study of globalization and neoliberalism in rural Bangladesh. It examines how globalization and neoliberalism are brought to the grassroots—the most intimate sphere of the social, the home and women—through the modernist discourse of women's empowerment through microcredit.

Arjun Appadurai has defined grassroots globalization as:

> ... new forms of social mobilization that proceed independently of the actions of corporate capital and the nation-state system . . . these social forms rely on strategies, visions, and horizons for globalization on behalf of the poor . . . this kind of globalization strives for a democratic and autonomous standing in respect to the various forms by which global power seeks to further its dominions. (2001: 3)

The grassroots globalization, I studied in Bangladesh, is contrary to Appadurai's model. It works through and not against corporate capital, donors, state, NGOs, and members of civil society, and creates complex new maps of social interdependencies that are laden with the financial investments of multiple actors at the local, national, and global levels. Grassroots globalization weakens the sovereignty of the patriarchal home, family, and replaces it with the sovereignty of the market through NGOs, contracts, courts, juridical subjects, and the remaking of subjects as a community police to safeguard their investments. The developmental NGO is the purveyor of this new economic sovereignty that is represented by corporate capital interests and local institutional interests (NGOs), and is an architect of neoliberalism within a modernist developmental discourse of poor women's empowerment through the market.

According to David Harvey neoliberalism believes that "Human well-being can best be advanced by liberating individual entrepreneurial freedoms and skills within an institutional framework characterized by strong private property rights, free markets and free trade. The role of the state is to create and preserve an appropriate framework to such practices" (Harvey 2005: 2). The role of the state should be to create an environment that unleashes these entrepreneurial urges and to withdraw from the management of public life. Bangladesh offers the paradigmatic site for an analysis of neoliberalism and women's roles as entrepreneurs. It is home to some of the most innovative NGOs in the world including the 2006 Nobel Prize winner the Grameen Bank and Building Resources Across Communities (BRAC), the largest NGO in the world.

Microfinance is the extension of small loans to poor women to start income-generating activities. Microfinance *aka* the Grameen model is also the promoter of the figure of the celebrated rural female entrepreneur—the cell phone lady, the chick breeder, egg-seller and dairy-cow owner. In this new climate of neoliberalism and shrinking funds, many NGOs were driven more by profit and financial viability than by concerns about the welfare of their poor female clients. Signalling this transformation from social work to for-profit motives, and the use of their members as internal markets has been termed as NGO "poverty enterprise" (Mannan 2009).

Thus, what had started out as the welfare of the poor had, over time, transformed into the capitalist welfare of NGOs. When the US Congress passed the Percy Amendment 1973 it required all USAID offices to integrate women into all aspects of their programmes. The idea was to increase women's participation in national economies and to reduce gender-related obstacles to education, work, healthcare and legal rights. This was followed by the United Nations declaration of 1975-1985 as the Decade of Women. For the next decade, UN and its affiliates prioritized women in all spheres of their development efforts. As a part of that the UN also declared 2005 as the year of microcredit since it seemed to be helping women financially. NGOs were the first responders to this call for the integration of women into development policies. They worked in the rural areas with direct access to women.

In this new rhetoric of Women-in-Development (WID), later called Gender and Development (GAD), the third world woman was conceptualized as an autonomous, sovereign subject who freely made rational choices in the market. She was thrifty, hard working, entrepreneurial and a competent manager of resources. The idea that NGOs were seamlessly introducing millions of marginalized women, majority of them borrowers of microfinance into the economy as 'entrepreneurs' and 'rights-bearing subjects' with very few adverse effects, fed into the aspirations of Western donors to create societies similar to European democracies. NGOs and their sponsors alike invoked this mantra of empowering poor women (Hashemi, Schuler and

Riley, 1996). Research from WID feminists also demonstrated that investing in women was an investment in children and families (Mayoux, 1999). NGOs were at the forefront of translating this WID idea into practice. Termed as the "add women and stir," approach, feminists critiqued this policy as essentially window-dressing that did not challenge existing gender dynamics and inequalities, and in some instances even exacerbated them.

At an epistemological level, there was no discussion of what it meant to frame development programmes and policies in terms of gender and not women. This "third world woman" was a "hyperreal" woman. Her abilities and incredible entrepreneurship was so celebrated and inflated *aka* Grameen Bank that the idea of this woman was substituted for the real woman on the ground. In development discourse, little attention was paid to men's social roles and labour, or how South Asian women were embedded in social relations with their husbands, in-laws, and kin, and how those relations circumscribed their behaviors. Besides women were also responsible to observe rituals relating to births, death and marriages for which they need money and were likely spend that loan for those rituals instead of income-generating activities. NGOs and their sponsors alike invoked this *mantra* of empowering poor women. What this rhetoric did not take into account was how inequality, caste, class, social hierarchies, rituals and feudalism, circumscribed and influenced social relations differently across the South Asian spectrum.

The question of how power relations shaped women's lives was restricted to a narrow analysis of rural patriarchy with scant attention to how NGOs themselves and their agents appropriated existing gender roles and power relations to exercise their will over their female members. Unlike rural men, women worked in the domestic sphere. They could join NGO groups and attend meetings, a regular feature of these rural development NGOs. Many thought by doing so, Muslim women became empowered.

They were also sought as 'credit-worthy' and reliable members because they were easier to police and dominate than rural men who would speak back to NGO managers. Men also had more physical mobility to leave the village if they could not pay the loans. These features of rural social life remained largely unaddressed in NGO-sponsored research. As long as NGOs increased women members in their programmes and hiring practices, and publicly promoted their fight against gender discrimination, the money flowed in from their Western donors.

At the centre of this global success story stands the lone female entrepreneur, often a poor, illiterate homemaker, who supposedly makes free choices in the market and excels with her entrepreneurial skills in spite of risks. The Grameen Bank model rests on the idea of the individual entrepreneur who, with the help of microcredit, becomes self-employed, owns private property (the assets she builds with the loans), and sells her fruits of labour in the market.

This out-of-the-home entrepreneur links seamlessly with neoliberal ideas of self-help and ownership ethics. In rural areas, in practice, it is the men control the loans, and it is rare to find a female entrepreneur unless she already has some marketable skills (Fernando 1997; 2006; Karim 2011; Rahman 1999). While new studies dispute the claims of microfinance proponents quite effectively (Roodman 2012; Bateman 2010; Karim 2011; Dichter 2007; Rahman 1999), microfinance still continues to thrive and attract followers who are like "evangelicals" for microfinance (Kristof and Wu Dunn, 2009). Hence one often finds people affiliated with MFIs and development organizations (World Bank, DFID, CIDA for example) writing in support of the work of MFIs. The fact that such a close relationship between the author and the organization poses conflicts of interest (does one bite the hand that feeds it?) is seldom addressed.

Yet there is another aspect to the widespread support for microfinance programmes, and that has to do with idea of altruism. Many people in the West support Grameen Bank and microfinance programmes and are reluctant to hear negative findings from research because these narratives of empowerment make people feeds into an innate need for altruism among those who are privileged. One can help the world's poor from the comfort of one's office or living-room through donations made to MFIs that show glossy images of happy "third world women" with the businesses they have started a sewing machine, a cow, a chicken farm, a tea-shop, and so on. Increasingly, MFIs have turned to individuals to sponsor their programmes in the developing world (see Kiva.org[1] for example). What is less known is what happened to these women and the businesses a year down the road. It has been well-documented that the majority of NGOs working with microfinance loans do not do market surveys before extending loans. Now that so many organizations extend them loans, the NGOs try to fulfil the targets. So they forget basic principles of the microcredit namely, if raw materials are available or not, cohesive of the group, etc. Further studies are not carried out to see how many chick farmers, cell phone operators, dairy cow breeders a rural economy can sustain. Bateman has termed this the "displacement" problem of microfinance (2010). That is, when new entrants come into the market place purveying similar goods and services and drive down prices, existing businesses lose money, and the overall net effect on the economy is usually zero. Thus, in economic terms microfinance businesses can be termed as zero-sum games. Thus the author concluded that microfinance did pose a major barrier for sustainable development and to the sustainable poverty reduction. He has analysed many cases studies in different parts of the world. Further women do not get a chance to become empowered!

The question still remains, why has microfinance galvanized so many people around the world, and why does it continue to be such a powerful instrument of poverty alleviation in spite of all these hurdles? The pioneering institution of microfinance, the Grameen Bank, made its reputation through targeting poor Muslim women in Bangladesh. The targeting of women, especially Muslim women as entrepreneurs, has been key to the wide success of the Bank and its microfinance programme in its initial phase. The image of Muslim women in Bangladesh walking in public without a scarf on head, meeting in group at loan centres, go to the bank alone, handling money are considered to be positive images. The Bank has shown to the west how poor and illiterate Muslim women form a bulwark against Islamic patriarchy. Here patriarchy refers to Islamic notions of seclusion for women and religious proscriptions against women's work in the public sphere. By dissolving the private/public distinction, women's work can gradually begin to weaken the patriarchy from within and enable market forces to penetrate rural communities. Thus, microfinance becomes an instrument of remaking Muslim societies into market societies that are similar to Western societal norms. The important role of Muslim women in the Grameen Bank/ microfinance story must not be underemphasized.

In addition to the above, there are three key reasons for its wide reception that I have outlined below that are both economical and ideological.

Female Entrepreneur

Microfinance is based on the idea of individual female entrepreneurship, and it makes the individual, and not the State, the driver of economic change (Bateman and Chang, 2012). The microfinance model seamlessly links up with current neoliberal ideas of development that sees the role of the state as limited. If we replace the term credit with debt, microfinance is reconfigured as a relationship of power and inequality between the creditor (the lender) and the financially-strapped woman (the borrower). Let us now ask, what happens to poor women when they are entangled in relations of debt? What are the social realties within which these women and loans operate? Most of the women borrowers live in extended family structures with kin and social obligations. These women's identities are relational, and are shaped by a number of factors such as marital, kinship, ethnic, and tribal allegiances. However, the microfinance literature tends to conceptualize women borrowers as autonomous subjects who independently make choices in the market.

There are several categories of women who can use microfinance loans productively. They are usually women who have marketable skills, own small businesses, have a certain market savvy, or are widows, abandoned or divorced, that is, they do not have a husband who will lay claim on their income. Yet this is an insignificant number within the vast pool of borrowers. Women, even if they have marketable skills but do not possess market access, often find themselves beholden to their husbands and male relatives. Thus, microfinance has to be located within the social constraints that poor people, particularly women face.

Grameen Bank has claimed that its work has reduced moneylending in Bangladesh. In fact, the opposite has occurred. Through these loans, formerly asset-less women and their families now have access to disposable cash that the moneylender can recoup. So, the traditional moneylender, who usually lends at 120 per cent interest rate, has expanded his net of financially-solvent customers that he can lend to. More interestingly, an innovative entrepreneurial subject that has emerged from this contact between loans and women is that of the petty female moneylender. Thus, instead of becoming small business operators, an activity that was not always encouraged by their husbands and families, women could stay at home and lend to traders, richer farmers and others in the community. In fact, there are very few female entrepreneurs in rural society. In majority of cases, their husbands use the loans. Thus, loans circulated from the women to a wider group of people, and if they could invest successfully, they paid the female moneylender the principal plus interest. Thus, instead of creating entrepreneurs, microfinance in Bangladesh has reproduced moneylending as a profitable and less-risky option for these rural women, which was not the intent of the Grameen and other MFIs working in this area.

Although the women were the borrowers of loans, I found that in almost 90 per cent of cases, men controlled the use of the loans, often with adverse effects on women. Moreover, they borrowed from five to six MFIs, which led to an accumulation of debt that many could not manage over time. When defaults occurred, and they occurred routinely for a variety of reasons, it resulted in heightened shame and pressure on the defaulting woman. Women who could not pay due to unforeseen circumstances (illness, poor investment decisions, theft of property) were subjected to public shaming by group members who were pressured by microfinance institutions to recover the money. MFI managers would threaten group members that if they could not recover the defaulted sum, either they would have to pay, or they would lose future loans. Thus, the defaulter woman would face the ire of the community who now saw her as the person who had broken faith with the group. Instead of developing social solidarity among the members, these loans led to an increase in intra-group friction. In a face-to-face society like Bangladesh, the conduct of women is strictly controlled, and women are the custodians of family honour. Shaming women publicly brought dishonour on the men, and by extension on the family. Hence, poor women bore the social costs of microfinance often with very adverse effects on their lives.

98 Per cent Rate of Loan Recovery

The Grameen Bank with its much-celebrated 98 per cent rate of loan recovery has effectively demonstrated to the financial community that the poor are 'bankable,' that is, the poor form a large pool of credit-strapped people who desperately need access to capital and they will repay those loans. In other words, it has demonstrated that the poor constitute a viable market for commercial banks. MFIs through high rates of loan recovery have shown that the poor have a need for loans, and that they pay back their loans. This has led to a profusion of dollars from aid organizations, corporations, and investors who see MFIs as combining profit with social good. Yet many MFIs depend on high interest rates and fees, often with many hidden costs, to sustain their operating costs. Thus, the poor borrowers pay for the salaries and overhead costs for many MFIs through the fees and interest charged to them. Often these overhead costs are out of sync with local community standards, and one often sees jarring images of MFI officers driving in SUVs while their borrowers walk bare feet.

A key function of loans is consumption smoothening for its borrowers, and often loans do not go into activities that they are intended for. In fact, many borrowers pay for medical expenses, dowries, home repairs, etc. with loans. Yet loans continue to be recovered at phenomenal rates, and these MFIs operate successfully. So, what is the story behind these phenomenal rates? First, it is important to make a distinction between loan repayment, that is, loans that are voluntarily given, and loan recovery, that is, loans that are recovered by applying pressure on the borrower. In many instances, MFIs force their borrowers to repay by applying pressure through community members and other tactics available to them, the police and elites (Karim 2011). In face-to- face communities, people fear loss of face, and try to manage their affairs to keep public humiliation to a minimum. Often women, when they cannot pay, will borrow from other sources such as from each other, the traditional moneylender, or kin to cover the default sum. As noted in the previous segment, it ties individual borrowers with a wider group and when a default occurs it sends ripple effects through a wide range of people, which heightens tension and friction within the group.

Constructing Markets

Microfinance connects the most intimate sphere of private life, the home and women, with the larger world of markets. Through these loans, money, commodities, and ideas circulate within communities integrating the local economy with the global. For example, Telenor of Norway and Grameen Bank jointly created the Grameen Polli Phone (Village Phone) programme that sold cell phones to rural women. Called Grameen Phone Ladies, these women made an income by selling time on their cell phones to rural people to make calls. The making of women as phone operators had some positive social impacts on women's lives. Homes of women who had become Phone Ladies were called Phone Bari (house with phone). In the early 2000s, it denoted status to such families. Bangladesh has a large number of overseas workers in the Middle East, Malaysia, UK and US, so the majority of the calls would be made at night. If the husband was present, then he would handle the calls. In his absence, the woman would appear in front of strangers and engage in the financial transaction. Thus in some instances, women were able to occupy a new kind of a social identity.

But these women also bore the social costs of introducing cell phone technology to the rural economy. The phones with their paraphernalia (phone, antenna, batteries, charger, security deposit, pension scheme, connection fee) cost approximately $700 in the early 2000s (Karim 2011, 97), although prices later fell as the price of phones went down. While initially many of the Grameen Phone Ladies had made money, very soon other cell phone companies moved into rural areas, and undersold the Grameen Phone Ladies. Cell phones have become universal in rural areas as a reliable means of communication, and it costs very little to purchase a phone or to make phone calls. Many of the women who had taken loans to operate their phone business, saw themselves stuck with huge debts that they had to repay although their phone business had declined severely. The point here is that Grameen Polli Phone was able to use these poor women, who remained dependent on it for access to much-needed cash, to usher in new market forces. These women had little or no knowledge of how competition worked in an open market. Thus, I would argue that they were used instrumentally to create an environment hospitable for corporations to enter and corner new markets (Karim 2011).

Thus it can be argued that microfinance instead of helping women to become empowered and reduce poverty, makes them indebted and poor.

NOTES

1. Kiva.org or Kiva Micro funds is a non-profit organization that allows people to lend money via Internet to low income entrepreneurs in over 80 countries. Its mission is to connect people through lending to alleviate poverty.

REFERENCES

Appadurai, Arjun (2001). 'Grassroots Globalization and the Research Imagination', in Arjun Appadurai (ed.) *Globalization*, pp. 1–21. Durham, NC: Duke University Press.

Bateman, Milford (2010). *Why Doesn't Microfinance Work: The Destructive Rise of Local Neoliberalism*. London and New York: Zed Books.

Bateman, Milford and Chang, Ha-Joon (2012). "Microfinance and the Illusion of Development: From Hubris to Nemesis in Thirty Years," *World Economics Journal*, Vol.1, (October), pp.13-36

Dichter, Thomas and Malcom Harper. (2007). *What is Wrong with Microfinance?* Rugby, Warwickshire, UK: Practical Action.

Dichter (2007). 'A Second Look at Microfinance, The Sequence of Growth and Credit in Economic History', *Centre for Global Liberty* and Prosperity Development Policy Briefing Paper, pp. 1-17 https://object.cato.org/sites/cato.org/files/pubs/pdf/dbp1.pdf

Fernando, Jude (1997). 'Disciplining the Mother', *Ghadar,* Vol. 1, No. 1 (May), p. 30.

Fernando, Jude (1997). 'Nongovernmental Organizations, Microcredit and Empowerment of Women', *The Annals,* Vol. 554, No. 1, pp. 150-177.

Fernando, Jude (ed.) (2006). *Microfinance: Perils and Prospects*, London & New York, Routledge.

Harvey, David (2005). *A Brief History of Neoliberalism*, Oxford, UK & New York, USA: Oxford University Press.

Hashemi, S., S. Schuler, A. Riley (1996). 'Rural Credit Programmes and Women's Empowerment in Bangladesh', *World Development*, 24 (4): 635-653.

Karim, Lamia (2011). *Microfinance and Its Discontents: Women in Debt in Bangladesh*, Minneapolis & London: University of Minnesota Press.

Kristof Nicholas and Sheryl Wu Dunn (2009). *Half the Sky: Turning Oppression into Opportunity* (New York, Vintage Books).

Munnan, M. (2009). BRAC: Anatomy of a "Poverty Enterprise", *Non-Profit Management and Leadership*, 2 (2) :219-235.

Mayoux, L. (1999). 'Questioning Virtuous Spirals: Microfinance and Women's Empowerment in Africa' in Journal of International Development, Vol. 11, No. 7, December/November .957-984.

Rahman, Aminur (1999). *Women and Microcredit in Rural Bangladesh:An Anthropological Study of the Rhetoric and Realities of Grameen Bank Lending*. Boulder, Colo.: Westview Press.

Roodman, David (2012). *Due Diligence: An Impertinent Inquiry into Microfinance*, Washington, DC: Centre for Global Development.

6

An Illusion of Empowerment: The Impact of Microfinance on Women in Punjab, Pakistan

Mahlyah Laila Fahimuddin

Introduction

Microfinance is often lauded as a cure-all for the issue of widespread poverty in the developing world. Spurred by the early success of organizations such as the Grameen Bank in Bangladesh, microfinance programmes for the poor have spread across South Asia and the world. Since the institutionalization of microfinance policy in Pakistan in 2001, there has been an increased focus on microfinance as a state strategy to reduce poverty and increase economic growth.[1] Yet there have been varying degrees of attention given to the study of how microfinance systems affect women's empowerment, which is often assumed to go hand in hand with poverty alleviation efforts.[2] Even the poverty alleviation effects of microfinance are inconclusive when viewed within the context of more thorough evaluation methods. The studies that have been conducted on microfinance and microlending institutions in Pakistan lead to conflicting and unclear conclusions regarding the efficacy of microfinance in reaching the poorest of the poor and empowering women.

This chapter focuses on evaluating how effective microfinance institutions have been in reaching the poorest of the poor, and to a more limited extent, evaluating its impact on women's empowerment. Section II provides an overview of the theoretical framework on poverty and empowerment within which microfinance is situated. Section III reviews poverty trends within Pakistan. Section IV discusses the social limitations on women in Pakistan and the need for their greater social and economic empowerment. Section V introduces the methodology employed in the examination of the microfinance impact assessments. The different organizational structures of the three institutions this chapter examines are described in Section VI, while analysis of the data on each institution to assess its poverty alleviation impact are presented in Section VII. Section VIII offers some concluding remarks.

The intent of this chapter is to expose issues that microfinance donors and practitioners should consider in moving forward with developing institutions in a manner to best support the work of poverty alleviation for the most deprived sectors of Pakistan's society. I seek to assess through the data available if microfinance has had an impact on clients, if it has been successful in reaching the poorest of the poor, if support services offered by an organization have had an impact on overall quality of life, and to see if the social cohesion model that most microfinance organizations operate on is really the most effective approach at working to include the poorest in microfinance services.

Theoretical Framework

The Indian development specialist Amartya Sen, along with Pakistani economist Mahbub ul Haq, laid the groundwork for present-day human development and empowerment efforts. In the context of India, the philosophy of Sen and Jean Dreze provide the theoretical foundation for programmes like microfinance institutions and inform the theoretical lens through which we understand the meaning of poverty, poverty alleviation and empowerment. The work of ul Haq and Sen lend meaning to these measures through ul Haq's work to develop the UNDP Human Development Report, providing one of the principal frameworks for understanding the multiple dimensions of poverty.

1. Entitlements and Capabilities

One of Sen's foundational concepts, that has greatly influenced the understanding of development work is the idea of entitlements. Entitlement relations refer to the system of relationships and power that derive from ownership and the private property system. Ownership entitlements can be derived from trade, production, one's own labour or inheritance or transfer. These forms of acquisition then provide one with the ability to exchange and thus build relationships through the exchange of entitlements.[3]

While entitlements allow one to have access to power, not everyone has access to entitlements. Thus one understanding of poverty is the absence of entitlements or exclusion from the private property system. This connects to Sen's other concept of capabilities, which refers to the freedom to live an equitable lifestyle, be it in terms of living to the average life expectancy, or being literate, well nourished and safely housed.[4] Thus, in order to address poverty, one must address the issue of capability deprivation in order to build the capacity to have entitlement relationships.

2. Poverty Alleviation

While poverty has been traditionally understood in terms of basic caloric needs, an expanded concept of the greater basic needs that has developed in the modern globalized world makes it imperative to also take into consideration non-food needs. There are also generalization problems with using the basic needs approach, such as the assumption that any human being will eat only nutritious food, that the methods of eating nutritiously do not vary by region or culture and that prices, and therefore base income levels, do not vary by region. We must look instead at poverty as an issue of inequality, relative to its environment. To address its root causes an understanding of the environment and non-food as well as food needs are required.[5]

3. Women's Empowerment

The idea of women's empowerment is not clearly defined

because it is such a broad and diversely understood concept. But certain trends emerge with a few essential ideas that form a broad foundation for discussions on empowerment. In terms of empowerment and microfinance, it is clear that there must be recognition of class differences amongst women. Microfinance institutions assume women to be a homogeneous group, which translates to poor targeting in programme implementation. There is an assumption that providing women credit allows them to have independence, which leads to increased power in the household, and thus creates new generations of empowered females. But this 'virtuous cycle' is based on a series of assumptions that cannot be guaranteed. Studies show that women do not have an increase in household bargaining power past a certain loan size. Women's work burdens are increased through integration into the labour force, with a net decrease in leisure time while men's leisure time increases as they take female labour as a reason to decrease their work time. Women bear increased stress from the legal responsibility of a loan that many times male relatives squander away. Depending on the success of the small business, female children may be pulled out of school for help, thus disempowering another generation. The long-term impacts of microfinance on female empowerment cannot be clearly measured at this point, but current analysis provides a cautionary tale to the future.[6]

Poverty in Pakistan

1. International and State Indices

With 45.8 per cent of it's population subsisting on less than $2 a day, and 12.7 per cent living on less than $1.25 a day, poverty is a major issue in the state of Pakistan.[7] Poverty has been an ongoing, long-term issue for the country. Since the 1990s, Pakistan saw an increase in its impoverished population from 20 to nearly 35 per cent.[8]

The primary human development indices suggest that the impacts of poverty are felt more heavily by women than men. Pakistan is ranked 147 out of 187 on the Gender Development Index, which measures life expectancy, adult literacy and gross school enrolment, and income by gender[9]. It is 99 out of 109 countries on the Gender Empowerment Measure, which measures women's involvement in political and economic spheres.[10] Women earn less than a third as much as men, earning $1,056 to men's $3,607 annually, adjusted to purchasing power parity.[11] They have a very low adult literacy rate, with only 39.6 per cent of women over age 15 literate, compared to 67.7 per cent of men.[12] Women are primarily employed in the insecure and low income generating agriculture sector, followed by manufacturing and social services at 75 per cent, 11.8 per cent and 10 per cent, respectively, whereas only 36.9 per cent of men are employed in the agriculture sector, and 17.9 per cent in trade as compared to only 1.8 per cent of women in trade.[13]

Table 1: Composition of Male and Female Occupational Structure, 2007-08 and 2008-09

Industry	*2007-2008*			*2008-2009*		
	Total (%)	*Male (%)*	*Female (%)*	*Total (%)*	*Male (%)*	*Female (%)*
Agriculture	44.60	36.90	75.00	45.10	37.30	74.00
Manufacturing	13.00	13.30	11.80	13.00	13.30	11.90
Wholesale and Retail	14.60	17.90	1.80	16.50	20.50	1.60
Community/ Social Services	13.70	14.40	10.60	11.20	11.10	11.60

Source: *Pakistan Labour Force Survey, 2007-09*

Female poverty in Pakistan is characterized by not only disparities in employment opportunities and wages, but also by a distinct decrease in the ability to change women's position due to limitations such as low literacy, low household bargaining power, and lack of control over land and productive capital.[14]

2. *Public and Private Poverty Alleviation Strategies*

Since 2003, the government of Pakistan has been focused on developing poverty alleviation strategies to address the chronic and growing issues of poverty and its associated negative impact on human capabilities and development, including women's empowerment. The first Poverty Reduction Strategy Paper was developed around four pillars—"accelerated and broad based economic growth while maintaining macroeconomic stability, improving governance and consolidating devolution, investing in human capital, and targeted programmes with emphasis on social inclusion."[15] In consultation with various local and provincial leaders, it was deduced that poverty is most acute in rural areas, or when households have low education levels, poor access to health and social services, and/or unstable employment.[16] Thus, it is recognized that human capital and capabilities development is one of several essential components in addressing poverty alleviation.

In acknowledgement of the fact that poverty is most concentrated in rural areas, microfinance is one of the main strategies cited by the state in combating growing rates of poverty amongst rural farmers. The model of small female collectives, such as that used by lending groups under the Grameen system, is employed as a way to develop a space for women to come together and build their social capital in a safe and socially acceptable way.[17]

The Poverty Reduction Strategy Paper II of 2009 expands on the idea of empowering women by defining it as focusing on women's primary and reproductive healthcare, school enrolment and retention, and expanding their participation in the labour force.[18] It also notes that as of 2001-02, about 75 per cent of Pakistan's poor are hovering right above, or right below the national poverty line, which is calculated on the basic caloric needs model, a model that has been criticized by poverty assessment academics as a model that underrepresents the degree of poverty by neglecting the importance of indirect needs.[19]

Since 2002-03, microfinance disbursals for Khushhali Bank, the Pakistan Poverty Alleviation Fund and Zarai Taraqiati Bank Ltd. (ZTBL) have increased from 2.5 billion rupees for 218,000 clients to 13 billion rupees for over 1 million clients.[20] As coverage of microfinance is projected to grow to 3 million borrowers by 2010 and 10 million borrowers by 2015, the rapid growth is expected to be managed by the private sector Pakistan Microfinance Network in ensuring adequate outreach and sustainability of loans.[21] The Pakistan Microfinance Network developed in 1997 as a response to monitor the rapid growth of the microfinance sector. Following the 2001 Microfinance Ordinance passed by then President Musharraf, the number of microfinance firms rapidly expanded. This is excluding those enrolled in one of the National Rural Support Programmes, which has reached over 2 million rural borrowers in all provinces under a 35 million rupees portfolio.[22]

Status of Women

Women in South Asia are subject to numerous social, cultural, economic, political and physical restrictions. These restrictions play a role in reducing women's effective power over their individual agency, the household and the community. An overview of the existing constraints proves a frame of reference to measure the current and potential benefits that microfinance may have on women in the region.

1. Constraints to Women's Social Power

Historically, women throughout South Asia have experienced varying degrees of social power. In Pakistan, the rights of minority groups, including women, have been manipulated in the struggle for power between military, religious and civil leaders. In the early decades of the nation, women first saw the restriction of their rights through the power struggle between the military administration of General Ayub, and the ulema of the Jamaat-i-Islam, who were running for election in 1965. While General Ayub had passed the Muslim Family Law Ordinance, which guaranteed women's rights in marriage, he later took action to restrict women's rights in politics to prevent the Jamaat-i-Islam's candidate, who was a woman, from undermining his power. In this way, women's rights were subject to change if it could secure the power of the status quo.[23] The policies of General Zia-ul-Haq are a key example of the restricting of women's rights to secure political power. General Zia consolidated his power by allying with the conservative

Jamaat-i-Islam group. He criminalized all dissenters' actions against him, and legitimized it by having the Jamaat-i-Islam declare this to be Islamic. In the name of Islam, he passed the Shariah laws, the Hudood Ordinance, and created the Shariah court system—all of which diminished the rights and voices of women and non-Muslims in both legal and religious spheres. He succeeded in mainstreaming the idea amongst the population that "all citizens were not equal" by giving the Jamaat-i-Islam free reign over the media and schools to educate the populace with their highly conservative and discriminatory interpretation of Islam.[24]

Zia used the rhetoric of Islam to legitimize the already existing ethnic, cultural and tribal norms that restrict women's behaviour. Unlike previous leaders, who drew on the urban elite to fill the ranks of the army and leadership, Zia relied on rural and lower class men to fill his army. These were men who were educated and trained in the joint religious-military *madrassas* run by the Jamaat-i-Islam. This included men who had migrated from Pakistan into neighbouring Arab countries to work, and upon their return, brought back comparatively more socially conservative views towards women.[25] For example, the concept of *purdah*, which is a cultural norm throughout the subcontinent regardless of religious affiliation, was more rigorously enforced. It became a marker of social class for women to be segregated and secluded, as a social marker of male honour and financial stability. For women to work was a sign of low class and the inability of a male to provide for his household.[26] This was reinforced by Zia's policies restricting women from educational opportunities and from working, thus strengthening existing tribal and cultural norms towards women.[27]

The use of religious rhetoric should not be misunderstood to mean that constricting women's rights is characteristic of Islam, or Muslim societies. As Jejeebhoy and Sathar explain in their study of women's rights in Pakistan, northern India and southern India, the degree of women's empowerment varies by region rather than religion. Those in the northern regions of the subcontinent, which are traditionally patrilineal, are more likely to restrict women's rights across religious groups, whereas women in the matrilineal or bilinear south are more likely to be autonomous. Regional norms in Pakistan have been further legitimized by the application of religious rhetoric, which patriarchal men and uneducated women are unlikely to challenge.[28] Given the low literacy rate in Pakistan, it becomes clear how these norms continue to go uncontested. The application of religious rhetoric in Pakistan under Zia's reign was no more than a political manoeuver to strengthen his relationship with the powerful Jamaat-i-Islam, a political move that has had long lasting repercussions for Pakistani women, in terms of their social, political and economic progress.

2. *Constraints to Women's Political Power*

While military governments created policies that restrict women's power and mobility in social spaces, they interestingly were responsible for providing a space for women in politics. It was under General Ayub that the local government system was created, albeit as a mechanism to legitimize his political power. General Zia built upon the model under his reign, creating the divisions of Union Councils (village level), Tehsils (sub-districts) and Zila (district) councils, as well as beginning the idea of reserving seats for women on each council level. He also sought to legitimize power by developing the local government system, thereby pacifying the elite as well by making power concessions to women from elite families.[29] While all women were subject to the restrictions of *purdah* as a social construct, the evidence of women's participation in local government councils during Zia's time indicates that *purdah* was not enforced as strictly for women in upper class families, and women experienced varied degrees of disempowerment, with the elite feeling the least impact.[30]

The system of reservations for women fell out of use during the period of civil government, even under Benazir Bhutto, and was not reintroduced till Musharraf came to power. He expanded reservations to 33 per cent of seats for women and 20 per cent of seats for workers and peasants at the Union Council level. While there are reservations at the Tehsil and Zila Councils and the National Assemblies, trends show that it is still women from elite families who hold the higher power seats.[31] While legal reforms do create a space for women to access the political sphere, it is apparent that amongst women, class works to further stratify women's access to political power.

3. Constraints to Women's Economic Power

Women's ability to engage with the market and participate in the labour force is dependent on her class and community. *Purdah* rules can take the form of psychological cloistering, by socializing women and men to believe that women should occupy a separate space. It can also take a more literal form to mean that women are restricted to the four walls of the home. This places great restrictions on women's ability to engage in productive work. Women in rural areas who work in agriculture have more flexibility regarding to *purdah* since agriculture is so labour intensive that they are required to work in the fields to reduce costs.[32] The ability of rural women to maximize their productive capabilities is restricted, however, by their lack of control over productive resources. The majority of women in South Asia, and Pakistan, lack ownership and control rights over land, as well as capital for other production inputs. This lack of control, especially over arable land, prevents women from most efficiently using land since ownership, sale and control of the products belong to the males, both legally and socially. The lack of access to land particularly restricts women's power as it curtails their bargaining power within the male-dominated household.[33]

For urban women, especially the urban poor, *purdah* can restrict women to only pursue piecework. Since they lack mobility, the goods they produce are often sold below market value as they depend on male relatives or children to sell them. By failing to properly market their wares, women's piecework is often perceived to be useless, with many earning less than Rs. 5 per day.[34]

In order to increase women's place and power in society, there is a complex interrelationship of social norms regulating honourable behaviour and access to resources between males and females, tied to class divisions and urban-rural divisions to economic and political power amongst females that must be addressed to fully influence women's potential empowerment. And this is not by any means an exhaustive list of the barriers Pakistani women face, but rather a brief highlighting of some of the most pressing issues.

Methodology

1. Why Punjab

Pakistan is composed of four provinces, Punjab, Sindh, Balochistan, and the North West Frontier Province, and two federally administered areas, the Federally Administered Tribal Areas (FATA) and Asad-Jammu Kashmir (AJK). Unlike the other provinces, Punjab is the most developed in terms of its economy and infrastructure. The province is located in the most agriculturally fertile region of the state. The Indus, Jhelum, Chenab, Ravi and Sutlej are all major rivers originating in the Himalayas that flow through the plains of Punjab, forming a vital resource for its agriculture industry.[35]

Even though Punjab only constitutes 25 per cent of the land mass of Pakistan, it is home to 55.63 per cent of the population, with 68.7 per cent living in rural areas and 31.3 per cent living in urban areas in the last census enumeration in Pakistan.[36] It has one of the highest literacy rates, with 58.7 per cent of the total population over age 10 literate. In the urban areas this consists of 78.9 per cent of men and 67.4 per cent of women, and in the rural areas it is 63.1 per cent of men and 39.5 per cent of women.[37] Punjab's economic activity provides the backbone to the nation's economy, contributing to 58 per cent of the national GDP, with the majority of its activity derived from the service sector at 54 per cent, while only 20.3 per cent comes from agriculture, and the rest from industry. These figures reflect labour distribution issues in the various sectors, as the majority of people still live in rural areas and 44 per cent of Punjab's labour force works in agriculture.[38]

Given its relative economic strength and literacy levels, it may seem unclear why Punjab is the province with the highest level of microfinance activity. With the highest population density and the most internal support infrastructure, it has facilitated the spread of microfinance institutions. Sindh is the second province most penetrated by the microfinance markets, with Balochistan and NWFP severely lacking due to the difficulties in accessing individuals.[39] This is both due to geographical distribution, and cultural and educational barriers making it difficult to access and outreach to potential clients, especially women. Therefore, since it has the most microfinance activity and the most longitudinal data available, this chapter will focus on microfinance organizations operating within Punjab, Pakistan.

2. *Organizations for Analysis*

The microfinance market in Pakistan consists of various of microfinance service providers. There are microfinance banks, rural support programmes, non-governmental microfinance institutions, commercial microfinance institutions and government-owned microfinance institutions. Within Pakistan, the market is dominated by three of these types of institutions —microfinance banks, rural support programmes, and non-governmental microfinance organizations.[40] Since these are the primary providers of microfinance, this chapter will focus on one organization from each category operating in Punjab, specifically the organizations with the largest loan portfolio and active borrowers within each category. These organizations are the National Rural Support Programme, the Khushhali Bank and the Kashf Foundation.[41] These organizations have all been in operation for at least ten years and have had impact assessment studies conducted on their operations and perceived impact on borrowers which provide sufficient data for the analysis of this project. They also all have different structural approaches in delivering microfinance services. While they are each distinct in their purpose and services, looking at different types of organizations raises interesting questions about correlations between institutional structure and its impact on changes experienced by clients.

3. Control Group Biases, Methodological Limits and Critiques in Impact Assessments

There are many complexities in running and evaluating an impact assessment. Hulme describes some of the various approaches used in creating impact assessment modules.[42] Several well established researchers have developed critiques of the way that impact assessments are executed, and these critiques will inform and guide this project's examination of the impact assessments carried out in Punjab.

Most impact assessment studies use the cross sectional impact assessment approach, which analyses data from a single point in time. By evaluating measurements from the treatment group (the clients receiving loans) to a control group (either new borrowers or non-borrowers) and comparing the two measures, one can attribute the difference to the impact of the treatment, or enrolment in a microfinance programme. This approach has several shortfalls, which Karlan elabourates on in his work evaluating impact assessment methods. He notes that three biases arise from this approach—a drop out bias, selection bias, and an institutional bias.[43]

Drop out bias is problematic when the testing method accounts only for treatment members who continued throughout a time period and does not acknowledge those treatment members who leave early. Karlan demonstrates that inclusion of all those who initially enrolled in the treatment can provide insights into why members leave, whether it is because they were negatively impacted or had progressed to a point where they no longer needed the loan.[44]

Selection bias regards why members joined the treatment at one point in time versus a later point. Members' initial income and asset levels, as well as access to alternative credit sources, such as traditional ROSCAs (Rotating Savings and Credit Associations) or private loans, influence when and why members enrol in microfinance programmes.[45] Also, the fact that a person or group chooses to apply for a microfinance loan already reflects a certain level of entrepreneurship and community cohesion that may be a greater cause for success than the loan itself. Thus special care must be taken in crafting the control group as one of comparable initial status.[46]

Institutional biases can also have a significant impact on the pool of clients treated or reached. External factors such as fund availability or the organization's long term plan can affect who is targeted, and when. In its infancy, an organization may be inclined to reach out to more stable small businesses before outreaching to the poor as it works towards financial sustainability.[47] This last bias can be one of the most difficult to control. Karlan, Asim and others offer methodological ways to offset the effects of selection and drop outs on the sample.[48] But external institutions such as the World Bank via the Pakistan Poverty Alleviation Fund (PPAF); the International Fund for Agricultural Development (IFAD); the United National Development Programme (UNDP); the European Commission (EC); Department for International Development UK (DFID); Swiss Development Corporation (SDC); the Asian Development Bank (ADB); and USAID have all contributed millions of US dollars to support Pakistan's microfinance market's development to strengthen women's empowerment, institutional efficiency, outreach, banking expansion and other factors.[49] This has had an impact on how the organizations operate based on the intent of the funding and the need to satisfy donors in order to have funding renewed. Till these organizations are completely self-supporting, the donors whom they are receiving funding from will have an impact on who and how organizations reach clients.

Considering that very few impact assessments have been executed to date, the data available on the organizations we will be examining are very limited. Much of it is provided by donor agencies such as the European Commission and the Asian Development Bank. Thus institutional bias will be most fully discussed when reviewing the data available.

4. Measures for Analysis

Barnes and Sebstad note that caution must be exercised in examining data for impact assessments as it takes different time frames to see changes in different categories. For instance, a change in income can be seen in a shorter period of time than changes in children's school enrolment, and both do not take as long to see changes in literacy and female empowerment.[50] This caution should be kept in mind when examining longitudinal data, which this project did not have access to.

There are several standard measures we will examine in trying to assess impacts on socio-economic status. These measures include income, expenditures, age, gender, and occupation of the lendee. We will also look at housing, education levels and school enrolment, health and perceived empowerment where the data is available for more long-term social impacts. In an effort to control external influences on respondents' answers, we will also compare changes to regional and national trends to consider if changes are due to microfinance or to more macro forces. White, Sinha and Flanagan cite this as an alternative method to use when a clean control group may not be available.[51]

Overview of Organizational Structures

1. Kashf Foundation

The Kashf Foundation was first created in 1996 as a research programme designed to assess the need and impact of microfinance services for poor women in Pakistan. It was inspired by the work of Muhammed Yunus, who founded the Grameen Bank in Bangladesh. The project began in Lahore, Punjab, backed by funding from the Pakistan Poverty Alleviation Fund, the Department for International Development, UK, and the Aga Khan Foundation. Over time, as it became increasingly financially stable, Kashf has expanded its branches throughout Punjab and recently entered Karachi in the Sindh province. The majority of its branches are in urban regions, addressing the urban poor.[52]

The organization's mission is to "alleviate poverty by providing quality and effective microfinance services to low income households, especially women."[53] In light of this mission, the organization has developed several products tailored to the needs of low income households. The products that they offer have changed over time.[54] All loans and savings products operate on a group model, where women create groups consisting of 25 community members whom they are not related to, and use their social capital as collateral to take out the loan, based on the concept Yunus used to build the Grameen Bank.[55] Kashf is funded through the Pakistan Poverty Alleviation Fund, the Grameen Trust, MCB and Acumen.[56]

Since 1996, Kashf has offered a General Loan, which ranges from Rs 6,000-50,000 for a one-year period to be repaid at a flat 20 per cent interest rate in 12 monthly instalments. In order to be eligible for this loan, each group member's household income must be between Rs. 3,000 and 10,000 a year. An Emergency Loan is also available for emergency consumption, educational, health or utility needs. It is available to those who have a General Loan and is set at Rs. 4000 with a flat 10 per cent interest rate to be repaid in 6 instalments within 6 months. The Emergency Loan was introduced in 1998. By 2001, the Life Insurance element developed, which is now a mandatory insurance component for all General Loan clients. 1.5 per cent of the base loan amount is held in insurance with an additional 5,000 rupees credit to families to mitigate costs associated with the passing of a family member. 2005 saw the development of the Business Loan, 2007 the Home Development Loan and 2008 the Health Insurance component with a low Rs. 350 annual premium. This programme has been especially effective in beginning to broach subjects such as reproductive health with women and families, an area that is difficult to approach given local cultural norms and sensitivities towards the propriety of the topic.[57] In the past, the Kashf Foundation also offered a voluntary savings component to which clients could contribute whatever amount they felt appropriate. Since the setting up of the Kashf Bank in 2008, management of savings services and the Business and Home Improvement Loans have shifted to be administered through the Kashf Bank.[58] Kashf proclaims to have a special focus on lending only to women. And it does—from 2004 through 2007, all its clients were women. Beginning in 2008, it made loans available to men as well. While only a small portion of men took out a loan—389 men to 316, 002 women it may mark the beginning of a trend that could be worrisome for those focused on the female empowerment aspect of the Kashf

Foundation.[59] As it is, the structure of the organization's microlending groups restricts access to only married, widowed or divorced women, excluding single women from access to microfinance services. It also allows male relatives to join in on group meetings and even to control financial assets. While a loan can only be taken out in a woman's name, it is common practice and understood by district and local staff that often the money of the loan is used by male household members to support their own businesses.[60] Even though 65 per cent of borrowers have their own business, only 20 per cent use the loan on their own business. The rest defer the loan money to their male relatives.[61]

As of 2008, Kashf had an active borrower base of over 313,512. It has seen rapid growth in clients from 2002-2008 (See Table 2). In an effort to develop women's social and human capital, Kashf has integrated skills training workshops into the bimonthly group meeting curriculum. These lessons have been seen to have a variable effect, with DFID remarking that many women could not recall what had been taught in the workshops.[62] However, the inclusion of these trainings marks Kashf as different from other microfinance service providers in the region.

2. *The Khushhali Bank*

The Khushhali Bank was formed in 2000 with the help of the State Bank of Pakistan and funds from the Asian Development Bank. Its primary purpose is to create a retail market for microfinance services directed to the poor. It operates under the Microfinance Sector Development Programme, which is focused on raising the income of poor households, outreaching to women and building social capital.[63]

The Khushhali Bank offers a variety of loan services targeted to the non-poor and the poor. In order to qualify for any Khushhali loan, a client must have been a resident of the area for two years and have an annual income under Rs. 300,000. While this limit effectively includes all poor households, it also opens the market for the poor to have to compete with the not so poor for loans: There are loans available for Agriculture,

Table 2: Kashf Foundation Borrowers by Type, 2002-08

	2002	*2003*	*2004*	*2005*	*2006*	*2007*	*2008*
Number of Borrowers	29,655	59,389	67,552	75,520	133,690	295,396	313,512
Gross Loan Portfolio (US$)	2,263,536	5,849,770	8,068,394	12,956,833	25,190,461	51,603,641	44,230,466
General Loan (US$)						32,870,667	41,151,513
Consumption Loan (US$)						13,849,264	
Housing Loan (US$)						4,883,700	304,988
Education Loan (US$)							2,773,966

Source: MIX Market, Kashf Foundation 2002– 08

Table 3: Khushhali Bank Borrowers, 2003-08

	2003	*2004*	*2005*	*2006*	*2007*	*2008*
Number of Borrowers	91,532	168,105	227,172	236,917	283,965	312,851
Percent Women Borrowers	37.64%	26.56%	33.33%	21.20%	15.43%	
Gross Loan Portfolio (US$)	11,924,316	23,542,172	32,177, 436	35,351,635	43,066,815	39,280,453

Source: MIX Market Survey Khushhali Bank Ltd., 2003-08

Livestock, Asset Purchase, New Business start ups and Working Capital. Like Kashf, all loan clients are organized into groups with social accountability serving as a proxy for material collateral. All loans are available for Rs. 3,000 to Rs. 15,000 a year to be repaid over a variable period, but loans are limited to 18-58-year-old clients. There is no gender preference for Khushhali customers. Like Kashf as well, there is a mandatory insurance component that safeguards borrowers against death or disability liability.[64]

In order to address the gender equity component of its mission, Khushhali has developed a special initiative called the Jafakash Aurat Project, which works towards training women in small cottage business skills and technological skills. The programme encouraged some women to take out loans to further develop their own businesses themselves.[65] Beyond this programme, the Bank does not offer supplemental training or support; it primarily supplies loans for a variety of business supports, available to both men and women. Yet a review of their loan usage trends indicates that women underutilized the loans at a steadily decreasing rate, even as the Bank's overall loan portfolio rapidly increased.

3. The National Rural Support Programme

The National Rural Support Programme (NRSP) grew out of a series of rural development programmes that date back to state-directed initiatives to address rural poverty during the post-Partition period. As early as 1953, the military and civilian governments have sponsored a variety of programmes aimed towards the rural and urban poverty situation. The NRSP was established in 1991 as a derivative of the older Aga Khan Rural Support Programme that was developed in northern Pakistan in the 1980s.[66] Like many microfinance service providers, the NRSP operates on a group model, through the utilization of Community Organizations (COs) which consist of members from poor households who come together to build on one another's social capital to leverage support and access credit. Initially, the role of the NRSP was simply to facilitate relationships between COs and service agencies, but over time, it has evolved to offering support services for rural development, as well as educational services, health services and protection for children against forced labour through various partnerships with national and international agencies.[67]

The NRSP offers a variety of formal products to clients, including savings and loans, health and life insurance, and skills training for agriculture, managements and technical skill development. There is a component of the programme that focuses on urban poverty, but we will not be examining that in detail here. Like the Khushhali Bank, the NRSP does not have an explicit mission directed towards female empowerment. Thus, of the over 41,000 COs operating in more than 40 districts throughout the nation, 70 per cent are for men only, 25 per cent for women only and 5 per cent are mixed. The low prevalence of mixed COs is due to *purdah*, the social and cultural restrictions on gender interactions that are especially dominant in rural areas. But the raw number of women taking out loans through the NRSP has increased from 39.2 per cent in 2002 to 42.7 per cent in 2006.[68] It should be noted that with the presence of female- only COs there has been a steady increase in female staff working with the NRSP over 2000-06. The majority of women taking out loans use it for livestock or small enterprises.[69]

Much of the NRSP is funded by the Pakistan Poverty Alleviation Fund, with various other international aid organizations contributing to the remaining operation funds.[70]

But it also continues to be funded by the endowment fund that it was started with, and so has remained a relatively stable provider.[71]

Data Analysis

In order to assess whether the studies that have been done on the three organizations are accurate in their positive evaluation of the role of microfinance on their clients, we will do a qualitative assessment reviewing the methods used in each impact assessment and the results obtained from the perspective of the biases reviewed in the Methodology section as well as comparing results to national trends. Due to the unavailability of raw data, we are limited to a qualitative assessment.

1. Kashf Foundation

There have been two impact assessments on the Kashf Foundation within the past five years, as well as a less rigorous study on the impact of microfinance on female empowerment.[72] We will be reviewing the data from the European Commission and Kashf Foundation for the majority of the indicators.

- ***Housing Type***

One of the preferences Kashf has for new lendees is that they own their home rather than rent their home.[73] While there is a significant difference between pipeline borrowers and active borrowers in terms of housing ownership, the profile of both pipeline borrowers and area non-borrowers is rather high, perhaps as a reflection of the preference noted in loan disbursals. Likewise, there are distinctive aspects regarding housing quality that present barriers to access for the very poor. Both pipeline and active borrowers are likely to have their homes made of baked bricks, revealing a greater social stability and house value than area non-borrowers. Zaidi combines pipeline borrowers and non-borrowers in his analysis comparing housing components, which skews the analysis to appear that active borrowers have made significant progress when in fact the non-borrowers and pipeline borrowers have such distinct profiles that they cannot be considered to be comparable in this case. Interestingly, non-borrowers are nearly as likely as active borrowers to have an RCC roof and cement floors than pipeline borrowers. In this case, by combining the two groups, it inflates the housing value of pipeline borrowers and decreases the value of non-borrowers to inaccurately portray active borrowers as having made progress in housing quality. Thus, it cannot be clearly inferred that active borrowers have improved their housing quality through microfinance enrolment, nor can it be clearly stated that it remains accessible to the very poor as over 80 per cent of pipeline and area non-borrowers own their homes.[74]

- ***Income***

One of the greatest challenges in assessing if microfinance has had a positive impact on income is the lack of longitudinal data. According to the Official National Poverty Line of Rs. 1,000 per month, only 5 per cent of active borrowers, 18 per cent of pipeline borrowers and 22 per cent of non-borrowers are below the poverty line. But at the international standard of $1/day, which translates to roughly Rs. 2,490 a month, all Kashf's clients continue to live below the international poverty line. According to Kashf's internal assessment, only 16 per cent of active clients are living over $2/day.[75] This suggests that even though some clients have renewed their loans with Kashf up to seven times, they are still living below the poverty line, which raises questions about their ability to facilitate the rise out of poverty. Owing to the absence of longitudinal data, it is not possible to attribute the higher income for active borrowers to be a result of the loans as it is possible due to selection bias that they were comparably better off to begin with.

- *Occupation*

The sector that the lendee is working in is also an indicator of the relative poverty level via class indicators. The clear majority of non-borrowers are employed in cottage industries, the type of in-house piecework that women living in more highly segregated *purdah* communities engage in. Alternatively, active and pipeline borrowers can be found working in businesses with fixed retail locations, revealing a higher level of social capital in terms of mobility and independence, as well as economic capital such that they are able to hold a business property.

Table 4: Kashf Foundation Borrowers and Non-Borrowers Occupation by Sector

Occupation	*Active (%)*	*Pipeline (%)*	*Non-Borrowers (%)*
Respondents	239 (46.9)	91 (17.8)	180 (35.3)
Business (fixed outlet)	36	26.40	15
Business (vendor)	16.30	12.10	12.80
Personal Community Service Provider	10.50	23.10	14.40
Cottage Industry	23.80	22	51.70

Source: Zaidi, 2009

• ***Education Level of Female Lendees***

Interestingly, we find that non-borrowers are more likely to have pursued higher education than active or pipeline borrowers. For example, the percentages of respondents belonging to the active category as well as that of the pipeline are 85 per cent and 78 per cent respectively, but that of non-borrowers is 76 per cent. By the same token, the low educational attainment by borrowers may indicate that they are less privileged.

• ***Education of Children***

Between non-borrowers and borrowers, there was little difference in net child enrolment. The main increase was in male child enrolment. Pipeline borrowers had the lowest enrolment overall, which may be correlated with their much lower expenditure on education than active or non-borrowers. There was a slight decrease from non-borrowers to borrowers in terms of female child enrolment. This raises the concern that as production increases in the home or around female labourers, female children may be more likely to be removed from school to support the business as that is seen as a more useful function for the child.[76]

• ***Health***

Health is one aspect that Kashf has clearly made a positive impact on. Active borrowers are much more likely to have had their children fully vaccinated than either pipeline or non-borrowers. For instance, in the case of active borrowers, 81 per cent of the children have had their vaccines completed. In the case of the non-borrowers, it is only 74 per cent.[77] This can likely be attributed to the phasing in of health education and services in conjunction with the microfinance products.

• ***Perceived Empowerment***

Women's empowerment, according to Zaidi, appears to have decreased with access to microfinance services, as suggested by Mayoux. The vast majority of active and pipeline borrowers defer control over their loan to their husbands. For instance, in the case of active respondents, only 28 per cent of the females control the loan in contrast to the 65 per cent of the cases in which the spouse controls the loan. Similarly, in the case of pipeline respondents, 77 per cent of the spouses control loans. In returning to the business/occupation component, the reason for higher prevalence of fixed businesses amongst borrowers may be attributed to the fact that the husband or other male family members is the owner of the business. Thus, microfinance, while increasing a woman's value in terms of how much loan money she can bring in, may instead be further marginalizing her as an income source without agency to control the money she is responsible for repaying.[78] Asim finds that microfinance for Kashf borrowers in Lahore has made no difference in household bargaining power. Instead, it can place a woman in a dangerous position, for if her male relatives are unable to make a return on the loan, she is personally liable to her lending group to find a way to repay it, which in some cases can lead to violence.[79]

Kashf has had an interestingly mixed impact. In examining implicit markers of poverty, such as housing quality, field of employment, and education level in addition to income, it does seem that while all borrowers are poor in an absolute sense, in terms of their capital wealth, borrowers are clearly better off than non-borrowers. The fact that these disparities are apparent in the case of active and pipeline borrowers compared to non-borrowers suggests, perhaps, a bias in terms of who has access to Kashf's services. It was also interesting to note that there was no perceived increase in empowerment, and perhaps greater marginalization. However, Kashf has made noteworthy progress in health services, which is no small task.

2. The Khushhali Bank

The Khushhali Bank has only had one impact assessment conducted on its operations throughout its ten-year existence. This single impact assessment has several methodological flaws which greatly distort the picture that the analysis portrays. Others have tried to use that data and re-present it in a different light, but have found that to be of limited utility.[80] The greatest flaw with the Montgomery impact assessment lies in its selection methodology. There are clearly outlier clients who are included in the sample that skew all analyses run on the data set. This can be observed by the widespread standard deviations on most income and asset indicators. Thus, this data and the positive conclusions that the initial assessor suggested, must be re-examined:

- ***Housing Type***

While there was no measure available for housing quality, type or ownership, it is critical to note that only 32 per cent of borrowers are land owners. Considering that 75 per cent of those surveyed are rural, this suggests that most Khushhali borrowers are indeed of the poorer sections of society, since wealth and access to productive labour is directly linked to safe access to land for the rural labour force.

- ***Income and Occupation***

There was no measure for overall income, but there was a measure for profits and outside income. The average profits amounted to Rs 81,884.8, but the standard deviation exceeds the average, at 710,166. This is to account for clients who accrued losses up to Rs. 51,300 and those who made significant gains up to Rs. 2.7 million. Thus averaging clearly does not provide an accurate representative profile of how borrowers are affected and a mode would have offered a more clear understanding. The external household income averaged to be Rs 8915, which leads to a net household income of about Rs 90,000. It would appear that Khushhali borrowers are faring extremely well, but due to the high standard deviation, it is unclear what the true distribution looks like without being about to exclude the outlier data sets. There was no measure in this assessment of what field the lendees were employed in.

- ***Health and Education Level of Lendees and Their Children***

The education level of lendees was pretty low for both males and females. Men had on average 5.76 years of education and women had 2.41 years of education. There is no measure of change in education levels, so it is not possible to see if access to loans has had an impact on lendees' educational attainment. Children have a 44 per cent chance with at .44 standard deviation to attend school. This does not provide any clear insight into a positive or negative change regarding student enrolment. Likewise, those who are likely to use health services in case of illness is around 57 per cent for oneself and 60 per cent for children, but the standard deviation is 0.48 which raises questions about what range of the sample surveyed would actually use health services, and if that reflects a change due to loan access or if it is a reflection of prior wealth status.

- ***Perceived Empowerment***

There was no way to measure for female empowerment in this case. A survey schedule was administered to ascertain women's perceptions of empowerment, but there is nothing to empirically establish conclusions on issues such as control over loan usage. Subjective perceptions, while valuable, do not provide a consistent or comparable measures for assessment in this case.

The greatest issue with evaluating the role of the Khushhali Bank on borrowers is that not much good data are available. Yet, as the largest microfinance bank in Pakistan, it is of great concern that to date there has still not been a rigorous study of its potential impacts.

3. NRSP

The National Rural Support Programme has had several impact assessments performed throughout its existence, yet most of these studies are not readily available. Again, we will reference the data from the European Commission's recent study on the NRSP. Unlike Kashf, NRSP does not have requirements or preferences regarding the economic status of potential clients. While they target the poor and their mission continues to focus on poverty alleviation, they do not have set parameters for defining poverty. Their district or village officers perform an assessment of those applying to be a CO, and if 75 per cent of the CO sign to take out the loan, they become responsible for repaying it. While it also operates on a social capital model, the NRSP encourages new lendees to contribute to savings as a safety, though the level is left to be determined by each person or household.[81]

- ***Housing Type***

There was no significant difference in housing ownership or type between active, pipeline and non-borrowers. All had a high level of ownership, with many having baked bricked housing as well. Interestingly, pipeline borrowers (98 per cent) and non-borrowers (99 per cent) were more likely to have RCC roofing.[82] Thus, it is inconclusive what role, if any, microfinance played on raising the quality of living in terms of housing.

- ***Income***

The income of borrowers has increased over time. Active borrowers have a significantly higher income than either pipeline (Rs. 1268) or non-borrowers (Rs. 1318), suggesting that being a part of NRSP has had a positive impact on increasing income. It is also interesting to note that 89 per cent of loanees control their own capital, in contrast to 9 per cent of spouses controlling it.[83] It should be noted that here all the people surveyed, though over the national poverty line, are again still living below the international $1 a day rate.

- ***Occupation***

As this is a rural support oriented organization, it is of course expected that the majority of lendees are in the agricultural industry. The next highest areas include livestock management and fixed business. Likewise, these are the highest areas for pipeline and non-borrowers, suggesting that NRSP has continued to target a similar profile of clients.

Table 5: NRSP Borrowers and Non-Borrowers' Occupation by Sector

Occupation	*Active (%)*	*Pipeline (%)*	*Non-Borrowers (%)*
Respondents	324 (47.6)	108 (15.9)	248 (36.5)
Business (fixed outlet)	19.80	30.60	34.70
Agriculture—Crop Production	47.80	30.60	33.50
Livestock Management	18.80	19.40	14.90

Source: Zaidi, 2009

• ***Education Level of Lendees and Their Children***

A good third of women rural borrowers in all categories have not pursued education. Those who did have pursued education mostly till middle school levels. Active borrowers have a higher rate of taking their education to higher levels, which may be a positive effect of access to microfinance services or may be a reflection of a better human capital state at the beginning of the loan cycle that has allowed these women to continue. These measures also include male lenders' education levels. A positive correlation was found between active borrowers and pipeline borrowers in terms of the percentage of children going to school. No significant difference was found in comparing non-borrowers from active borrowers.

Table 6: NRSP Borrowers and Non-Borrowers by Education Level

Education	*Active (%)*	*Pipeline (%)*	*Non-Borrowers (%)*
Respondents	324 (47.6)	108 (15.9)	248 (36.5)
No Education	32.10	39.80	31.90
Primary	19.40	20.40	22.60
Middle	18.20	19.40	16.90
Metric	24.10	16.70	19.40
Inter	4.30	3.70	6.90
Graduate and Above	1.90		2.40

Source: Zaidi, 2009

• ***Health***

It appears that there is a positive correlation between borrowers' status and children's immunization. Borrowers are seen to have an increase in children who have completed their vaccine schedule and a decrease in those children with an incomplete vaccine schedule. This is a significant impact due to the lower access to services that comes with living in rural areas.

Table 7: NRSP Borrowers and Non-Borrowers' Health

Education and Health	*Active (%)*	*Pipeline (%)*	*Non-Borrowers (%)*
Respondents	324 (47.6)	108 (15.9)	248 (36.5)
School-going Children	91.00	85.00	91.00
Boy Students	90.00	85.00	89.00
Girl Students	73.00	65.00	72.00
Vaccines Completed	68.50	64.40	61.60
Vaccines in Progress	30.10	25.00	35.70
No Vaccines	1.40	10.60	2.70

Source: Zaidi, 2009

- ***Perceived Empowerment***

As empowerment is not a goal for the NRSP, it is difficult to assess from this data whether it had an impact on its women clients. Of all the borrowers surveyed, there was a higher percentage of self-control over the loan, as the majority of those surveyed were men. But the percentage of those who have control is greater than the percentage of total men surveyed, which does suggest that some women are retaining control of their loans. This could suggest a significant success for the NRSP, as working towards rural female empowerment can be one of the most challenging tasks.

Since the nature of the NRSP is so different from other microfinance providers, as it is focused on rural poverty alleviation and does not explicitly consider female empowerment, it must be examined in a different light. Here as well, it appears to have worked well in terms of capturing the poor as defined by income, yet it is still benefiting a more privileged poor as many of these people are owners of solidly constructed homes, which suggests a level of asset access and stability that the very poor lack. Due to the lack of significant female enrolment in NRSP programmes, it is difficult to assess what impact it has had on female empowerment.

Conclusion

Before offering any conclusions, it warrants noting that this is a qualitative assessment of very dissimilar organizations. The intent in looking at such diverse organizations was to try to get a sense if the services distinct to each type of organization might have an influence on how the effects of microfinance are felt amongst clients. The limitations in doing this are that we do not compare various organizations within each type and it is difficult to cross compare. But it does lay the groundwork for deeper examination into the differential impacts that are associated with the various support services.

In terms of the bigger question—to what extent does microfinance reach the poor, and does it reach the poorest of the poor, it appears from the indirect markers of poverty and wealth that it is only the marginally poor and not so absolutely destitute who have access to microfinance. This is inferred from the high rate of house ownership by lendees and the fields that lendees work in. Occupations such as fixed location businesses, agriculture and livestock maintenance assume a base level of capital assets, suggesting that microfinance is mostly helping those who already have means but only need slight assistance in moving their income-generating activities forward. Due to the model of community groups as a way to provide social capital as a material collateral substitute, it may be inferred that those who lack physical assets are socially excluded from lending groups and thus lack access to the market. This is a question that would warrant further investigation and analysis, as well as comparison to other microfinance institutions that loan directly to individuals.

There is some concern in the shift towards a banking model compared to the community centred model offered by Kashf and the NRSP. While on the one hand it may open opportunities for individual loans, it also has higher income requirements that may serve as an access barrier. Banks like Khushhali offer lower interest rates than Kashf does to borrowers, which may serve as an incentive to invite more impoverished clients, but that model will not last for too long as donors try to urge banks towards self-sustainability.

In terms of female empowerment, it remains to be seen what impact has been felt on women. The more qualitative indicators offer conflicting reports as they are based on women's subjective experiences, which will be influenced by their relative class, location, and other external factors. The best quantified measure that we currently have is that of women who retain control over the loans that they receive. In the cases studied here, they do not. But according to Kashf's records, that number is increasing with more veteran members. Whether that is a result of microfinance or a preexisting condition is again unclear.

In terms of recommendations for future work, it is that there is a clear and pressing need for a longitudinal study of microfinance institutions in Pakistan. While such studies are costly, they are the most accurate way to see if microfinance has truly made a difference or if donors and lenders are continuing to pour funding and efforts into a system that may not be entirely effective.

NOTES

1. State Bank of Pakistan. "Microfinance Institutions Ordinance 2001," *State Bank of Pakistan*, 2007. http://www.sbp.org.pk/l_frame/MF_Inst_Ord_2001.pdf.
2. Mayoux, L. "Tackling the Down Side: Social Capital, Women's Empowerment and Microfinance in Cameroon," *Development and Change* 32.3. (2001): 421-450.
3. Sen, A. "Poverty and Famines: An Essay on Entitlement and Deprivation." *The Amartya Sen and Jean Dreze Omnibus.* (Oxford University Press, USA, 1981): 1-216.
4. Sen, A. and J. Dreze. "India: Economic Development and Social Opportunity."*The Amartya Sen and Jean Dreze Omnibus.* (Oxford University Press, 1995): 1-229.
5. Sen, A. "Poverty and Famines: An Essay on entitlement and Deprivation." *The Amartya Sen and Jean Dreze Omnibus.* (Oxford University Press, USA, 1981): 1-216.
6. Mayoux, L. "Questioning Virtuous Spirals: Microfinance and Women's Empowerment in Africa." *Journal of International Development* 11. (1999): 957-984. Batliwala, S. "Taking the power Out of Empowerment: An Experiential Account." *Development in Practice* 17.4-5. (2007): 557-565. Agarwal, B. "Bargaining" and Gender Relations: within and Beyond the Household." *Feminist Economics* 3.1. (1997): 1-51. Siddiqui, R. "Modelling Gender Dimensions of the Impact of Economic Reforms on Time Allocation Amongst Market Work, Household Work and

Leisure." *Pakistan Institute for Development Economic Report* 185. (2004).

7. UN Development Programme. "Pakistan," *United Nations Development Programme.* 2015. http://hdr.undp.org/en/countries/profiles/PAK#
8. UN Development Programme. "Human Development Report 2009," *United Nations Development Programme.* 2009. http://hdrstats.undp.org/en/countries/data_sheets/cty_ds_PAK.html.
9. UN Development Programme. "Gender Development Index," *United Nations Development Programme.* 2015. http://hdr.undp.org/en/indicators/137906
10. UN Development Programme. "Human Development Report 2009," *United Nations Development Programme.* 2009. http://hdrstats.undp.org/en/countries/data_sheets/cty_ds_PAK.html.
11. UN Development Programme. "Human Development Report 2009," *United Nations Development Programme.* 2009. http://hdrstats.undp.org/en/countries/data_sheets/cty_ds_PAK.html.
12. UN Development Programme. "Human Development Report 2009," *United Nations Development Programme.* 2009. http://hdrstats.undp.org/en/countries/data_sheets/cty_ds_PAK.html.
13. International Finance Corporation. *Pakistan: Microfinance and Financial Sector Diagnostic Study.* (Frankfurt: Frankfurt School of Finance & Management, 2008).
14. Chant, S. "The Feminization of Poverty and the Feminization of Anti-Poverty Programmes: Room for Revision?" *Journal of Development Studies* 44.2. (2006):165-197.
15. Government of Pakistan. "Accelerating Economic Growth and Reducing Poverty: The Road Ahead." *Poverty Reduction Strategy Paper* (Islamabad: Ministry of Finance, 2003).
16. Government of Pakistan. "Accelerating Economic Growth and Reducing Poverty: The Road Ahead." *Poverty Reduction Strategy Paper* (Islamabad: Ministry of Finance, 2003).
17. Government of Pakistan. "Accelerating Economic Growth and Reducing Poverty: The Road Ahead." *Poverty Reduction Strategy Paper* (Islamabad: Ministry of Finance, 2003).
18. Government of Pakistan. *Poverty Reduction Strategy Paper II.* (Islamabad: Finance Division, 2009).
19. Jamal, H. "In Search of Poverty Predictors: The Case of Urban

and Rural Pakistan." *Social Policy and Development Centre, Pakistan.* (2004).

20. UN Development Programme. "Human Development Report 2009," *United Nations Development Programme.* 2009. http://hdrstats.undp.org/en/countries/data_sheets/cty_ds_PAK.html.
21. UN Development Programme. "Human Development Report 2009," *United Nations Development Programme.* 2009. http://hdrstats.undp.org/en/countries/data_sheets/cty_ds_PAK.html.
22. Pakistan Microfinance Network. *Microfinance Connect,* 2007. http://www.microfinanceconnect.info/au_intro.php.
23. Shaheed, F. "Gender, Religion and the Quest for Justice in Pakistan." *United Nations Research Institute for Social Development.* (2009): 1-42.
24. Shaheed, F. "Gender, Religion and the Quest for Justice in Pakistan." *United Nations Research Institute for Social Development.* (2009): 1-42.
25. Shaheed, F. "Gender, Religion and the Quest for Justice in Pakistan." *United Nations Research Institute for Social Development.* (2009): 1-42.
26. Shaheed, F. "Purdah and Poverty in Pakistan." *Women, Poverty and Ideology in Asia.* (Hong Kong: Macmillan Press Ltd., 1983). 17-42.
27. Shaheed, F. "Gender, Religion and the Quest for Justice in Pakistan." *United Nations Research Institute for Social Development.* (2009): 1-42.
28. Shaheed, F. "Constructing Identities: Culture, Women's Agency and the Muslim World." *UNESCO.* (1999): 61-73.
29. Shaheed, F. "Constructing Identities: Culture, Women's Agency and the Muslim World." *UNESCO.* (1999): 61-73. Munawar, R. "Towards Women Empowerment in Pakistan." *Women and Empowerment: Experiences from Some South Asian Countries* (2005): 88-108.
30. Shaheed, F. "Constructing Identities: Culture, Women's Agency and the Muslim World." *UNESCO.* (1999): 61-73. Munawar, R. "Towards Women's Empowerment in Pakistan." *Women and empowerment: experiences from some South Asian Countries.* (Chandigarh: Unistar Books Pvt. Ltd., 2005). 88-108. Singh, D. and M. Singh. *Women and Empowerment: Experiences from Some South Asian Countries.* (Chandigarh: Unistar Books Pvt Limited, 2005).

31. Munawar, R. "Towards Women's Empowerment in Pakistan." *Women and Empowerment: Experiences from Some South Asian Countries.* (Chandigarh: Unistar Books Pvt. Ltd., 2005). 88-108. Singh, D. and M. Singh. *Women and Empowerment: Experiences from Some South Asian Countries.* (Chandigarh: Unistar Books Pvt Limited, 2005).
32. Shaheed, Farida. "Purdah and Poverty in Pakistan." *Women, Poverty, and Ideology in Asia: Contradictory Pressures, Uneasy Resolutions.* (1989). Afshar, H. and Agarwal, B (Eds.). *Women, Poverty and Ideology in Asia.* (Hong Kong: Macmillan Press Ltd., 1983). 17-42. Hunt, J. and N. Kasynathan. "Microfinance and Transformation in Gender Relations in South Asia." *Gender and Development* 9.1. (2001): 42-52.
33. Agarwal, B. "Gender and Command Over Property: A Critical Gap in Economic Analysis and Policy in South Asia." *World Development* 22.10. (1994): 1455-1478.
34. Shaheed, F. "Purdah and Poverty in Pakistan." *Women, Poverty and Ideology in Asia.* (Hong Kong: Macmillan Press Ltd., 1983). 17-42.
35. Government of Punjab. "Punjab Portal," *Punjab Government*, 2010. http://pportal.punjab.gov.pk/portal/portal/mediatype/html/user/anon/page/default.psml/js_panename/ContentViewAdmin/portal/306/nav/right/punjabcms/servlet/PunjabCMSServlet?CMDCMS=V_D_BROWSER&CMDDOCTYPE=1&txtDocID=7394&txtVersionID=1.
36. Government of Pakistan. *Area, Population, Density and Urban/Rural Proportion by Administrative Units.* (Islamabad: Population Census Organization, 1998).
37. International Finance Corporation. *Pakistan: Microfinance and Financial Sector Diagnostic Study.* (Frankfurt, Frankfurt School of Finance & Management: 2008). 1-40.
38. Government of Punjab. *Punjab Economic Report*. (Punjab: Punjab Economic Research Institute, 2007).
39. International Finance Corporation. *Pakistan: Microfinance and Financial Sector Diagnostic Study.* (Frankfurt, Frankfurt School of Finance & Management: 2008). 1-40.
40. International Finance Corporation. *Pakistan: Microfinance and Financial Sector Diagnostic Study.* (Frankfurt, Frankfurt School of Finance & Management: 2008). 1-40.
41. MicroWatch. "January–December 2009 Annual Report." *MicroWatch* 14. (2009): 1-16
42. Hulme, D. "Impact Assessment Methodologies for Microfinance:

Theory, Experience and Best Practices." *World Development* 28.1. (2000): 79-98

43. Karlan, D.S. "Microfinance Impact Assessments: The Perils of Using New Members as a Control Group." *Journal of Microfinance/ ESR Review* 3.2. (2001): 75-85.
44. Tedeschi, G.A., and D. Karlan. "Cross-Sectional Impact Analysis: Bias from Dropouts." *Perspectives on Global Development and Technology* 9.3-4. (2010).
45. Karlan, D.S. "Microfinance Impact Assessments: The Perils of Using New Members as a Control Group." *Journal of Microfinance/ ESR Review* 3.2. (2001): 75-85.
46. White, H., S. Sinha, and A. Flanagan. "A Review of the State of Impact Evaluation." *International Workshop on Impact Evaluation for Development, Paris.* (2006): 1-24.
47. Karlan, D.S. "Microfinance Impact Assessments: The Perils of Using New Members as a Control Group." *Journal of Microfinance/ ESR Review* 3.2. (2001): 75-85.
48. Karlan, D.S. "Microfinance Impact Assessments: The Perils of Using New Members as a Control Group." *Journal of Microfinance/ ESR Review* 3.2. (2001): 75-85. White, H., S. Sinha, and A. Flanagan. "A Review of the State of Impact Evaluation." *International Workshop on Impact Evaluation for Development, Paris.* (2006): 1-24. Hussein, M., and S. Hussain. "The Impact of Micro Finance on Poverty and Gender Equity: Approaches and Evidence from Pakistan." *Islamabad: Pakistan Microfinance Network* (2003).
49. International Finance Corporation. *Pakistan: Microfinance and Financial Sector Diagnostic Study.* (Frankfurt, Frankfurt School of Finance & Management: 2008). 1-40.
50. Barnes, C., and J. Sebstad. "Guidelines for Microfinance Impact Assessments." *Washington, DC: Assessing the Impact of Microenterprise Services, Management Systems International* (2000).
51. White, H., S. Sinha, and A. Flanagan. "A Review of the State of Impact Evaluation." *International Workshop on Impact Evaluation for Development, Paris.* (2006): 1-24.
52. Kashf Foundation. "KASHF Foundation - Our History." *KASHF Foundation - Our History.* Kashf Foundation, 2007. http://www.kashf.org/site_files/display_content.asp?id=4.
53. Kashf Foundation. "KASHF Foundation - Our History." *KASHF Foundation—Our History.* Kashf Foundation, 2007. http://www.kashf.org/site_files/display_content.asp?id=4.
54. Kashf Foundation. "KASHF Foundation – Annual Reports 2005-

07." *KASHF Foundation - Our History*. Kashf Foundation, 2007. http://www.kashf.org/site_files/publications.asp.

55. Kashf Foundation. "KASHF Foundation – Products and Services." *KASHF Foundation - Our History*. Kashf Foundation, 2007. http://www.kashf.org/site_files/products.asp.
56. Zaidi, S.A. (et al). "Social Impact Assessment of Microfinance Programmes." *Islamabad: European Union-Pakistan Financial Services Sector Reform Programme. Enabling Poor Rural People to Overcome Poverty International Fund for Agricultural Development Via Paolo di Dono* 44. (2007).
57. Kashf Foundation. "KASHF Foundation – Annual Reports 2005-07." *KASHF Foundation - Our History*. Kashf Foundation, 2007. http://www.kashf.org/site_files/publications.asp.
58. Kashf Foundation. "KASHF Foundation – Annual Reports 2005-07." *KASHF Foundation - Our History*. Kashf Foundation, 2007. http://www.kashf.org/site_files/publications.asp.
59. Mix Market. "KASHF Foundation - Data." *Microfinance Information Exchange Inc.*, 2007. http://www.mixmarket.org/mfi/kashf/data.
60. Kashf Foundation. "KASHF Foundation – Annual Reports 2005-07." *KASHF Foundation—Our History*. Kashf Foundation, 2007. http://www.kashf.org/site_files/publications.asp.
61. Kashf Foundation. "KASHF Foundation—Impact Assessment Report." *KASHF Foundation—Our History*. Kashf Foundation, 2005. http://www.kashf.org/site_files/display_content.asp?id=15
62. Kashf Foundation. "KASHF Foundation – Annual Reports 2005-07." *KASHF Foundation—Our History*. Kashf Foundation, 2007. http://www.kashf.org/site_files/publications.asp.
63. Mix Market. "KASHF Foundation—Data." *Microfinance Information Exchange Inc.*, 2007. http://www.mixmarket.org/mfi/kashf/data.
64. International Finance Corporation. *Pakistan: Microfinance and Financial Sector Diagnostic Study*. (Frankfurt, Frankfurt School of Finance & Management: 2008). 1-40.
65. Khushhali Bank Limited. "Jafakash Aurat Programme," *Khushhali Bank Limited,* June 5, 2013. http://www.khushhalibank.com.pk/special_initiatve/jafakash_aurat.php.
66. Khan, M. *Participatory Rural Development in Pakistan: The Experience of Rural Support Programmes*. (Oxford University Press, 2009).
67. Khan, M. *Participatory Rural Development in Pakistan: The*

Experience of Rural Support Programmes. (Oxford University Press, 2009).

68. Mix Market. "National Rural Support Programme–Data." *Microfinance Information Exchange Inc.,* 2007. http://www.mixmarket.org/mfi/nrsp/data.
69. Khan, M. *Participatory Rural Development in Pakistan: The Experience of Rural Support Programmes.* (Oxford University Press, 2009).
70. Khan, M. *Participatory Rural Development in Pakistan: The Experience of Rural Support Programmes.* (Oxford University Press, 2009).
71. Mix Market. "National Rural Support Programme–Data." *Microfinance Information Exchange Inc.,* 2007. http://www.mixmarket.org/mfi/nrsp/data.
72. Zaidi, S.A. (et al). "Social Impact Assessment of Microfinance Programmes." *Islamabad: European Union-Pakistan Financial Services Sector Reform Programme. Enabling Poor Rural People to Overcome Poverty, International Fund for Agricultural Development Via Paolo di Dono* 44. (2007).
73. Zaidi, S. Akbar, (et al.). "Social Impact Assessment of Microfinance Programmes." *Islamabad: European Union-Pakistan Financial Services Sector Reform Programme. Enabling Poor Rural People to Overcome Poverty, International Fund for Agricultural Development Via Paolo di Dono* 44. (2007).
74. Zaidi, S.A. (et al). "Social Impact Assessment of Microfinance Programmes." *Islamabad: European Union-Pakistan Financial Services Sector Reform Programme. Enabling Poor Rural People to Overcome Poverty, International Fund for Agricultural Development Via Paolo di Dono* 44. (2007).
75. Barnes, C. and J. Sebstad. "Assessing the Impact of Microenterprise Services." *Guidelines for Microfinance Impact Assessments.* (2000).
76. Mayoux, L. "Questioning Virtuous Spirals: Microfinance and Women's Empowerment in Africa." *Journal of International Development,* 11. (1999): 957-984.
77. Zaidi, S.A. (et al.). "Social Impact Assessment of microfinance programmes." *Islamabad: European Union-Pakistan Financial Services Sector Reform Programme. Enabling Poor Rural People to Overcome Poverty, International Fund for Agricultural Development Via Paolo di Dono* 44. (2007).
78. Mayoux, L. "Questioning Virtuous Spirals: Microfinance and Women's Empowerment in Africa." *Journal of International*

Development, 11. (1999): 957-984.

79. Mayoux, L. "Questioning Virtuous Spirals: Microfinance and Women's Empowerment in Africa." *Journal of International Development,* 11. (1999): 957-984. Chant, S. "The Feminization of Poverty and the Feminization of Anti-Poverty Programmes: room for Revision?" *Journal of Development Studies* 44.2. (2006): 165-197.
80. Setboonsarng, S. and Z. Parpiev. *Microfinance and the Millenium Development Goals in Pakistan: Impact Assessment Using Propensity Score Matching.* (Asia Development Bank Institution, 2008).
81. Zaidi, S.A. (et al). "Social Impact Assessment of Microfinance Programmes." *Islamabad: European Union-Pakistan Financial Services Sector Reform Programme. Enabling Poor Rural People to Overcome Poverty International Fund for Agricultural Development Via Paolo di Dono* 44. (2007).
82. Zaidi, S.A. (et al). "Social Impact Assessment of Microfinance programmes." *Islamabad: European Union-Pakistan Financial Services Sector Reform Programme. Enabling Poor Rural People to Overcome Poverty International Fund for Agricultural Development Via Paolo di Dono* 44. (2007).
83. Zaidi, S.A. (et al). "Social Impact Assessment of Microfinance Programmes." *Islamabad: European Union-Pakistan Financial Services Sector Reform Programme. Enabling Poor Rural People to Overcome Poverty International Fund for Agricultural Development Via Paolo di Dono* 44. (2007).

7

Decentralization and Community Governance in India: A Gender Perspective

Bidyut Mohanty

Introduction

The decentralized system of grassroots level governance introduced by the Indian government in 1993 included the mandate that a certain critical percentage of women, Scheduled Caste (SC) and Scheduled Tribe (ST) members—persons placed at the lowest rungs of society—be ensured representation with an aim to making governance more representative, participatory, and inclusive. But being first timers the women in general, and those belonging to SC and ST in particular, though formally partners in governance, have not performed well in these roles. This may primarily be due to a lack of confidence, among other factors. At any rate, in most cases they work as dormant members. Coupled with the 1993 measure, another action facilitated by the Indian state whose primary beneficiaries are women has been the introduction of small loans to microcredit groups aimed at putting additional income in the hands of poor women.

The Government of India introduced these two measures with the expectation that women would become more visible in politics and the economic sphere, and thereby improve their position and bargaining power in the family as well as in society. Both measures have created a huge impact in terms of numbers. While roughly one million women get elected into the local system of decentralized governance every five years, about twenty million women have come under the umbrella of microfinance groups since the mid-1990s. Thus about twenty-one million women are interacting among themselves in public institutions and in the market place. Such an unprecedented number of women working in arenas other than the home has led to substantial social mobilization in India.

Given favourable conditions the effects of the two measures converge. This in turn has led to the opening of a new front through which "women's collectives" have been formed and lively interaction is taking place in the public arena. A women's collective works not only as a pressure group to advocate the implementation of women-friendly programmes channelled through local government, but also to support elected women representatives in carrying out their responsibilities within the local government system. The cementing factor that binds them together is an element of social capital—namely, trust and cooperation—since most of these women belong to common clans and come from similar socio-economic backgrounds, and face similar kinds of discrimination in the family and society. These collectives also try to transcend the barriers of inter-caste conflict by forming women's federations covering larger geographical areas. Under this changed scenario, women leaders have been successful in fulfilling their responsibilities as public leaders. In the process they have been able to strengthen the institutional structure of the local government system and have thereby acquired agency to negotiate, carving out a place for themselves in society from a position of strength. The results of such strengthened agency are reflected in increased life expectancy and literacy. Nevertheless, caution needs to be voiced regarding the longer-term effectiveness of such agency since it has not yet led to an intergenerational change that raises the status of the girl child.

In this chapter an effort will be made to assess the institutional framework of the local government system and its partners with particular regard to elected women representatives and their background. The second section will be devoted to various aspects of microcredit, followed by a section highlighting the synergistic impact of the microcredit and local government systems on the performance of women. In order to substantiate our position, both primary and secondary source materials will be used.

Status of Women in India

Even after over two decades of economic reforms and high growth rates, Indian women lag behind their sisters in neighbouring countries in terms of access to healthcare and education. The infant mortality rate in India far exceeds that of Bangladesh even though India fares much better in terms of per capita income. Similarly, life expectancy is better in Bangladesh compared to India, and the female literacy rate is also much higher there compared to India.[1] Unfortunately, the "female deficit" is much more extensive in India compared to her neighbour,[2] and recent census data on the sex ratio (females per hundred males) shows that areas which had earlier enjoyed a favourable sex ratio now manifest a female deficit, particularly in the age group of 0-6.[3] The child sex ratio shows a declining trend, dropping from 927 to 914 between 2001 and 2011. Moreover, the incidence of dowry-related deaths and domestic violence has not decreased[4]. In other words, women are still treated as second class citizens even after seventy years of freedom.

The reasons for the female deficit are not difficult to trace. First of all, it is to be noted that the total fertility rate has declined all over India,[5] as women are opting for fewer children. Coupled with this is the idea of "son preference," which in a patriarchal societal structure like that in India is still very strong among the rural people owing to lack of old age security in any other form than sibling support. Secondly, the customs of Indian society dictate that daughters are destined for marriage and are bound to go to their husbands' households, while sons stay at home and inherit parental property. As a result, women who have sons get more attention in the family than those who have only daughters. Thus women try to have only sons and might not opt for a second child if their wish is fulfilled in having a son in the first birth. Thirdly, with cheap technology easily available women are able to plan better and opt for a male baby rather than a female. As globalization allows more low caste people to move above the poverty line, communities that previously refrained from neglecting their daughters have started emulating the values of the higher castes. Thus nowadays, low caste communities do not allow their women to work in public. Nor do they give bride price,[6] which earlier had been prevalent among them. On the other hand, low caste communities are adopting the practice of dowry. In addition, they practise sex selective abortions. As a result of these trends, women in general and girl children in particular are devalued. In order to rectify these structural factors, two gender-friendly measures have been taken up and it is to these that we turn next.

Women's Status-Enabling Government Policies

In recent decades two major developments at the policy level have taken place in India to redress women's concerns by gendering political and economic institutions. In politics, women used to be very poorly represented before the introduction of the local government "quota" system. That lacuna has been removed by giving a certain critical percentage of seats to women in those institutions. This has been characterized as the "jump-start" as against "slow start" that would enable women to proceed along the path of women's empowerment.[7] The second development is gendering the money market to deliver small loans to poor women so as to augment income by allowing them to use their hidden entrepreneurial potential. This policy is modelled after the microcredit programme of the Grameen Bank of Bangladesh. While the first initiative was designed to remove the political vacuum in terms of representation, the second one aimed at putting more income into the hands of cash-strapped women, particularly rural women belonging to the SC and ST communities.

In terms of numerical values, the first development has given rise to slightly more than a million elected women leaders per 5-year term at the grassroots level. These are women with diverse social and economic backgrounds. The second measure has drawn roughly twenty million women into Self Help Groups (SHGs). Before proceeding further, we shall look at the institutional set up of the local government institutions in order to depict the real situation in so far as the structure is concerned.

Local Government Institutions and Women's Representation

Till 1993, policies were formulated in the Planning Commission in Delhi and were implemented in the villages by district and block-level administrators. Policies did not reflect the ground reality of local areas that present diverse situations, so there was a dire need for smaller political units not only in order to conceptualize but also to implement relevant policies that would affect the lives of millions of people living in rural areas. Thus in 1993 it was decided at the policy level to give more power to local government units, and thus establish an era of decentralized governance in rural areas. Even though the number of administrative units keeps changing every year as per the size of population and other administrative purposes. According to the latest data there are about 0.65 million village panchayats (village political units), 5,564 block-level panchayats, and 687 district panchayats according to the Government of India[8]. The panchayats are supposed to plan, implement, and monitor almost all local developmental projects, ranging from livelihood issues to food security and other aspects of poverty alleviation, which is much broader than the targets set by the Millennium Development Goals (MDGs).

Although these institutions are given important responsibilities, they are not given an autonomy of untethered funding, dedicated functionaries, nor power to autonomously plan and execute. As a result, panchayats are reduced to mere implementing agencies. Most of their funding comes from the central or state governments and it is allocated at the programme level. These institutions are also burdened with another set of problems, inasmuch as they are superimposed on an already-stratified social structure in terms of power relations, even though the structure shows signs of weakening in certain parts of village India.[9]

Nonetheless, while these institutions have not completely met the goal of Gandhi's *Swaraaj*[10]—the Little Republic—a large number of people do get involved in deciding how to implement the welfare programmes in a more targeted and efficient way. In other words, the local government institutions have opened up potential for villagers to take part in local administration, even though such participation remains somewhat limited.

Opportunities have increased considerably for villagers in general and women in particular since the introduction of a 2005 rights-based livelihood act called Mahatma Gandhi National Rural Employment Guarantee Act (called MG NREGS for short).[11] This scheme, for all its transparency and accountability, is mostly targeted at Scheduled Caste (SC) and Scheduled Tribe (ST) populations as well as other marginalized sections of the people. Its objective is to provide able-bodied labourers with physical work—particularly in the agriculturally slack season that lasts a hundred days—by paying the prevailing minimum wage. The programme is implemented through the panchayats. About 100,000 rupees (Rupees 62.00 = $1) come into panchayats every year to be spent by these elected representatives. Because of this scheme, villagers have shown considerable interest in attending the once purely formal village assemblies (gram sabha).[12]

The Uniqueness of the New Panchayat Setup

The panchayat system has enabled a large number of people to be elected every five years and, in the process, has facilitated the building of human capital. For example, in each five -year-term, there are about three million elected representatives at the all-India level, out of which 75,000 are women. It is because not less than one third of the total seats in each tier of panchayats, both at the ward and headship levels, are reserved for women. Recently the quota was increased to fifty per cent, so that the number of women representatives has risen above the previous level. But unlike "slow track" methods seen elsewhere,[13] the Indian representation model creates conditions in which women often get elected with the support of male family members. As a result, women's own choice of standing for elections is sometimes in doubt, and that may lead to the creation of "dummy" women chiefs in the local government institutions.

The quota has been extended to all groups of women, ranging from SC and ST to general castes. Many micro studies have been conducted in different parts of India to show the impact of such large numbers of women in public space. Some of the studies qualified the success of the quota system, indicating that women do not contest elections on their own and are prompted by male family members and village elders.[14] Others, like Duflo and Chattopadhyay (2004), have noticed that the quota has indeed helped women's visibility in the panchayats.[15] Dwelling briefly on these studies allows us to examine the impact that the quota system has had on women's status in society.

Bardhan et al. (2010) have studied all the districts of West Bengal for the period of 1998 to 2004 and have examined the welfare schemes targeting SC and ST as well as households headed by SC women chiefs.[16] The authors noticed that access to benefits worsened among female-headed households in those panchayats where women are heads of the panchayats. The authors explain this phenomenon as reflecting the relative ignorance of existing benefits among elected women representatives and the exploitation of this ignorance by the elite class. By not sharing information on the existence of other types of benefits available the SC population through panchayats, the elites appropriate benefits for themselves such as agricultural mini kits and irrigation facilities. The authors also pointed out that SC villages gained a lot in terms of access to benefits whenever SC male chiefs were present. However, the study does not take into account the impact of caste and family patriarchies, which are prevalent among the Dalit (SC) women. It is a well-known fact that SC men and women work together in public places. If a SC male is literate, his knowledge of the functioning of the panchayats often becomes evident through elected women. In other words, literate SC men trying to improve the situation of their co-villagers might seek to work through their women, making themselves visible in the process. But it is equally important to point out that women do not form a homogeneous group. For instance, some of them may not have the aptitude to go into politics or are not interested in pursuing it. In others castes, male family members might also have wanted to use women to further their political ambitions. Nevertheless, given a chance, some women do get an opportunity to express their leadership ability through the panchayat system.

On the other hand, Chattopadhyay and Duflo (2004) have studied the national level impact on women of the reservation system in panchayati raj and have noticed a positive correlation between the quota and women's empowerment.[17] These authors have experience in several states and have come to the conclusion that, for example in West Bengal, the elected SC women have invested more on roads and drinking water which are essential for women. In Rajasthan, on the other hand, they invested more on water because it is a desert state. The authors are also of the opinion that because of the reservation system, the SC community has achieved significant representation. Similarly, Beaman, Pande and Topalova (2006) have studied 24 states and have noted that elected women representatives are targeting welfare schemes in a focused manner, while fewer bribery cases are reported. But still the general impression among villagers is that women leaders are not capable of performing well. The authors attribute this to gender bias towards women leaders. Jaffri and Singh (2006), who have been working in a tribal-dominated district of Madhya Pradesh, observe that it is not unusual to find "natural community leadership" among the SC and ST.[18] Some may require exposure to the political environment in order to grow as political leaders and the quota gives them an opportunity to do so. Thus, to dismiss all elected women representatives as rubber stamps or door mats of men would be far from the truth. Finally, even if women do not show leadership quality at the initial stage, their mere presence of them in political institutions has had an empowering impact.

It may therefore be concluded that women's presence in political institutions has shown mixed results. In the next section we discuss the impact of micro-loans in strengthening women's economic power.

Microcredit/Microfinance Groups

As noted earlier, women in India have traditionally been denied both political and economic power leading to the denial of social power as well. To overcome these barriers, various welfare policies were initiated by the government with participation of civil society members and donor agencies. As a result, along with political representation, women in India also gained an opening in the economic sphere. Starting in the 1990s a policy shift in the development paradigm took hold. Till then, developmental policies targeted only male family members, ignoring women's needs and their integral role in household management. But from the 1990s onwards, women's needs were given relatively greater emphasis. Since women are resource strapped and no commercial bank would give them loans without economic collateral, the government decided to start a microloan programme through the Department of Women and Child Development, which got reinvented in the 1980s and 90s a as microcredit programme modelled on the Grameen Bank in Bangladesh.[19] According to one estimate of the National Bank for Agriculture and Rural Development (NABARD)—the nodal agency supporting microcredit groups through various programmes—the microcredit programme has reached 86 million poor households in India alone and the SHGs had bank accounts with outstanding savings of $1.23 billion in 2009. Furthermore, the report also showed that about 4.2 million SHGs are linked with bank loans.[20] According to the latest figure, it has declined to 3.9 million in 2016 informed by 166 MFI ranging in 29 states of India[21]. It is to be noted that the after the crisis of MFIs and resulting in the famers' suicides all over India it was expected to decline drastically. Nonetheless it seems that the vitality of the sector has been regained to some extent particularly after the regulations and introducing the flexibility in the interest rates both for MFIs and for the clients. Though we do not know if it is being implemented or not. According to the Economic Survey of India (2011-12), the SHGs model has been designed in such a way that it encourages women to be linked to the bank not always as a provider of loan services but as a means of saving. The report also points out that of the total number of SHGs, women constitute at least 76 per cent of members. These women contribute 72 per cent of saving and 82 per cent of the outstanding loans in this sector. In the Bharat Microfinance Report, 2016 of which we have referred to in this paragraph, the total women borrowers constitute 97 per cent of the total of which again SC/ST constitute 30 per cent and that of minorities 27.In so far as the urban and rural outreach is concerned the urban one clientele has declined from 67 per cent to 62 per cent between 2015 and 2016. The same report also tells us about the zonal situation. For example, like the previous situation, the southern zone shows the highest growth followed by the east. However, the growth rates are higher in the northeastern and central regions. Further it also reports that the average outstanding loan per borrower turns out to be Rs. 11,429 out of which 94% are used for income generation.

Before microcredit groups are formed, lender agents ("animators") travel from village to village informing villagers about the benefits of microcredit. Women are encouraged to save out of their meagre earnings. Group membership is usually constituted on the basis of shared socio-economic characteristics. For example, sometimes women belong to the same caste or community and are often related to each other. In fact, civil society members try to encourage group formation from within one individual ward to encourage homogeneity, either in terms of belonging to one group of kin or of persons facing similar socio-economic hurdles. It is also important to repeat that the membership of microcredit groups is generally recruited from marginalized sections of the society, such as from SC and ST communities. Further the members also focus on the locally available raw materials and skill as well as market.

Impact of Microcredit on the Status of Women

Many studies of diverse scale and scope have been conducted to gauge the impact of microcredit on the financial, social, and political status of women. Yet few illuminate the improvement of women's economic status after they join SHGs. The majority of the studies do show that access to microcredit reduces "vulnerability" to disaster at the family level.[22] Kabeer (2006), for instance, has examined several microcredit groups comprising of ST and SC and Other Backward Caste (OBC) communities located in remote areas in India, and came to this conclusion. She also pointed out that microcredit has made a very perceptible impact on the social status of women who are slightly above the poverty line. She has studied many non-governmental organizations (NGOs) situated in tribal areas of India and Bangladesh, concluding that women participating in microcredit groups supported by these NGOs are able to manage practical needs such as access to healthcare services and children's education, though not the strategic needs of challenging the power structure embedded in the family. Yet these types of needs overlap. The SHGs studied are mostly engaged in cattle and poultry rearing, paddy husking, and the processing of minor forest products and selling them in neighbouring markets. These types of economic activity require very low capital and a short gestation period, particularly in India. Devika pointed out that the Kudumbashree programme, which is also a microcredit programme, has enabled women to become agents of change, but that it has not gone beyond this point.[23] Specifically, the author analysed the most important government programme on microcredit in Kerala, observing that women have become successful social audit personnel who efficiently live up to their responsibilities, yet still fail to challenge the oppressive power structure in the family.

Both Karim (2011) and Fernando (2006), on the other hand, argue that empowering women should be pursued rather than helping them get microcredit, which leads to indebtedness in cases where they fail to repay their loans on time and shaming for their failure to fulfil family honour.[24] Karim, for example, points out that the logic of microcredit works under the assumption that women are autonomous actors, yet rural women in Bangladesh—as in any feudal society—are bound by several kin relationships including the spouse, in-laws, etc. In many instances family members compel women to borrow from lending institutions, but if they are unable to repay for unforeseen reasons they become the victims of humiliation since they are the prime borrowers. Fernando, discussing contributions to his edited volume, pointed out that the empowerment of women through microcredit became a new orthodoxy after it was introduced in the 1990s.[25] However, in this process women's interests were subordinated to the priorities of mainstream development in a way that became detrimental to the NGO-led empowerment model.

Sharma, on the other hand, suggests that inadequate attention has been paid to assessing through multi-variable analyses the gender impact of microcredit, and she is of the opinion that it does hold potential for microenterprise development and the strengthening of women's capacity provided that strategies shift from the present narrow vision of these programmes, especially in terms of the performance yardstick. She also points out that there is enough evidence to support the notion of "dynamics of collective responsibility" by means of which women have emerged from the poverty trap, citing India-based organizations including Self-Employed Women's Organization (SEWA) to support her argument. Nevertheless, she feels that not much research has been done to determine the chain of causality among crucial variables.

Synergy Between Women's Roles in Microcredit, Panchayats, and Community Governance

In the sections above it was noticed that neither political representation nor microcredit measures have led to unbiased empowerment of women. In many instances the institutional constraints have become obstacles. Fortunately, these barriers have been partially overcome by women combining the opportunities presented to them through the panchayats and microcredit. In such instances women are emerging as successful leaders. In order to demonstrate this success, we will use both secondary and primary source materials.

Pant, for example, has conducted a study of three states and four organizations which have facilitated sixty Self Help Groups, and these NGOs' involvements in twenty-six panchayats.[26] Pant noticed that members of SHGs being facilitated by the NGOs became interested in taking up issues of public concern. For instance, women started disseminating information in these communities about matters such as deliberation in public forums and gram sabha, where basic issues like shelter, pensions, and drinking water are discussed. Through such participation they act as pressure groups to leverage access to resources, agenda setting, and altering rules and norms which can engender better policies. Some of the women got elected to panchayati raj institutions and proved to be effective in these roles. By taking part in various forums their self-confidence increased, as did group solidarity. But in all these cases the women needed the help of NGO members through the entire process. Both Lindberg and Jeyaraman, who have focused on the synergy between the SHGs in Tamil Nadu, reached the same conclusions.[27] For his part, Lindberg pointed out that a "silent revolution" in the form of women's empowerment is slowly taking place in the rural areas of Tamil Nadu. He has been revisiting the same set of households over a span of twenty-five years, and noticed that along with the diversification of occupational structure beyond agriculture, pro-poor policies by the state—including microcredit—have empowered women to become agents of change. He also noticed that SHG members were becoming very vocal and taking part in local elections.

Jeyraman has highlighted trends similar to those observed by Lindberg but has also studied the benefits of the Employment Guarantee Act, which, he adds, has led to women's empowerment but not to the creation of permanent infrastructures in the villages. A similar case is that of the Kudumbashree programme which started in the 1990s as a community-led poverty identification programme in the state of Kerala. At that time, the NABARD had promoted SHG linkages to banking programmes, establishing itself as a viable microfinance model. Kudumbashree, a programme for neighbourhood members, was launched in 1998 as a community network that would work in tandem with local government for poverty eradication and women's empowerment. The programme aims for universality, so it has tried to reach out to each and every poor woman in every village. Its spread has been phenomenal, and made possible only because women are taking charge. The programme includes not only welfare dimensions but also rights-based employment provisions which are routed through the local government system. In this way the programme strives to convert a microfinance-led financial security model into a more comprehensive model of local economic development.

A study taken up by the Institute of Social Sciences (ISS), New Delhi evaluating a UNDP-funded project which had tried to increase the capacity-building measures of elected women representatives from panchayats in ten states revealed that the implementing partners in those states concentrated on building women's networks to carry out community governance, particularly relating to the delivery of basic services among their own villagers. The project ran for five years from 2003 to 2008. The women's networks are active not only at the village level but also at the block and district levels. These women came to know the strength of a women's collective as they went together to the gram sabha village assembly to put pressure on the *sarpanch* (the panchayat chief) to get electricity or drinking water for their villages. Similarly, the women's collective also tried to energize the newly elected women representatives to speak up in the panchayat meetings—so successfully that the women's network could extract the concession that 20 per cent of the panchayat's own revenue would be spent on women-related events. The women's network members were recruited mostly from SC, ST, and OBC. In one of the states the women panchayat chiefs along with some SHGs formed a network to implement a scheme that enabled pregnant women to visit hospitals for delivery of their babies. In the process, the incidence of both maternal and infant mortality decreased[28].

Yet another study conducted by the Institute of Social Sciences, New Delhi which ran from 2003-05 and covered seven states was designed to investigate whether intersections between local government institutions and microcredit groups existed. The project was funded by Plan International, which routes its welfare activities through NGOs and Community Based Organizations (CBOs). One finding was that wherever synergies between the women in panchayats and those in CBOs took place, the benefits of welfare-oriented activities got maximum attention.[29] In one case, a women's collective was determined to implement a project on total sanitation in their panchayat, and with much effort the collective was able to attain this goal. As a result, the panchayat received an award for achieving total sanitation. In all these cases, concerned civil society actors were demonstrative in encouraging the women to organize their collectives so as to realize their goals.

Enabling Factors

In the examples above it becomes apparent that whether women become empowered or become victims of oppressive lending system depends very much on the nature of the NGOs with which women's groups are affiliated. From the studies of Kabeer, Karim and those of the ISS, it has become clear that the nature of microfinance institutions largely determines the kind of results to expect.[30] Kabeer studied organizations working among the tribal groups in remote areas of India. Similarly, the evaluation conducted by the ISS also focused on organizations working with groups of poor SC and OBC women on microcredit initiatives.

But it is also important to find out what kind of women's networking is taking place. For example, in most of our cases women belong to poor families for whom "governance" essentially means delivery of basic services, such as drinking water, a school nearby for their children, and electricity. They also realize that it is the role of local government to provide them with these basic services and that it is these institutions through which they can lobby to get things done. Thus the principle of social capital in the form of bonding, trust, and group solidarity become the crucial factor. Pai has also shown how the chiefs of local government institutions recruited from Scheduled Castes in one Indian state have targeted welfare programmes very effectively among their own members.[31] Importantly, they belong to similar socio-economic backgrounds. The author was trying to show the strength of social capital formation among the most downtrodden groups of society, but she also pointed out that in another setting social capital became inoperative because of intra-caste rifts.

For her part, Karim has observed big microfinance institutions of Bangladesh working with a pure profit motive and trying to adopt arm-twisting measures to recover loans at any cost. Needless to say, some of the microfinance institutions working in India are employing similar kinds of pressure tactics and women are falling into debt by borrowing money from multiple organizations, and in turn lending it to other, poorer women. This problem reached a crisis stage in 2006 in one Indian state culminating in 2010 and drew the attention of the Reserve Bank of India to regulate the microfinance industry.[32] But to judge all microfinance organizations and all microcredit groups as equally fraught would be a mistake. To quote Sharma: "There is no one grand model which will work across different contexts. The outcomes will be determined by many factors, including the microeconomic policy framework, the role of mediating organizations, different stakeholders' group dynamics, and so on."[33]

Concluding Remarks

With the low economic and political status of Indian women as a backdrop, two gender-friendly measures—women's representation in local government institutions and microcredit loans to poor women—were introduced by the Government of India with the objective of increasing women's visibility in the public sphere. The immediate results of these two measures have been to bring a large number of women into the public arena, leading to tangible social mobilization. Owing to institutional and other social barriers, women have not been able to achieve the full potential of these two measures. But they have enabled women benefiting from the measures to come together and form women's collectives, and attempt to manage the governance of basic services at the community level. In many places these groups have made a difference in opening access to those services through the use of collective strength and social capital. Such collective networks should be mobilized to their full potential in order to achieve the maximum gains from the government measures. It may be also argued that if the women's networks are encouraged, other social ills such as deliberate sex-selective abortions might also be reduced.

NOTES

1. Sen, Amartya K. "Growth and Other Concerns. Reservation to Participation: Capacity Building of Elected Women Representatives and Functionaries of Panchayati Raj Institutions." (*The Hindu*, February 2011).
2. Klasen, S. and C. Wink. "Missing Women: Revisiting the Debate." *Capabilities Freedom and Equality, Amartya K. Sen's Work from a Gender Perspective.* (New Delhi: Oxford University Press, 2006).
3. Interestingly, the problem of sex ratio (females per thousand males) has become very complex. The result of the recent census shows that the overall sex ratio has increased from 933 to 940 between 2001 and 2011.This reflects that women in the age groups of 7+ and above are living longer than that of men. Biologically this is more logical than the other trend that is decreasing sex ratio in the age group of 0-6. At another level, the total fertility rate of Indian women has decreased from 2.9 to 2.6 within a decade but this figure masks regional variations. In many states the fertility rate has decreased to just one per cent and the fertility rate of the high growth rate states particularly in the northern states has also decreased though at a lower rate. (*Indian Express*.com/news/). So many families are opting for a smaller family norm, and hence the maternal mortality rate is also declining. It has implications for the status of women in the older age groups but the declining fertility rate is taking place at the expense of the girl child, which should be taken note of.
4. http://www.firstpost.com/india/crimes-against-women-up-34-in-four-years-most-reports-from-up-maharashtra-west-bengal-2991754.html
5. http://www.thehindu.com/data/india-to-reach-replacement-levels-of-fertility-by-2020/article6717297.ece
6. Bride price in contrast to dowry is paid by the son's family, particularly in SC, ST and OBC communities. It was so because women in those communities used to participate in economically useful work such as working on the field or selling the fishermen's catch in the market or selling milk products in the market. But once these communities climb the economic ladder, they try to withdraw their women folk from public and practice sex selective abortions.
7. Dahlerup, D. "Introduction." *Women, Quotas and Politics.*

(London: Routledge Taylor & Francis US, 2006).

8. https://www.google.co.in/?gfe_rd=cr&ei=HM_kV5-UMpPy8AeE6bboCg#q=Total+number+of+Districts%2C+India+2016
9. Lindberg, S. "A Silent Revolution? Women's Empowerment in Rural Tamil Nadu." *Economic and Political Weekly,* March 26, 2011. http://www.epw.in/special-articles/silent-revolution-womens-empowerment-rural-tamil-nadu.html
10. Swaraaj, the Little Republic was first conceptualized by Mahatma Gandhi in 1909 to mean self-rule by the community.
11. Dreze, J. *National Rural Employment Guarantee Act.* (Delhi: National Book Trust, 2005). Government of India. *Economic Survey 2011-12* (New Delhi, Oxford University Press, 2012). http://www.grameen.com/index.php?option=com_content&task=view&id=782&Itemid=751.
12. In the new 'avatar' the functioning of the gram sabha is quite essential for the healthy functioning of the local government or panchayats. Since the introduction of the above mentioned Act, even women who used to shun the meetings for the presence of the village elders started trickling into the meeting. As will be seen later, women are the major beneficiaries of this scheme.
13. Dahlerup characterized the high percentage of women's representation in political institutions, particularly in the context of Nordic countries, as "slow track," pointing out that the process took at least forty years to reach a critical mass of forty per cent. Nowadays nobody wants to wait that long so some countries are attempting to "fast track" the process, whereby the quota provision would increase the number of women in the political institutions overnight. Dahlerup, D. "Introduction." *Women, Quotas and Politics*. (London: Routledge Taylor & Francis US, 2006).
14. Bardhan, P., D. Mukherjee and M.P. Torrado. "Impact of Political Reservations in West Bengal Local Governments on Anti-Poverty Targeting." *Journal of Globalization and Development* 1.1. (2010). Beaman, L., E. Duflo, R. Pande and P. Topalova. "Women Politicians, Gender Bias and Policy Making in Rural India" UNICEF, *The State of World's Children,* New York (2007).
15. Jafri, A. and V. Singh. "Gender Mainstreaming in District Plans in Madhya Pradesh." In Niraja Gopal Jayal, Amit Prakash, Pradeep K. Sharma (eds.) *Local Governance in India; Decentralization and Beyond*. (New Delhi: Oxford University Press, 2006).
16. Bardhan, P., D. Mukherjee and M.P. Torrado. "Impact of Political

Reservations in West Bengal Local Governments on Anti-Poverty Targeting." *Journal of Globalization and Development* 1.1. (2010), pp. 1-34.
Beaman, L., Esther Duflo, R. Pande and Petia Topalova. "Women Politicians, Gender Bias and Policy Making in Rural India", UNICEF, *The State of World's Children,* New York (2007).

17. Chattopadhyay, R. and E. Duflo. "Women as Policy Makers: Evidence from a Randomized Policy Experiment India." *Econometrica,* 72.5. (2004).
18. Jafri, A. and V. Singh. "Gender Mainstreaming in District Plans in Madhya Pradesh", op. cit.
19. In India also there is a model of self help which is really a bottom up approach, unlike the Grameen Bank or later microcredit programmes in India. The Self Employed Women's Association or SEWA is an organization in which women from the informal sector set up a cooperative and saved their own resources, then took loans from that. But it is not scaling up like the microcredit program, perhaps because every woman has a skill but she may not require capital to start; the objective of the microcredit programme is that it ignites the hidden skill of the poor women.
20. According to the website of Grameen Bank there are about 8 million members, and 1,253,160 groups working with the bank, which has a $648.68 million balance as a single bank. There are other large microfinancing institutions such as BRAC, ASA whose membership also runs into millions of women in the countryside of Bangladesh.
21. Ramesh, Sowmya. "Highlights of Bharat Microfinance Report." (2016) <se-mf@solutionexchange-un.net.in>
22. Naila, K. "Microfinance, The MDGs and Beyond: What Difference Can Financial Services to Low-Income Women Make?" (New Delhi: IFAD and UNIFEM Gender Mainstreaming Programme in Asia, 2006).
23. Devika, J. "Between 'Empowerment' and 'Liberation' The Koodumbasree Initiative in Kerala." *The Indian Journal of Gender Studies,* 14.1. (2007): 33-60.
24. Karim, L. *Microfinance and Its Discontents: Women in Debt in Bangladesh.* (Minneapolis & London: University of Minnesota Press
25. Fernando, J. (ed.). 'Introduction, Microcredit and Empowerment of Women in *Microfinance, Perils and Prospects* (New York: Routledge, 2006). pp. 1-36.
26. Pant, M. "Self Help Groups as Change Agents in Enhancing the

Political Participation of Women in Local Self Governance." In Sumi Krishna (ed.) *Women's Livelihood Rights Recasting Citizenship for Development.* (New Delhi, Sage, 2007): 318-44.

27. Lindberg, S. "A Silent Revolution? Women's Empowerment in Rural Tamil Nadu." *Economic and Political Weekly,* March 26, 2011. http://www.epw.in/special-articles/silent-revolution-womens-empowerment-rural-tamil-nadu.html
28. UNDP (2009) *From Reservation to Participation ; Capacity Building of Elected Women Elected Women Representatives and Functionaries of Panchayati Raj Institutions,* Unpublished Report.
29. Ghosh, B., B. Mohanty, and N. Jacob (eds.). *Local Governance: Search for New Path.* (Concept Publishing Company, 2011).
30. Karim, L. *Microfinance and its Discontents: Women in Debt in Bangladesh.* (Minneapolis & London: University of Minnesota Press, 2011). Fernando, J. (eds.). Introduction: *Microfinance, Perils and Prospects* (New York: Routledge, 2006). Kabeer, N. *Microfinance, the MDGs and Beyond: What Difference Can Financial Services to Low-Income Women Make?* (New Delhi: IFAD and UNIFEM Gender Mainstreaming Programme in Asia, 2006).
31. Pai, Sudha (2004). "Social Capital, Panchayats and Grassroots Democracy: The Politics of Dalit Assertions in Two Districts of Uttar Pradesh" in Dwaipayan Bhattacharyya, Niraja Gopal Jayal, Bishnu Mohapatra (eds.) *Interrogating Social Capital: The Indian Experience.* (New Delhi, Sage), pp. 35-70.
32. Sriram, M.S. "Microfinance Industry in India: More Thoughts", *Economic and Political Weekly* 46.50. (2011): 110-12.
33. Sharma, K. "Small Loans, Big Dreams: Women and Microcredit in a Globalized World", *The Economic and Political Weekly,* 46.43. (2012): 58-63.

8

Microcredit: An Indian Experience

Annapurna Pandey

Introduction

This chapter is based on an ethnographic study of alternative microcredit initiatives introduced in select villages in the eastern Indian state of Odisha and the town of Puri, a major pilgrim centre on its eastern coast. With detailed case studies of marginalized and destitute women who are excluded from the conventional microcredit programmes, it provides new insights on very small-scale assistance programmes, also called 'nanofinance', for these women. It outlines an alternative model for financial support for the economic activities started by these women and compares it with the microcredit schemes promoted by banks and microfinance institutions in the neoliberal economy. In this chapter, I analyse programmes adopted for widows and abandoned women living in the Swadhar home in Puri town and interest-free microcredit schemes promoted by an organization called Amara Biswas, through which rural women have created a new social and economic space for themselves with the help of microfinance.

Over the last thirty years, microfinance has emerged as an important model of development of small enterprises, especially for women in South Asia. In 2009, more than 128 million of the world's poorest families took microloans, up from just 7.6 million in 1997 and investment funds for microfinance totalled over $11 billion, according to a Microcredit Summit Campaign report released in March 2011.[1]

As stated in a UN report of 1997: "Microcredit is a critical anti-poverty tool—a wise investment in human capital...[W]hen the poorest, especially women, receive credit, they become economic actors with power. Power to improve not only their own lives, but in a widening circle of impact, the lives of their families, their communities and their nations."[2]

Recent case studies of microcredit initiatives, however, have been deeply sceptical of their problematic and sometimes violent outcomes.[3] As reported in the print media, these days the picture of microcredit programmes carried out in India looks anything but rosy. A recent report on microcredit observed that microcredit moneylenders have become a new source of exploitation,reportedly charging anywhere from 23 per cent to 60 per cent interest on the loans (*Washington Times*, October 30, 2010). Such behaviour causes endless grief among poor villagers, often with fatal consequences to the borrowers of microcredit loans.

Why Odisha?

Odisha in eastern India is known for its abundant natural resources but is, ironically, one of the poorest states in India with 32.6 per cent of its population defined as living below the poverty line (BPL) compared to the all India average of 21.9 per cent[4]. The tribal communities or Adivasis, officially called Scheduled Tribes (ST), who constitute 22.85 per cent of the state's population, and the historically disadvantaged 'Dalits' or Scheduled Castes (SC, the former outcastes) who constitute 17.13 per cent, together form nearly 40 per cent of the total population of the state. Further, the poverty level among the ST is 63.52 per cent while it is 41.39 per cent for the SC. For another large population group of farmers, landless tenants, husbandry men and artisans called Other Backward Classes or OBC the BPL level is 24.16 per cent (ibid). Since independence, despite constitutional protections for these groups, various development programmes of industrialization and mining leading to deforestation and displacement have impoverished tribal and other communities dependent on natural resources for their sustenance. Manoranjan Mohanty (2014) aptly describes

Odisha to be a case that presents a crisis of democracy with upper caste and patriarchal domination that has been consolidated through the formation and expansion of an educated middle class that provides services to the capitalist extractive economy, while vast sections of the population, especially Adivasis, the indigenous tribes, Dalits and agricultural workers remain marginalized.

Women and the girl child have suffered the most from these policies because of inadequate opportunities for education and employment and the structural constraint of being both unpaid labour on family farms and the primary caregivers at home, especially of children and the elderly. As per the 2011 Census, women's literacy stands at 64.36 per cent, whereas the overall literacy rate is at 73.45. There is a wider gap in ST and SC literacy rates as girl children in many rural and tribal areas drop out of school at an early age. There is a huge disparity between the general masses and indigenous people. Women from the ST communities remain excluded and though enrolment is increasing, dropout is very high. About 75 per cent of tribal women are engaged in agriculture and in the unorganized sector such as mining, *bidi* manufacturing, NTFP collection and construction work. The female labour force constituting one-third of the rural workers in India "face serious problems and constraints related to work such as lack of continuity, insecurity, wage discrimination, unhealthy job relationships, and absence of medical and accident care" (Hans and Patel, 2012).

The Role of Microcredit and Women in Odisha

It is widely recognized that financial independence is the key to women's empowerment. The role of microfinance in giving credit to the women in rural and tribal areas who do not have any access to mainstream banking institutions has been widely acknowledged (Arnopoulos, 2010; Ghate, 2006; Kingsolver, 2009; Dhanabhakyam and Mufliha, 2013). As an effort to make loans more accessible to poor and low-income women, the United Nations launched the International Year of Microcredit in 2005. In Odisha, microfinance has emerged over the last ten to fifteen years as one of the fastest growing and most promising interventions addressing the issues of women's empowerment and poverty reduction. There are twenty-three major microfinance institutions (MFIs) actively working in rural Odisha. Some of them are very well known, such as Annapurna, Gram Utthan, SMCS, Adhikar, Bandhan, SKS, Ujjivan, among others. In a study comparing four low income states in India, it is observed that even though Odisha claims to have 32.02 lakhs (3.2 million) borrowers, only 10.09 lakhs (1 million) are active constituting 38 per cent of the total borrowers[5]. The decrease in active borrowing is obviously a deterrent for the growth of microfinance institutions in the region.

In order to empower poor and marginalized women, the state government has introduced a programme called Mission Sakti, linking women's self-help groups (SHGs) with microfinance institutions. The network of women SHGs across the state and reservations for women in the three-tier local government system of elected panchayats in rural Odisha provide some visibility and work opportunities to large numbers of women. However, statistics suggest that a majority of economically active but poor women remain deprived of any economic gain from microcredit loans. As per government records there are 3.87 lakhs (.38 million) WSHGs with 46.5 lakh (4.6 million) women as members having a credit link (Hans and Patel, 2012). In contrast, the microcredit loans are very low though knowledge of microcredit has been found to be high. Data indicate that the concentration of microfinance amongst economically active women across all the states including Odisha is minuscule. There appears to be very little correlation between female literacy and the extent of microlending in Odisha.[6] However it is known that women find microcredit loans a high risk, low safety strategy and stay away from MFIs solely run for profit who do not take into account the personal constraints of the borrowers or the natural tragedies that borrowers are often subject to.

What is Wrong with Microcredit? Reports from Various Studies

Reports from various studies like that of Jude Fernando (2010) paint a grim picture of the microcredit scenario: women borrow money to start income-generating initiatives that may fail miserably due to such factors as excessive or insufficient rainfall necessary for the sustenance of a crop,[7] or the objects of the loans like goats and cattle dying of illness. Another major problem is social and political pressure such as the humiliation and shame people face in case of default.[8] For example, some microfinance lenders take advantage of uneducated women and charge exorbitant interest rates, creating strong pressure to make timely payments. Fernando reports that MFIs in the Asia-Pacific region charge interest rates ranging from thirty to fifty per cent a year.[9] It is noteworthy that borrowers are typically not aware of the overall interest rate. They only know how much they have borrowed and how much the interest per week is. The biggest incentive for them is that the microcredit interest is definitely less than that of loans they had been taking individually from the local village moneylenders.

Compared to the usual complicated loan process through banks and other major lending institutions, the microcredit system is supposed to make the loan process very simple. Lendees are required to provide photographs of the husband and wife and must sign the loan documents.[10] The signed document is simply collected and about 10,000 to 15,000 rupees are handed over to each family for a period of fifty weeks. They have to return an amount plus interest every week (technically, equated weekly instalment or EWI).[11]

In the conventional microcredit model, as an incentive for women who successfully pay back the loan in fifty weeks, the loan amount to each of their group members is doubled. If a member has not been able to pay on time the other members will not get a new loan unless the pending amount is cleared. If any one of the members is unable to pay back their loan, other members pressure her to repay by whatever means—whether by selling her household utensils, land, domestic animals, or even children. In many incidents not reported in the media, a family had to give away their child to get money to pay back a loan, and after arranging money from elsewhere (at five to ten per cent interest per month) got the child back. Peer pressure is the most shameful for a woman. If she is in default on her loan, the other members in the village will hound her. Even if she leaves the village, they will trace her and make life very difficult for her.

In many instances, the microfinance loan trap leads to distress migration. Even though provision of insurance for crop loss or loss of life on the part of the lendee exists among some microfinance corporations, it is not disbursed as common practice. Programme members are often not aware of it. When asked the question of how a woman should repay the money in case of total loss of the investment due to natural causes like untimely rain, fire, storm, diseases or any kind of accident, an answer like this one is typical: "[T]hat is not our business; whatever they have to do, they have to return our money. They may borrow it from the local people or arrange it which ever way they can." In the eyes of one reporter, "A microfinance loan is like slow poison, worse than alcohol or drugs. These companies are luring the people and getting them addicted to loans and then telling them that they are unsocial, illiterate poor."[12]

Various studies on microfinance institutions report that poor village women have become embroiled in debt, with forty to fifty per cent interest rates and the constant fear of losing their home and land due to the compounding interest added to their principal. As Bidyut Mohanty, an activist engaged in the Right to Food Campaign in tribal areas of the Koraput district, notes: "There is no difference between moneylenders and MFIs. Both are exploiting the poor."[13] Defaulters are subjected to mental torture, social pressure and even physical violence when they cannot repay these loans.[14]

Recent news from Odisha confirms some of the observations made above. Amitabh Patra has reported on suicides due to the burden of microfinance debts.[15] In April 2011 there were several such suicide cases—one male, one female, and one entire family of six people including small children—within a single week, all the residents of Bargarh District. Families in this region had received loans from the World Bank-funded, government supported SHG programme with agent NGOs as well as microfinance companies like Swayam Krishi Sangam (SKS), Spandana, Asmita, VISWA, a few more companies backed by ITC (Indian Tobacco Company), and Vedanta-like corporate entities that are causing havoc across the country. Focused on charging higher interest, these companies are primarily committed to profit making and are increasingly becoming less concerned in the well-being of the borrowers. Many families originally took the loans for animal husbandry but the goats died of illness. Having no agricultural land such families now survive as casual labourers. One of the husbands is a deaf-mute. The wives are being regularly threatened and told to sell their homes. They are no longer able to live in their own villages. They are even abused by other members of the SHG when seen at a workplace, while going out to bathe, or when visiting a relative in the village on any occasion.

Microfinance is regarded by many observers as a disease that has spread into every nook and corner of Odisha. Besides the just mentioned recent suicides in Bargarh, there are reports of suicides in Kalahandi among cotton farmers after distress selling and the burden of the loan traps created by such microfinance companies. Meanwhile, there has been massive competition among various private corporations promoting money transfer in the name of microfinance.[16] In a different example, about twenty families from backward castes moved to an area of Andhra Pradesh to work at brick kilns as migrant labourers. Most of the families in this village have taken loans from the five to seven microfinance companies operating nearby.

The poor are not the only people who have been afflicted by microfinance drudgery and suffering at the hands of corporate moneylenders. As a result of loan default, even better-off families are moving away from their villages, leaving behind houses which get registered with the lenders. For example, after being trapped by microfinance loans, four well-to-do families were ruined and fled from their village after selling or mortgaging their homes. The homes were later transferred to their lenders (Patra, 2011).

There are several instances of microfinance lenders entering a village and assembling groups of fifteen to twenty-five women who take the loans. Several companies have invested rupees four to six lakhs each ($9,200 to $13,800 respectively) in a village and effectively collect more than thirty-six per cent interest, most of it from illiterate people. The loans have spread to families engaged in many other occupations besides agriculture.

Even if loan recipients are able to start small-scale production enterprises, they often have difficulty bringing goods to market,[17] and any increased contribution to household income they achieve is often met by a corresponding decrease from other household members.[18] Studies in Africa suggest that the benefits of microfinance loans seem to accrue to women who are already of high status.[19] In summary, even though researchers find microcredit to be the sure route out of poverty it is claimed to be, the gap between the rhetoric and the reality of microcredit is wide.[20] From the examples above, I conclude that microcredit, in the model of the neoliberal economy introduced in India in the 1990s, has given rise to a tremendous disparity between the haves and have-nots.

The microfinance institutions that emerged as a pro-poor social enterprise in the 1980s, turned into commercial ventures with a "market model" within a decade. An eyewitness account narrates a day with microfinance loan agents in one village:

> Yesterday I went to Jatlaa Village, under Sarkanda Gram Panchayat in Bargarh District to observe the process of money transfer from the women's SHG to the loan agent. The SKS (Swayam Krishi Sangham) finance agents start their day at about 7 am, when women are busy with their daily housework. The microfinance companies schedule a weekly collection for each group of about 20 women. They arrive sharply at the discussed time: if they come late, they pay a fine of ten rupees; if the women borrowers are late, they pay a fine of ten rupees each. In this way timely collection is ensured. The agents get a salary of about five thousand rupees per month and an incentive percentage of the collection. Women start gathering at the group collection centre from about 7 am, and keep waiting for the agent.[21]

The microfinance groups supported by foreign agencies have refigured the Hindu cultural values of women in the villages.

A model of relationship has developed between the agencies and their local women clients. The village women are looked upon as a culturally distinctive "Indian consumer" and are entiçed in the name of Shakti (goddess of power and strength) to take loans from these microfinance institutions.[22]

MFI agents treat the members of the women's groups with great respect when initiating the programme. The women, who are used to normal treatment at home, are addressed as "mothers" and elevated to the status of "Goddess Laksmi." The respect shown to them is reciprocated by the women. A few local men who witnessed these proceedings said that as husbands they never received such respect from their wives as the loan agents receive from the women.[23]

An Alternative Programme to Microcredit: A Conceptual Analysis

What opportunities might exist for women who do not qualify for microfinance? What are possible alternatives to the profit-based microcredit programmes popularized by international organizations and promoted by the state? Despite negative images of various microfinance programmes, my preliminary study documents the success of an alternative model: local, indigenous efforts to reach out to women who do not qualify for microcredit from international programmes and local NGOs, and the impact of these local initiatives in creating a sense of empowerment among women that propels them to improve their personal situation and build up strong social networks.

One group of women, rejected or abandoned by their families, namely, widows, deserted women and destitute girls have found it difficult to access any form of financial assistance even for their survival. In this chapter, I will focus on two alternative programmes focusing on such women and addressing some of the above issues, that were initiated for widows, destitute women and girls separated from their families—Swadhar and Aamar Biswas in the state of Odisha. The women at the centre of my research are framed as victims by both the state government and international monetary organizations. Existing microcredit programmes would not qualify them for any kind of loan. The state perpetuates their victimhood and dependency by placing them in shelters. But in order to achieve a fair assessment it is imperative to set aside the standard criteria and look deeper, and in unlikely places. I would argue that the increasingly commercialized microcredit programmes may be helping women to become economically independent, but the poorest of the poor are left out in the microcredit profit-making model. Many studies of microcredit emphasize its social benefits, which of course are far more compelling than the pessimistic perception of why it fails.[24]

Based on my fieldwork among the women of the Swadhar Widows Home in Puri, India, I aim to show how women who are looked upon as social outcastes, having neither capital nor assets in their name and without even the means to survive, have taken advantage of an alternative to conventional microcredit and not only managed to change their self-image, but also found new meaning in their lives through their entrepreneurship ventures. On the basis of a few case studies, I will analyse the success of these alternative microcredit programmes. I will emphasize what is unique and innovative about the case studies in terms of the methods that the women have used to make their business ventures a success and the challenges they continue to face in this effort.

I first met the women residing in Swadhar (literally translated as "Self Sustenance") in 2006. This home was set up by social activist Chandrika Mohapatra in 2006 under a scheme for 'Women in Difficult Circumstances" launched by the Department for Women and Child Development of the Government of Orissa in 2001-2 in cooperation with reputed non-government organizations (NGOs). After hearing about the life-altering accounts of these women from Chandrika Mohapatra, president of Vijaya, a non-profit women's organization headquartered in Odisha's capital, Bhubaneswar, I visited Swadhar again in the summer of 2007 and in 2011. Primary data was collected using qualitative methods, including key informant interviews, focus-group interviews, field observation, and informal interviews. This chapter is based on research conducted between 2007 and 2011.[25] Conversations with officials of various NGOs facilitated cross checking of information supplied by respondents. I also informally interviewed a key woman leader who founded Amara Biswas (Our Faith), an alternative microcredit programme, which she calls Nano Finance, to be discussed later in this chapter and some of its women participants.

Two Alternative Microlending Models: Swadhar and Amara Biswas

My study of the widows' home "Swadhar" in Puri, and Amara Biswas, in the state of Odisha, provide unique accounts. First, these women are not model microcredit consumers. They do not belong to typical families and hold no collateral. The women in Swadhar are not from the same village, do not belong to a Self Help Group (SHG), nor do they have the money to invest in a cooperative. The widows do not have a co-signer to avail of any loan. The Swadhar Home run by the NGO Vijaya is devoted to their rehabilitation and empowerment in a patriarchal society. Chandra Talpade Mohanty notes, "struggles for gender justice and women's rights are multifaceted, and focus on psychic, socio-political, economic and cultural aspects of patriarchal relations." (Mohanty, 2013). With a change of space and some financial assistance, these women who have been subject to grave physical and sexual abuse and economic deprivation, have found new opportunities in their life, by exploring their capabilities and developing their social networks challenging the social stigmas and taboos associated with their marginalized status in Hindu society.

My focus is on marginalized, destitute women who may not qualify to become clients of typical microfinance organizations, and my investigation involves an alternative microcredit model and its impact on the lives of these widows. I explore the networking relationship of the women availing themselves of microcredit, rather than looking at the latter as a purely financial initiative. Few studies have focused on the women who slip through the microcredit net, so to speak, due to financial and social constraints or to how they make use of alternative sources of support and sustenance.

Looking at microcredit as a social project rather than a financial one, especially for socially marginalized women, I have observed that the women do not consider themselves to be victims. In so many instances they face their adverse situations with tremendous courage and dignity, and always come forward to fight for their fair share in society and demand social justice. The women of the widows' home I researched are deriving new meaning through their intra-group networks as a loan group. My experience shows that the widows of Odisha, rather than being completely removed from or oppressed by economic and social relationships (as wives, daughters, mothers, and sisters), are engaged in different kinds of negotiations with each other as well as with various institutions of the larger society and the state. In the process, these women dispel the widely held view that they are among the least empowered and most marginalized women in India. With the help of a loan, this collective of women was able to find niches to explore their capabilities, trying out their entrepreneurial capacities against the social stigmas and taboos associated with their status as widows and destitute.

Among the Hindu majority in India, widows are looked upon as inauspicious. On the death of a husband whatever role a wife had played—as daughters, sisters, and mothers—suddenly becomes problematic. All relevant studies show that widows continue to be the most despised among women in India, and their dismal condition even in modern Indian society has attracted the attention of several scholars.[26] Their studies confirm that widows are treated as a separate social category irrespective of age and are subject to discrimination in terms of class and property holdings.[27]

Odisha is known as one of the most backward states in India. Compared to the national average, women have lagged behind in education, employment in organized and unorganized sectors, and in health. As a result, the state government has been promoting the Women's Development Programme (WDP) since the mid-1980s in collabouration with various non-governmental organizations. Microcredit has been popularized through SHGs (self-help groups) and has been introduced as part of WDP in Odisha and in many other states. The WDP epitomizes the shift towards both empowerment and the greater participation of poor, rural, and tribal women in the wider women's movement project. Here I would argue that even though microcredit as part of the WDP was introduced and strongly implemented in the state of Odisha with the collabouration of the Indian state, NGOs, and various foreign funding agencies (the World Bank and the Ford Foundation, among others), it has failed to reach a certain section of women—especially widows, who constitute an integral segment of the most marginalized group of women in Indian society.[28]

Swadhar: The Widows' Home

In 2006, Chandrika Mohapatra started Swadhar under a government initiated programme, to give shelter to widows and other women deserted by their families.[29] What follows is a brief overview of what Swadhar is and what it has done since its inception, relying first on a self-description of the organization appearing in its official brochure.

Swadhar is a national level model, yet an innovative rehabilitation centre for widows, women affected by domestic violence, sexual harassment, physical handicaps and women in distress, including elderly women seeking emotional support, love, affection, care, and protection. The innovation finds expression in caring for these women by way of inculcating human values in life and promoting social justice. Since July 2006, over 150 widows, elderly, and destitutes have been provided shelter; however, the number at times goes beyond 200 and fluctuates throughout the year. The high density of women at this home may be because it is located in Puri, the land of Lord Jagannath, where widows conglomerate from all corners of the state in search of *mokshya* (salvation), to find ultimate meaning in their life. This home is under an approved scheme of the government but the funds provided are inadequate for the maintenance expenses (only a sum of Rs. 500 per month, per person is available under the scheme). The government does not provide any other resources to enable these women to contribute meaningfully to the society.[30]

When I visited this home, I was struck by the range of women representing different socio-economic strata as well as different age groups living together. The residents comprised elderly women in their seventies and eighties, middle-aged women in their forties, fifties and sixties, and some young women in their twenties and thirties. In 2006, there were ninety-eight women living in this home. Even though they belonged to different age groups, their commonality was that they were all suffering from the loss of a partner due either to death or to extended absence.

Compared to the United States, the Indian state does not have adequate institutional mechanisms to provide care for old people and unfortunates like these widows. Traditionally, they are expected to be taken care of by family members. But in a changing economy, families are shying away from the moral responsibility of taking care of their widows and other unfortunates, and as a result, the latter simply end up on the street. The neoliberal economy and privatization of vital resources have compelled the state to shrink its social welfare policies and programmes, causing destitute women deserted by their families to seek protection through non-governmental organizations. Families under financial constraints are pushing their mothers, wives, and sisters to NGOs that are doing what families were doing previously, so that the NGOs have taken over some of the functions, responsibilities and obligations of the state to take care of its marginalized citizens. These women are therefore doubly marginalized: first they are widows, and second, they are poor.

I was persuaded by Mrs. Mohapatra to get involved with Swadhar, and so periodically I would spend some time with these women when I went to Odisha. From my conversations with them I learned that they were enthusiastic about starting a catering business that could make them economically independent, and give them a chance to use their skills and feel good about themselves. The real challenge was where to find funds. Some of my enthusiastic friends and I got the idea to conduct a fundraising campaign in 2007, tapping the local talent available in the San Francisco Bay Area of California among

Odissi and Bollywood dancers, *Bhajan* (Hindu devotional songs) singers, and others. My family and students distributed pamphlets and invitations through E-vite, we rented a communal kitchen and cooked a sumptuous Indian meal. Sixty people from different parts of our community came to attend the performance, and in all we raised $6,000 to contribute to the Swadhar organization.

In 2008, I travelled to Odisha and spent a day at Swadhar, discovering that the women had invested the money we raised in 2007 to buy a refrigerator, a commercial stove, a grinder, and pots and pans to start their business enterprise. Now, they employ their skills making puris, allo dum, chutneys, and pappads, as well as spices and chhatu and badi, all popular food items, and supplying the local women's college and tourists coming to the Jagannath temple with these foods. Through this enterprise they have discovered new strength in themselves. This endeavour has helped them in developing a new sense of identity as independent, self-assured, and productive members of the community. Entrepreneurship has given a new meaning to their lives.

On my visit to Vijaya-Swadhar Home in the summer of 2011, I met Sabita, a demure and pretty twenty-four-year-old with an easy smile on her face. When asked, she quipped: "Apa, I am the first one in my village who studied till class ten. I always wanted to do something for the neglected women. I used to listen on radio and was inspired by women leaders who would discuss women's issues and about various programmes to help women out."

Sabita had an arranged marriage at the age of eighteen in 2005. Her father had agreed to give Rs. 30,000 (about $500) in dowry. He did not give the entire amount because he had heard that her husband was not a reliable person and wanted to make sure that her in-laws were treating her right. From day one of her marriage, she was tortured regularly by her mother-in-law and her husband and was treated worse than a servant. She claims that her father-in-law was a decent person but her mother-in-law was a tyrant. She had several broken fingers and toes and was in despair. To add to her travails, Sabita had two children in quick succession, a six-year-old daughter and 5-year-old son. Her husband would lock her up in the house and would not allow her to interact with anybody. One day she escaped from the house and left without knowing her destination. Only with the faith in Lord Jagannath, she landed up at Vijaya, Puri. When asked how she feels being here, she said:

> I am at peace here. Since I got married, I suffered so much! I do miss my children. But Jagannath is my only refuge. When I left home, I did not know where I would land, whether in the jungle or the ocean! Yes, my husband was very unfair and did not treat me well. But I do not want to punish anybody. It is up to Jagannath. I am very happy. Ma, the supervisor of the programme, has given me saris to wear and has taken me to see my Lord Jagannath. Whatever work I am asked to do, I chip in. I help with the sale of milk, our little store and the catering. Till I breathe my last, let Jagannath keep me at his feet.

In the summer of 2011, ninety-two women were living at the home, a rented house with ten spacious rooms and thirteen bathrooms spread out on three floors. A retired nurse supervises the residents as the in-house director. They receive a weekly visit from a local doctor who provides his services free of charge. When I asked the residents what the main attraction of coming to Swadhar was, their spontaneous response was: "its proximity to Lord Jagannath.[31] We feel so close to Him living in His majestic abode, just walking distance from here." The women lead a very austere life in the home; everything is cooked *sadha* (vegetarian) without even any onion or garlic. They generally eat *prasad* (consecrated food) from the Jagannath temple as sweets. The cooking is done by a few Brahmin women residents (with a small stipend of Rs. 350, equivalent to $8), while cleaning is managed by the residents of the house and is done by them in turn. The old people are spared of any chores; they spend time with each other and are engaged in their Jagannath worship. Safety is another major reason why most of the women feel comfortable here. One of the residents, Bhuta (the name literally means "ghost," her acquired name at this home because she walks in and out of the home at will), is quite content where she is, claiming that she stays in a beautiful home where she is safe and can do what she loves, going to the temple. "What else can I ask for?"The women in this home share a sense of personal freedom and are constantly encouraged to learn income generating skills like making spices, snack food, garland-making etc. as well as marketing to become small-scale entrepreneurs.

A Few Case Studies of Women at Swadhar

Let me share a few voices from the few case studies I collected during my visits to this home. Pramila, now in her seventies and one of the older residents, came here approximately five years ago when she became a widow. In her words:

> My son and his wife were very mean and abusive. Even though I did all the household chores, they would not give me enough food or clothing. I did not even have any warm clothes for the winter months. When I asked my son for a little money to do my *habisha* (the winter months of November-December in the lunar calendar when widows move to Puri to spend a month of austerity and penitence[32] in the presence of Lord Jagannath), he taunted me saying, "you are a widow and be thankful that at least you have a roof over your head. If you want money, go and earn it. We do not have enough money to take care of our children and ourselves. On top of it, you are an extra mouth to feed." From that day on, I decided that I would never see them again. (Personal conversation in Odia, translated by the author)

She came to Swadhar on her own and has decided to live the rest of her life there. Even though she has another son and two daughters, they hardly visit her. She does go to see her daughters occasionally. Pramila is one of the most active women in Swadhar. Being a Brahmin widow, she helps out in the kitchen (giving/handing out food, and collecting *thalis*) and is eager to participate in any income-generating programme such as making incense sticks and paper bags as well as food catering undertaken by the residents of the home. I was amazed to see her positive spirit, even sharing her limited space with other women in the home. She seems to be very content and says, "everything we get here is adequate and we are treated like a family." She says that the motto she recites is, "If there is a will, there is a way."

Bharati Das is in her fifties and has been staying in Swadhar for about four or five years. Her children and their spouses were cruel and unjust to her. They would deny her food, and proper living conditions, among many other deprivations. She feels elated that recently her grandchildren discovered her after a long time. They were told by their parents that she was dead. She loves helping out with the making of incense sticks and paper bags. She has knee problems, which interfere with her ability to sit down on the floor and getting up, and sometimes she needs assistance. About living in Swadhar Home she says, "This is my home. I will die here. Where else will I go?"

Sashigali, a Bengali around seventy years of age, has been staying in Swadhar for almost five years, having arrived in Puri nearly seven years ago from her hometown of Keonjhar. She too helps out with all the activities. Her son and daughter-in-law were mistreating her and she could not tolerate it any more, so she came to Swadhar. She says, "Everybody treats me well here and loves me so much!" She does not go to visit her home and realizes that Swadhar is her only home now. She loves staying together with the others when they are not working, and reading books with them. She agrees that the catering business is great, serving not just college students but also tourists coming to the Jagannath temple.

Bimala is a very feisty seventy-year-old, resident at Swadhar for almost three years. Being childless, when she became a widow she had no one to turn to. She first went to live in an ashram (spiritual retreat) but came to Puri emotionally destroyed. She has since given all her money to the Jagannath temple. She says, "I feel at home here. I really like it... everybody treats me well. Now this is my family. My only desire is to die at the footsteps of Jagannath." She discovered a new family in Swadhar and made new bonds with the women and girls who stay here. She says that they learn from each other, and there are not any scheduled turns. Everything works by a voluntary process in the house.

M. Tandra, forty-five years old, has a familiar story—beaten and abused by her husband, she left home emotionally and physically battered. She has been at Swadhar since 2007, and though her mother tongue is Bengali, the language of the neighbouring state of West Bengal, she has learnt to speak some Odia. She enjoys being at Swadhar. In spite of the language barrier, she claims that everyone gets along well and she helps out with whatever there is to do at the home. Even though she has two brothers and has been in contact with her mother, she sees this as her only refuge.

Manju Sripanda, about sixty-five years old, has been at Swadhar for five years. She is the head cook and is paid a small stipend for her service. She came here as a destitute, having no one to stay with. She is quite content where she is now. She claims that she stays at a beautiful home where she can do what she loves (cooking), and is safe. "What else can I ask for?"

Sunanda, age around forty, had been staying at Swadhar for just a month when I met her. She is originally from Bengal and has two children, but landed here after being thrown out of her own home. She admits that she was scared when she first arrived at Swadhar, but everyone has treated her well and she has made it her home.

Women in Swadhar: A Home Away from Home

On my visit to Swadhar in July 2011, I was surprised to see a few teenager girls living in the home. It is against the rules since the facility is meant for the widows or adult women abandoned by their families. Basanti Sabru is fifteen years old, and had been at Swadhar for a few months, having come here in May 2011. She says: "Both my parents are alcoholics. I lived with them in the forest area in Ganjam." She along with a couple of other girls were taken to Goa to be sold as maidservants, but they were rescued by an NGO, Apana Ghar (engaged in rescuing abandoned girls and women) and brought to Puri by the police. She is currently an "orphan" since the organization has no contact with her family and is not even sure if she has one. She says that she wants to go to school but feels embarrassed because she is too "old." She goes to the Jagannath temple with everyone else but confides, "It would be nice to have some toys to play with. Since the kids are not involved in anything else, I do not have much to do." Girls from the interior parts of Odisha have been lured into sex trafficking out of utter poverty. Two other girls, Anju Gomango from Ganjam (South Odisha) and Mini Mullick from Gajapati district, have also been rescued from sex trafficking by the police and are residing in the home.

Suita Hembrum is a shy thirteen-year-old, originally from Kolkata, who has been at Swadhar since August 2009. She came to live in the home after the police found her aunt trying to sell her. The sad part is that her father, who worked as a coolie (baggage carrier) at the Kolkata railway station, orchestrated the whole business of selling her. She used to live with her father, mother, three brothers and sister, but currently has no connection with her family. She attends a school in Puri, and is in the third grade. Her parents did not let her study or go to school, demanding instead that she take care of her siblings in the village. She appreciates the opportunity to attend school and has friends there, but does not stay in contact with them once school is out. Everything is good for her at the shelter, although like every other child she wishes there were toys to play with. She enjoys studying science and wants to become a medical doctor. Of course, she yearns to be with her mother and misses her the most.

The sisters Rajeswari (14) and Sugyani (12) both joined Swadhar in June 2009. Their mother died when Sugyani was one-year-old and their father died when she was four. Their maternal uncles (mother's brother and aunt's husband) dropped them at the home and signed a declaration saying that they "are unable to take care of them and we have no right over them." They share in common a desire to get out of their helpless situation and aspire to study and become independent. In 2011 Swadhar housed a wide range of women who had suffered all sorts of abuse, abduction and mental and physical torture.

A space at this home has given these women a new meaning and purpose to their lives. When they joined the home, they were shattered, emotionally drained and completely broken, suffering from low self-esteem from being disowned and deserted by their family members. For example, on a Sunday in July 2007, I saw two elderly women delivered to this house by government staff. In a personal conversation, Chandrika Mohapatra explained to me that "they were abandoned by their families and left on the streets in Puri to fend for themselves. The district collector sent an order to bring them to this home." Their identities had been tied to the roles of mother, wife or a daughter, but once forced out of their homes they had nowhere to go. In the home they live and work together and take pride in being with others just like themselves, which reflects the depth of the women's solidarity given that they come from different castes, ethnic groups, economic classes, and educational backgrounds. Chandra T. Mohanty (2003) observes that solidarity involves "mutuality, accountability, and the recognition of common interests as the basis for relationships among diverse communities."[33] The women have adapted to their new surroundings. This opportunity of living together has made them feel useful to themselves and others. Instead of feeling marginalized and victimized by their circumstances, they have developed a new zest for life. They have come a long way from a sense of worthlessness to a purposeful life. They are reenergized and feel useful to each other. In short, promoting skill building and entrepreneurship among these women has made a visible difference in their lives.

Based on my research findings, I argue that this unique development initiative, specially spearheaded by the residents of Vijaya's Swadhar Home, has helped them to find both a new purpose in their personal lives and empowerment through their role of entrepreneurs financed by individual charitable contributions. These women have made use of new opportunities by exploring their capabilities and developing their social networks challenging the social stigmas and taboos associated with their marginalized status in Hindu society. Women who are despised as social outcastes and do not even qualify for microcredit loans take advantage of an alternative to the conventional microcredit programme and change their self image. I also wish to emphasize what is unique and innovative about the case studies in terms of the methods that the women have used to make their business ventures a success, and what can be learnt from the challenges these marginalized women have faced in microcredit and how they have learned to cope with their social and economic constraints.

Aamara Biswas: An Innovative Microcredit Model

The second success story related to the microcredit model concerns the project called NanoFinance, which was initiated by Ranu Mahanty, founder of a non-profit organization called Aamar Biswas (Our Faith). Ranu Mahanty, an Odia and a longtime resident of the USA, observes: "I started with four lakhs and three thousand rupees. Now it is sixteen lakhs and ninety thousand rupees. Since 2008, about 5,000 women are availing themselves of nano-finance and are involved in the programme. It started in Sambalpur but has spread to Cuttack, Puri, and other areas in Odisha."[34] She explained to me how it started:

> One day I saw the girl who worked at our home helping with my ailing mother suddenly run out of the house. I asked her what was so urgent. She answered, "Apa, I am going to pay the interest on my microcredit loan. If I do not pay by 4 pm today, the loan of five hundred rupees will become five hundred and fifty rupees [one hundred and ten per cent interest]. I will have to pay interest on the principal of five hundred and fifty rupees." She could not get out of the loan unless she managed to pay the entire principal of 500 rupees all at once. This was not possible for her family of five members (husband, wife, two school going children, and her mother) with a joint income of 2000 rupees a month. I gave her five hundred rupees to pay off the loan, but it made me think. At that time, I was working with BISWA (Bharat Integrated Social Welfare Agency) in developing a microfinance institution in Odisha. The next day I went to BISWA where a group of women were working in a unit producing petticoats for sale. I asked them whether they had any experience borrowing money from the microcredit organizations charging excessive interest. A majority of them said yes and explained how they were subjected to perpetual indebtedness to the moneylenders. I lent them money personally, to get out of the clutches of the microcredit lenders and became intrigued to know more about the plight of poor women in my area.

One day, I was watching a very frail woman hawker walking in my neighbourhood with a basket of vegetables on her head.

I asked her, "how do you manage to run your livelihood?" She told me it was very difficult. She needed three hundred rupees to have a few more vegetables and in turn generate a manageable profit. I lent her the money with the promise that she had to return it within a year so that somebody else could use it. She returned me the money in four months. This is how it started and spread in the region. I was amazed to see that now five thousand women are benefiting from this project. Since I deal with very small amounts of money, interest free, I asked my husband Vanu, what was smaller than micro. He said, "nano." This is how the programme came to be known as NanoFinance.[35]

Ranu Mahanty explains the difference between microfinance enterprises (like SKS, Asmita Foundation, BISWA) and NanoFinance thus:

> The basic difference is in the policy. The [typical microfinance] loan is supposed to be for fifty-two weeks (one year). In the first week they will give a loan and will ask for payment next year. On top of it, all the other costs like the administrative and insurance costs put a heavy toll on the borrowers, especially, the lower class women who do not have any other means to support themselves and their families. If the borrowers cannot pay, they will be standing over their dead bodies. Many instances of harassment are cited. Alcoholism of the male family members is also very common. Women of the lowest earning group cannot handle a loan of Rs. 5,000. Their husbands may snatch it away from them. Whereas, they can hide Rs. 500 easily since it is a small amount. They may conceal it in their saris. For its return in a woman's day-to-day life, the growth of 500 rupees is very significant and empowering.[36]

Ranu Mahanty goes on to explain some other projects enabling women to strengthen their businesses and help improve their social and economic situation. The projects she is promoting include rope-making, tailoring, and providing filtered water, among others. Describing one example she says: "In Puri, we have helped a group of women process the coconut fibre. I have bought them a machine to manually extract the fibre and bind it into rope in order to make doormats. It cost Rs. 21,000. Once they repay the loan, the machine will be theirs." Another example involves tailoring groups, which she explained thus:

> I saw many girls who were not in school. They do not have the means to attend school to help themselves to become self-dependent. I am lending them Rs. 500 to buy materials and sew petticoats. Also, I am doing fundraising in my hometown to buy some sewing machines and other accessories for this tailoring project. My main aim is the empowerment of women at the grassroots level.

A much needed water filter project has women buy a water filter for Rs. 450 and sell it for Rs. 480 just to cover the shipping and handling cost. It is done purely on a non-profit basis specially to cater to the needs of the poor who cannot afford to buy a water filter in the market. Regarding the success of NanoFinance, she had this to say:

> We do not have a brochure, no publicity, no advertisements, no office, and no telephone. If you work at the grassroots level, you do not need a fancy office. I do not get involved with the state government. People know that I am a tough worker. I do not take any money from anybody. Whatever money I raise through friends and family, I invest it in nano-finance. Without biswas (faith/belief), it would not run. I may go, but biswas will keep it going. I have started an organization in the USA called Our Biswas that expresses our belief in the services of women of all societies.[37]

Conclusion

In summary, let me re-emphasize the point made by many scholars working on microcredit in South Asia and elsewhere: even though it has not succeeded in making a measurable change in women's economic lives, it certainly can provide new meaning for them socially. It has also enabled the emergence of new kinds of alternatives to microcredit, which are rectifying some of the inadequacies of traditional microfinancing institutions. Experience suggests that microcredit entails not just economic transactions for women, but provides a new opportunity for many of them to interact with other women and establish new social connections. My preliminary observations of Swadhar and Aamara Biswas suggest that even dispossessed and marginalized women need to be viewed on their own terms. I stumbled upon both these unlikely groups who show tremendous potential and capabilities. A broader implication of this study is that we must look into unusual places, with unlikely groups and structures that might turn out to reveal little noticed examples of human agency and subjectivity even in the midst of seemingly overwhelming constraints. Microcredit programmes might not be empowering women economically, but it is worth looking at the alternative models generated by women that strengthen their economic base, restore their self-esteem and give a sense of dignity and purpose to their lives. Women develop a new psycho-social space, a sense of self-worth, a new connection with the community, and a new lease on life.

Being social outcastes, rejected by their families, widows are deemed to be unfit for their cultural roles as daughters, wives, mothers or mothers-in-law. Since they are shunned by family members, they already experience a debilitating loss of self-esteem. Microcredit provided by Swadhar and Aamara Biswas provides them a new opportunity for sustenance and gives them a sense of dignity. They also develop a new self-confidence, the realization that their lives are not all about their relationships to male family members. They can create a positive niche for themselves, and in the process become role models for women with similar life experiences.

Postscript

As I had mentioned earlier, Vijaya's Swadhar Home was introduced under the auspices of the Union Ministry of Women and Child Development in 2002 for providing institutional support to destitute women without any family support. In 2015, this scheme has been renamed as Swadhar Greh in order to accommodate women of various age groups suffering from physical, emotional, financial, social and psychological crises. It has been converted into a temporary accommodation programme till women get rehabilitated and find an alternate source of support. Pursuant to current arrangement, women cannot stay there longer than three years. The provision is slightly different for the older women over 55 years of age but they too cannot continue to stay in the home beyond the age of 60. This has created a challenge at Swadhar Home in Puri. Women in their 60s and 70s have stayed here since 2006 and have accepted it as their permanent home. Now they have been forced to relocate elsewhere, to the less friendly environment of old-age homes, perhaps. The central government provides Rs. 1,800 ($25 approximately) per resident for vocational training per year. The younger women attended skill development training for entrepreneurship and have started their own small businesses. With the business initiative started in 2011, some women have formed a cooperative assisted by Vijaya to sell handmade food products and handicrafts for a living. It will be useful to study the entrepreneurship of women under the present Swadhar scheme.

Aamara Biswas is a good example of a self-initiated microcredit programme. With its help, women in rural areas have worked together to avail of the no-interest loans to undertake business initiatives and have become successful entrepreneurs. These cooperatives transcend the caste and tribe divide that prevails in Indian villages. Working together, these women have developed a sisterhood; have helped empower themselves and their families; and have taken up social issues like dealing with emergency services during floods and drought, or abuse of women and children in the name of dowry or child abduction. Nirupama, in her 40s, coordinator of Aamara Biswas in Jajpur has a pukka house, rides her bicycle all over the village to give loans and collect them. In the village, riding a bike for a married woman is not a common sight, so this is definitely a taboo she has broken. In 2013, as a loan coordinator, she earned $200 in salary and from harvesting black lentils on her own small patch of land. Her daughter was studying in her third year science in college and she wanted to be an optometrist. Nirupama said, "I do not want my daughter to marry early and be a housewife. I want her to be a doctor and serve the community." Sabita, a mother of two children, aged 7 and 8, is a successful entrepreneur. Along with 11 women borrowing Rs. 1000 each ($20), she bought a threshing machine to process paddy after the harvest and they rent out the machine for additional income. "Now our cooperative has $2000 in the bank. We would love to buy a tractor next." Sabita loves her economic independence. "Before I asked my husband for all my needs even to buy a sari and stuff for the children. Now he asks me for his expenses." When I was visiting the village with Ranu, Sabita's group requested her to take a third loan in order to buy a tractor. Ranu asked her group to wait and let other women get a chance. They readily agreed.

The goal of Aamara Biswas is to economically empower women without imposing any set boundaries. Unlike other corporate microcredit schemes, it promotes trust and fellow-feeling among women. Ranu agrees that they have lost money in some instances because of the personal problems of the coordinator and the members who have borrowed from Amara Biswas. Some of the defaulters succumbed to illness and suffered from personal loss in the family. But the organization has flourished mainly because of the mutual responsibility taken up by women who are borrowing money. The nature of Indian rural society is such that women have a sense of moral obligation and pride to pay back the loan they take from the organization. I learn from several of my respondents that they feel a sense of connectedness and moral obligation towards their sisters who are in the same or worse situation and need help. Besides, the attraction of an interest free loan is an additional reason that they feel compelled to return the money so that they can avail of the loan again and a more disadvantaged person can get help.

Recently the Clover organization (situated in Concord, Massachusetts, USA, which runs an NGO in Uganda) have started a collabouration with Ranu Mahanty of Aamara Biswas and have launched the Kisoboka Initiative: Nano Finance Programme on April 18, 2016.[38] The programme is based in Kampala, Uganda, and focuses on improving the livelihoods of needy mothers struggling with small businesses or women interested in starting a new business who lack even small capital or a collective of mothers to start an income-generating initiative like a poultry farm, a greenhouse, a clean water remediation facility, or a village store.

It is heartening to see that the Aamara Biswas model has

been replicated in other developing countries where women do not have capital of their own, and are the principal bread earners, often being in a similar situation as their Indian counterparts. Whether it is going to work out in those countries or not, only time will tell.

NOTES

1. Kinetz, E. "Microfinance Struggles to Restore Its Reputation." *The Economic Times*. Bennett, Coleman & Co. Ltd., March 7, 2011. http://articles.economictimes.indiatimes.com/2011-03-07/news/28665801_1_sks-microfinance-vikram-akula-loan-sharks. [Mention "quoted in" *Economic Times*, March 7, 2011.
2. Annan, K.A. *Renewing the United Nations: A Programme for Reform: Report of the Secretary-General*. (United Nations, 1997).
3. Moodie, M. "Enter Microcredit: A New Culture of Women's Empowerment in Rajasthan?." *American Ethnologist* 35.3. (2008): 454-465.
4. Census Report, 2011. The central government defines anyone earning Rs. 27.20 or less per day in rural areas as Below Poverty Line (BPL), while those earning up to Rs. 33.30 a day in urban areas are classified as poor, though these benchmarks vary from state to state. *Times of India*, July 24, 2013.
5. For details, please refer to a Report titled *Outreach of Microfinance Institutions in Four focus States, Poorest States Inclusive Growth (PSIG) Programme*, June 2015. https://responsiblefinanceforum.org/wp-content/uploads/MFI-outreach-in-PSIG-States-credit-bureau-anaysis1.pdf
6. Ibid., pp. 10-11.
7. Fernando, J. "The Myths Behind Microfinance." *Forbes*. December 9, 2010. http://www.forbes.com/2010/12/09/microfinance-myths-muhummad-yunus-entrepreneurs-finance-jude-fernando.html.
8. As an example, there has been an "alleged" suicide by Bikala Garia, a *bhaaga chashi* (sharecropper). He had cultivated four and a half acres of land on a shared basis. But unseasonal rain ruined the entire crop, following which he fell into the SHG/microfinance loan trap and paid back the loan only partially. He had to again take a loan to cultivate a half acre of watermelon. The microfinance company repeatedly pressured him to repay, and following the pressure—which he could not bear—he consumed poison and committed suicide on April 15, 2011. He

is survived by both his parents, four brothers, his wife, two daughters aged 13 and 18, and a 9-year-old son. A report from Odisha details the harassment of two families including Garia's by the collection agents of a microfinance company and SHG members which forced them to sell all their belongings and leave their own village home with the children. In the process, they lost their land and become casual manual labourers.

9. Fernando, J. "The Myths Behind Microfinance." *Forbes*. December 9, 2010. Web. http://www.forbes.com/2010/12/09/microfinance-myths-muhummad-yunus-entrepreneurs-finance-jude-fernando.html.
10. Interestingly, the signature requirement helps increase the official rural literacy rate, as any person knowing how to sign a document is counted as a literate by the government.
11. Credit card companies do the bigger business, as EWI on credit card purchases in bigger cities at macro levels.
12. Patra, A. "Focus Odisha." E-mail Interview, April 18, 2011.
13. For more details, refer Mohanty, B. "Focus Odisha", April 28, 2011.
14. Rahman, A. "Microcredit Initiatives for Equitable and Sustainable Development: Who Pays?" *World Development* 27.1. (1999): 67-82.
15. A day after a farmer's suicide at Haldipali Village near Bargarh, another disturbing news appeared where a farmer's wife, Meera Bhoi, 55 years old, from Jatla village committed suicide following microcredit loans and crop loss. She had borrowed forty thousand rupees from three private microfinance corporations and was paying interest of seven hundred rupees per week. She has left behind her old husband and five children, a widowed daughter, an unmarried young daughter, two sons, and one married daughter. The family owned 2.7 acres of land only. Patra, A. "Focus Odisha." E-mail Interview. April 18, 2011.
16. Patra, A. "Focus Odisha." E-mail Interview. April 18, 2011.
17. Mahmud, S. "Actually How Empowering is Microcredit?" *Development and Change* 34.4. (2003): 577-605.
18. Mayoux, L. "Questioning Virtuous Spirals: Microfinance and Women's Empowerment in Africa." *Journal of International Development* 11.7. (1999): 957-984.
19. Mayoux, L. (1999). Ibid.
20. Isserles, R. "Microcredit: The Rhetoric of Empowerment, the Reality of 'Development as Usual.'" *Women's Studies Quarterly* 3.4. (2003): 38-57.

21. Patra, A. "Focus Odisha." E-mail Interview. April 18, 2011.
22. Mazzarella, W. *Shovelling Smoke: Advertising and Globalization in Contemporary India*. (Duke University Press, 2003).
23. Patra, A. "Focus Odisha." E-mail Interview. April 18, 2011.
24. Moodie, M. "Enter Microcredit: A New Culture of Women's Empowerment in Rajasthan?" *American Ethnologist* 35.3. (2008): 454-465. Arnopoulos, S.M. *Saris on Scooters: How Microcredit is Changing Village India*. (Dundurn Press Ltd, 2010).
25. In summer 2011, I returned to this organization to collect some life histories and observe the impact of the income-generating programme introduced in 2007-2008.
26. Giri, V. (eds.). *Living Death: Trauma of Widowhood in India*. (Gyan Books, 2002). Agarwal, B. "Widows versus Daughters or Widows as Daughters? Property, Land, and Economic Security in Rural India." *Modern Asian Studies* 32.1. (1998): 1-48.
27. Chen, M. *Perpetual Mourning: Widowhood in Rural India*. (Oxford: Oxford University Press, 2000).
28. A Ford Foundation report estimated that nearly forty-five microfinance institutions (MFIs) are working in the state of Odisha providing approximately fourteen hundred crore rupees in financial support in the last four years to sixteen lakh families for undertaking various vocations and meeting their consumption needs (2006). As per government statistics, Odisha is home to fifty-two lakh and eighty-nine thousand farming families of which forty-seven lakh and fifty-six thousand families are registered as members in primary agriculture cooperatives. But strangely, a mere fifteen lakh members demand loans to cover their agricultural expenses even at an interest rate of only five per cent per year. This could come down to three per cent for them if they make timely payments. While the cooperative department had fixed the total loan target for disbursement at Rs. 3076 crore by all agencies during the last kharif season, it was actually able to advance Rs. 2620 crore, lagging by 456 crore behind the target. This entails a very large gap between the requirements and provisioning, which creates ample opportunity for MFIs to jump in and make big money. To fetch such hefty profits, MFIs work on simple-looking, cleverly crafted operational guidelines. Charging high interest rates ranging from 20-28 per cent on a flat basis against the reducing bank interest actually accounts for a 40 to 50 per cent interest collection. MFIs working in Odisha (24 registered in Odisha and 21 registered out of state) now pay 40,000 to 50,000 Rs. to top officers, rent

palatial buildings at five or six locations in Bhubaneswar and other major cities, pay large sums for interior decoration, and spend on maintaining luxurious motorcades in order to demonstrate their power. In short, profits earned by exploitation of helpless borrowers are used at pleasure by MFI owners while the marginal loanees continuously perish in the debt trap. In 2010, forty-six farmers committed suicide because of this pressure. Currently this is considered as a passport to big money or could be dubbed as a *Kamadhenu* (the ever milking cow) to them. The irony is that with the increasing number of MFI-related suicides in the state, MFIs engaged in providing small ticket loans to the clients through Joint Liability Group (JLG) have swelled beyond imagination. In view of this it is essential to discuss the retail loan scenario of Odisha and expose the hidden agenda of MFIs. Again, weekly repayment schedule looks like a pro-poor strategy but ironically contributes to substantial profit build-up.

29. I have a long-standing association with this group called Vijaya, the NGO started by Chandrika Mohapatra who comes from a distinguished political family in Odisha. Her older sister, Nandini Satpathy, had served the Upper House as a member of Parliament from 1962-1970, and became the first woman chief minister of Odisha in 1972. During the early 80s while I was a graduate student in Social Science at Jawaharlal Nehru University, I conducted research on the socio-political background of women in politics. That gave me the privilege to interview both Chandrika Mohapatra and Nandini Satpathy. I have been observing Mohapatra's involvement with various women's organizations since that time. She runs two women's organizations: Swadhar, a project on widow's well-being in Puri, and a blind girls' home in Bhadrak, Odisha.
30. Mohapatra, C. "Focus Odisha." Personal Conversation, April 18, 2011.
31. Jagannath, the preserver of the universe, is the patron deity of the people of Odisha, India. His abode in Puri is one of the four centres of pilgrimage for the Hindus.
32. The *habisha*, like many Hindu rites, is a *brata* (or *Vrata)* rite—a vowed observance. Historically, vows have been an important part of Hindu ritual life for centuries. People make vows mainly to secure something in this world, such as progeny, wealth, good fortune, health, fame, or long life. Sometimes people make vows to secure something in the next world; and occasionally, as in the *habisha rites,* people make vows to gain something both in

this world and in the next.... Proper fulfilment of vows not only brings the vow maker the rewards that he or she seeks but also invests the person with great spiritual power. See James M. Freeman, "The Ladies of Lord Krishna: Rituals of Middle Aged Women in Eastern India." *Essays on Odishan Society*, Prafulla, 2009, p. 64.

33. See Chandra T. Mohanty, Feminism without Borders: Decolonizing Theory, Practising Solidarity. Durham and London: Duke University Press, 2003, p. 7.
34. Mahanty, R. "Focus Odisha." Personal Conversation. March 6, 2011.
35. Mahanty, R. "Focus Odisha." Personal Conversation. March 6, 2011.
36. Mahanty, R. "Focus Odisha." Personal Conversation. March 6, 2011.
37. Mahanty, R. "Focus Odisha." Personal Conversation. March 6, 2011.
38. Clover Foundation is a 501(c)(3) non-profit organization situated in Concord, Massachusetts, USA and an NGO in Uganda. Clover Foundation provides a safe, caring and engaging environment for Uganda's young children living in extreme poverty in the urban slums of Kampala by providing early childhood learning and preschool education to children who otherwise would not have the opportunity. Recently, Clover Foundation has collabourated with Aamara Biswas to economically empower poor mothers in Kampala, Uganda, in order to provide a safe and secure environment their children. For details, see their website, http://clover-foundation.org

REFERENCES

Agarwal, B. (1998). "Widows versus Daughters or Widows as Daughters? Property, Land, and Economic Security in Rural India." *Modern Asian Studies* 32.1. 1-48.

Aladuwaka, Seela and Momsen, Janet. (2010). 'Sustainable Development, Water Resources Management and Women's Empowerment: The Wanaraniya Water Project in Sri Lanka', *Gender & Development*, 18: 1, 43 -58.

Annan, K.A. (1997). *Renewing the United Nations: A Programme for Reform: Report of the Secretary-General*, United Nations.

Arnopoulos, S.M. (2010). *Saris on Scooters: How Microcredit is Changing Village India*. Dundurn Press Ltd.

Chen, Martha A.(1993). *Coping with Seasonality and Drought in Western*

India, New Delhi: Sage.

Chen, Martha A., and Jean Drèze (2000). *Perpetual Mourning: Widowhood in Rural India*. Oxford: Oxford University Press.

Elyachar, Julia (2002). Empowerment Money: The World Bank, Non-Governmental Organizations, and the Value of Culture in Egypt. *Public Culture* 14(3): 493–513.

Ferguson, James, and Akhil Gupta (2002). 'Spatializing States: Towards an Ethnography of Neoliberal Governmentality'. *American Ethnologist* 29(4):981–1003.

Fernando, Nirmal (2006). *Understanding and Dealing with High Interest Rates on Microcredit*. Asian Development Bank.

Fernando, J. (2010). "The Myths Behind Microfinance." *Forbes*. December 9, 2010. http://www.forbes.com/2010/12/09/microfinance-myths-muhummad-yunus-entrepreneurs-finance-jude-fernando.html.

James M. Freeman (2009). "The Ladies of Lord Krishna: Rituals of Middle Aged Women in Eastern India." *Essays on Odishan Society*, Prafulla, p. 64.

Ghate, Prabhu (2006). 'Microfinance in India: A State of the Sector Report', New Delhi: Microfinance India.

Giri, V. (eds.) (2002). *Living Death: Trauma of Widowhood in India*. Gyan Books.

Gupta, Akhil, and Aradhana Sharma (2006). Globalization and Postcolonial States. *Current Anthropology* 47(2):277–301.

Hans, Asha and Dr. Amrita Patel (2012). Women of Odisha: Status and Challenges, *Odisha Review*, February-March.

Harcourt, Wendy and Arturo Escobar, eds. (2005). *Women and the Politics of Place*, Bloomfield, CT, Kumarian Press, Inc.

Isserles, R. (2003). "Microcredit: The Rhetoric of Empowerment, the Reality of 'Development as Usual.'" *Women's Studies Quarterly* 3.4. (2003): 38-57.

Jeffery, Patricia, Roger Jeffery, and Andrew Lyon (1989). *Labour Pains and Labour Power: Women and Childbearing in India*. London: Zed.

John, Mary E. (1996). Gender and Development in India, 1970s–1990s. *Economic and Political Weekly* 31(47): 3071–3077.

Kingsolver, Barbara (2009). What Money Doesn't Buy: Microfinance and Women's Empowerment in South Asia", March 17, http://www.commondreams.org/view/2009/03/17-8

Lamb, Sarah (2009). *Aging and the Indian Diaspora Cosmopolitan families in India and Abroad*, Indiana University Press, Bloomington and Indianapolis.

Mahmud, Simeen (2003). "Actually How Empowering is Microcredit?"

Development and Change 34(4): 577–605.

Mayoux, L. (1999). "Questioning Virtuous Spirals: Microfinance and Women's Empowerment in Africa." *Journal of International Development* 11.7. 957-984.

Mazzarella, William (2003). *Shovelling Smoke: Advertising and Globalization in Contemporary India,* Duke University Press.

Mcleod Sheila Arnopoulos (2010). *Saris On Scooters How Microcredit is Changing Village India,* Dundurn Press Toronto.

Mohanty, Chandra Talpade (2013). "The Education of Gods and Men: A Feminist Reading of Lakshmi Purana", an unpublished article for a proposed book on the Lakshmi Purana.

Moodie, M. (2008). "Enter Microcredit: A New Culture of Women's Empowerment in Rajasthan?." *American Ethnologist* 35.3: 454-465.

Narasimhan, Sakuntala (1992). *Sati: Widow Burning in India,* New York: Anchor Doubleday.

Rahman, A. (1999). "Microcredit Initiatives for Equitable and Sustainable Development: Who Pays?" *World Development* 27.1. 67-82.

Sen, Mala (2001). *Death by Fire: Sati, Dowry Death, and Female Infanticide in Modern India,* New Brunswick, N.J.: Rutgers University Press.

9

Microenterprise Development and Women in the US: Perspective of a Microfinance Organization

Marsha Bailey

Background/History

In 1987, based on the phenomenon described as "the feminization of poverty," Women's Economic Ventures (WEV), a non-profit organization based in California, began offering workshops for women addressing issues such as pay equity, non-traditional employment and economic literacy.[1]

In 1988, with the help of a planning grant from the James Irvine Foundation, WEV began to research the feasibility of creating a more comprehensive economic development strategy for women. At the time, little research was available that identified barriers to economic development for American women. Existing studies identified four major obstacles:

1. Lack of access to capital
2. Lack of affordable childcare
3. Lack of educational opportunities
4. Social stereotypes that viewed women as incompetent to operate businesses

The passage of the Equal Opportunity in Education Act, (Title IX), in 1972 led to groundbreaking research sponsored by organizations such as the American Association of University Women (AAUW) which identified the negative impacts of systematic gender bias in education. During the same time period, the growth of women's organizations dedicated to helping victims of domestic violence, rape and sexual harassment increased public recognition of the high rates of sexual violence against women and its long-term, traumatic impacts. All these factors had serious economic impacts: women earned 56 cents for every dollar earned by a male and single mothers experienced the highest rate of poverty of any group measured.

Traditionally, women had been taught to defer to male authority figures rather than trust their own judgment, had been largely isolated from sources of emotional support and had few successful female role models. Based on these assumptions, WEV articulated an organizational philosophy that would permeate all our programmes:

1. Women should have access to quality education in an emotionally safe and supportive environment.
2. Programmes must emphasize empowerment, self-help, personal responsibility and peer support.
3. Programmes should help women build personal wealth and financial stability.
4. Programmes should be holistic in nature and acknowledge that reversing the effects of gender socialization, discrimination, lack of access to education, gender violence and poverty would require a significant, long-term commitment.

In January 1991, after two years of research, programme development and fundraising, WEV launched a self-employment programme based on the Grameen Bank model. Its goal was to help women increase their earning potential in an economy dominated by low-paying jobs in the retail, tourism and service sectors. Our programme began as a four-week business orientation and peer lending programme which provided loans of up to $1,500 to low-income women. Most of the women WEV served had no prior experience owning a small business; in the midst of a recession, many viewed self-employment as the last resort in a depressed job market.

Within a year, we realized that our model was not fulfilling the needs of our clients for a number of reasons including:

1. Peer group formation was slow and ineffective. WEV's service area was spread out over a large region with low population density. At the end of one year, we were been able to facilitate the formation of only five peer groups.
2. The backgrounds of peer group members were so diverse that clients were unable to benefit equally, leading to frustration and attrition. Because there were no longstanding relationships within groups, peer pressure had a limited effect.
3. The maximum loan of $1,500 was too small and, because of the stability and size of commercial credit markets in the US, most clients had access to small amounts of credit through credit cards or family members.
4. Doing business in a developed economy tends to be much more complex than in the developing world; consequently clients needed considerably more technical support and training than they were able to receive from their peers.
5. Conventional wisdom among early adaptors of the Grameen model was that the peer group structure was not labour-intensive to the organization and that organizational self-sufficiency was attainable. These assumptions proved to be wildly inaccurate.

As word spread in the community about WEV's self-employment programme, we began to receive increasing numbers of phone calls from women who communicated the same message: "I do not know how to run a business—I need training." In year two, WEV initiated a six-week business training class. One of our assumptions was that clients would get to know each other in the classes and borrowing group formation would increase. Demand for training was high and by 1994, WEV's self-employment training programme had expanded from six to fourteen weeks and some clients were travelling from over hundred miles away in order to participate.

But while training programmes were growing dramatically, WEV's loan programme was still not meeting our expectations. Another client phone call convinced us to abandon the peer lending model in favour of an individual loan programme that would provide loans of up to $25,000. A woman called for advice on how to finance her growing business. She had been operating out of her garage for seven years and had five employees. She wanted to move into a commercial location. "I went to the bank to apply for a $15,000 loan and was willing to put up my house as collateral," she told WEV's Executive Director. "The loan officer told me he could give me a loan to remodel my kitchen but not to grow my business. What should I do?" A year later, in 1995, WEV launched the Small Business Loan Fund with $75,000 in seed money from the City of Santa Barbara's CDBG[2] funds and $225,000 in investments provided by six local banks at 0 per cent interest. In 1999, WEV became a US Treasury certified Community Development Financial Institution (CDFI).

Programme evolution, insights and challenges:

Fees for Service

There has been much discussion in the US microenterprise field over whether poor clients should be charged fees for the services they receive. WEV decided to charge fees at the outset for two reasons: 1) We believed that women would be more committed to successfully completing their training if they invested their own money in it, and 2) WEV had no major funding sources when we started and we knew that we had to be able to generate fee income in order to survive.

Target Group Characteristics

While many organizations chose only to serve low-income women, given that WEV served an area of small cities and rural areas, we did not believe that we would be able to achieve sufficient scale if we limited our services only to poor women. WEV decided to target low-to moderate-income women for our services but to make services available to all on an income-based sliding fee scale. Historically, 95 per cent of WEV clients have qualified for some level of fee subsidy and all have made a financial investment in their future by paying a minimum fee for their training. In 1994, the minimum fee was $50. By 2010, the fee increased to $200. Clients have the option of paying fees in small increments. The full cost of training is approximately $2,500.

WEV's client base is consistent with local demographics: 56 per cent of clients are Caucasian, 37 per cent Latino, 3 per cent African-American, 2 per cent Native American, 1 per cent Asian, and 1 per cent other. Latino clients tend to be poorer than other clients. Ninety per cent are women and the average client age is 39. Historically, 69-75 per cent of WEV clients have been low-income according to local HUD standards[3]. WEV donors, after attending a class, often observe, "They all look middle class." This observation underscores the frequent misperception that the poor are uniformly uneducated, inexperienced in the work world and generally ill equipped. The majority of WEV clients are working poor. Most have some college, many have degrees, and some have advanced degrees. What they have in common is that they are often underemployed, going through major life transitions such as a divorce, illness or loss of livelihood and they have few or no assets beyond their own ambition.

Having a diverse range of clients has helped WEV to develop a curriculum that satisfies the needs of women with varied educational and employment backgrounds. Our experiential teaching methodology is effective with adult learners and more skilled clients help those who are less well prepared. We are convinced that the diverse participant makeup adds a richness and depth to the learning experience that would not be as profound if the clients all came from the same socio-economic background.

WEV believes that help should not be reserved only for the neediest and hardest to serve. Serving only the neediest is not only unjust; it limits us to creating costly interventions with only modest impact. By serving women along a continuum of need, we can provide more cost-effective services that result in more significant impacts, especially job creation. Research has shown that women employers provide better benefits and higher pay than male-owned businesses.

During the twenty-five years that WEV has been helping women start and grow businesses, we have seen distinct changes in our clients. Whereas in 1991, few women owned or thought of owning their own business; today the majority of WEV clients see self-employment as an end goal, not a stopgap strategy to earn money between jobs. Approximately one-third of WEV clients are already in business when they enrol in our self-employment training programme. But over half of WEV clients work full time in a low- to moderate-paying job while they start their business on the side. Straddling both worlds, their first major hurdle is the transition to full self-employment. The next hurdle is hiring employees and managing sustainable growth.

Economic development efforts in the developing world often target subsistence farmers who consume everything they grow. All too often, microenterprises are the first world equivalent: subsistence businesses whose owners spend everything they earn on basic family needs with nothing left to reinvest in the business. Although microloans are intended to help precisely these types of business owners, many, especially women, still lack the confidence or the financial sophistication or are too risk averse to incur debts in order to help their businesses grow. The same gender-related phenomenon is present in the venture capital market.

In every programme evaluation WEV has ever conducted, women have consistently indicated that in addition to the technical training they receive, they highly value the supportive environment and want to continue to be connected with the organization and their peers. They uniformly identify subjects in which they would like to receive additional training, yet once they complete the structured 14-week self-employment training program, only a small percentage continue to take advantage of the variety of ongoing services that are available to them.

WEV clients who do take advantage of ongoing services such as mentoring and coaching or who remain active in Mastermind peer groups swear by the results. One WEV client famously described our programme as "a cross between boot camp and an all-you-can-eat buffet." Yet some clients are still starving. We need to know why. Why do some clients avail themselves of every service WEV offers while others strike out on their own after completing only the core training programme? How do the elements of character, personality, life experience, behaviour, and external influences combine to enable or prevent success? Can we identify patterns and develop client profiles and by doing so, tailor our programme delivery methodology in a way that will better serve our clients and more effectively use our resources?

Challenging Conventional Wisdom

After twenty-five years—a generation—of experience, it is worth challenging some of the conventional wisdom upon which many women-serving programmes have been based. Among them:

1. We can only empower women by allowing them to define success on their own terms, set their own goals and move at their own pace.
2. We do not impose our own expectations on clients.
3. We do not judge clients' ideas.
4. Women will do better in an all-female environment.

WEV programme development has traditionally been shaped by client feedback gathered through programme evaluations and focus groups. As our pool of client outcome data has grown, we have begun to believe that client outcomes might improve if we were to better balance our approach between pull and push, i.e. having higher expectations of our clients. We have observed that teachers who communicate to their classes that everyone must complete a business plan have a much higher rate of business plan completion (95-100 per cent) than teachers who do not (40-60 per cent). Clients who "know what they do not know" might be better at directing their own learning than those who "do not know what they do not know." Client businesses might be more successful if we provided more ongoing structure and accountability for creating ambitious goals and growth strategies and supported them with more advanced financial training and analytic tools. By not encouraging clients to think bigger, we may be reinforcing their self-doubt and continuing to limit their horizons.

The story of the "Pet Rock," has been used as a cautionary tale for business counsellors as to why we do not judge our clients' ideas. Instead, we say, we teach our clients to do the research and figure out on their own whether or not an idea has potential. This is also a convenient excuse for not telling the truth when an idea is poorly executed or incompletely thought out. We must find a middle ground in which we can encourage clients to distinguish between possibility and fantasy. This includes helping them to make decisions about when to cut their losses and restructure or close a business to avoid further losses.

WEV has observed that, depending on their life experience, many women still need and indeed thrive in an all-female learning environment, while others enjoy it but do not find it necessary. The women who do not find it necessary are often frustrated and feel held back by clients who need more emotional and social support and are unable to "stick to business." Some women may be better served by being "pushed out of the nest." WEV is currently developing an accelerated track for such clients and looking for opportunities to create partnerships that will expose them to greater opportunities for investment and significant growth.

Since 1999, WEV has been developing services focused on business growth. These services have often been underutilized by clients who could most benefit from them—particularly services such as coaching that provide valuable 1:1 support that is tailored to the client's unique challenges. WEV believes that we must do a better job of helping micro-entrepreneurs understand that establishing a successful business does not happen in just one or two years. To that end, WEV launched a pilot project in 2010 entitled Thrive in Five® that is based on an individual case management model and focuses on the first five years of business. The goals of the programme are to help micro-entrepreneurs:

1. Establish businesses that create equity and assets beyond the value of their labour.
2. Create larger and more sustainable businesses that generate more jobs.

3. Look beyond service sector businesses to businesses that create tangible products and increase their profit potential.
4. Achieve long-term financial security.

Measuring Programme Impact and Effectiveness

Since 1994, WEV has conducted follow-up client surveys to evaluate individual and economic outcomes. Since 1999, WEV has participated in Microtest, a performance and outcomes evaluation conducted in partnership with the Aspen Institute's FIELD programme. WEV's random survey consistently shows that client business success is distributed across a wide continuum from businesses that generate only a few thousand dollars in revenues to at least one business in each cohort that generates close to $1 million in sales.

Since 1999, WEV has dedicated considerable time and resources to developing follow-up services that continue to provide training and support after clients have completed the core self-employment training programme. The purpose of the follow-up services is to help clients build sustainable and profitable businesses that meet their income goals. Till 2010, follow-up services were not structured in the same way as WEV's core training programme. Advanced training conferences and workshops were provided in targeted subject areas three to four times each year. Clients who joined WEV's alumni organization, WEV Got Business, were provided with discounts on training and consulting and also with ten free coaching sessions. Clients were also encouraged to continue meeting in Mastermind (peer) groups that were formed during core training.

Although clients uniformly report that they highly value the training, support and accountability WEV's core programme provides, many do not take advantage of follow-up services. The random nature of client participation in ongoing services made it difficult for WEV to evaluate the effectiveness of those programmes or their impact on client success.

It is anticipated that Thrive in Five's®individual case management model will enable business consultants to monitor client behaviours, business practices and external challenges and provide timely and focused assistance that will lead to better client outcomes. The case management model will provide a platform for the ongoing evaluation and continuous improvement of the programme, its content and delivery methods. Concurrent with the programme launch, WEV is implementing a research study to evaluate Thrive in Five's effectiveness.

Research Objectives and Thesis

A crucial resource for the design, implementation and development of the Thrive in Five® programme was a systematic qualitative study of current and former WEV clients. It features depth interviews carried out with Thrive in Five® programme participants as well as with micro-entrepreneurs who completed WEV's core programme.

The main objectives of this aspect of the research and development project are:

1. To identify critical business events and outcomes experienced by clients over the period since completing WEV's core training programme.
2. To explore clients' perceptions of and attributions for their experience and outcomes over time.
3. To elicit clients' evaluations of WEV's core training provision and its usefulness over time and to explore *what kinds of further support*, at *what points in time* and *delivered in what manner* would have been beneficial.
4. Through assessment both of *variation* and *overlap* in client experience and outcomes, to further understanding of how support can best be *tailored* to particular circumstances and needs.
5. To translate findings and insight gained from the study into *product* through development of recommendations for revising and improving the design and implementation of the five-year Thrive in Five® programme.

The thesis of this element of the research is that *an in-depth, systematic understanding of the experiences and assessments of current and former clients, with differing levels of business outcomes, can yield critical information about the types and timing of longer term support that will be effective in enhanced microenterprise training programmes*. The thesis is explained and justified below, followed by a discussion of the method, outputs, scope, duration, and implementation plan of this aspect of the research.

Client-Focused Data

The first premise of the research study is that clients themselves are (or should be) the most crucial source in the identification and development of Best Practice. Much of the discussion and dissemination of Best Practice in the microenterprise training field rests on the views of providers and consultants. Case studies or other formats based on expert evaluation are important and useful tools for disseminating innovative models of training and development—and indeed WEV has participated in this kind of work. However, such studies often are descriptive rather than empirical and/or insufficiently informed by client experience and evaluation. The *targets* of training and development methods and their *lived experience* applying them in the real world must be a crucial source of evaluating provision and designating Best Practice. This is not controversial—however, undertaking high quality client-focused evaluation research is challenging. The particular timing, approach and method of collecting and analysing evaluation data from micro-entrepreneurs is important.

Timing of Research

Client-focused evaluation will benefit from a remove of time and opportunity for reflection. WEV, like most established microenterprise training providers, carries out post-training surveys of clients. In the parlance of many evaluation frameworks (see for example, Kirkpatrick's model below), these Level 1 'Reactions' assessments capture participants' immediate satisfaction with particular training experiences. However, the limitations of this kind of assessment are clear. Training programmes such as WEV's often are intense experiences for individuals and immediate evaluation will be heavily influenced (and perhaps reduced to) emotional reactions. Time and space for reflection can allow a more nuanced and thoughtful assessment by clients of the usefulness of different aspects of training provision.

Figure 1: Kirkpatrick's Four Level Evaluation Model

LEVEL 4: OUTCOMES
How has the training contributed to measurable business outcomes?
⇑
LEVEL 3: TRANSFER
To what extent did the training transfer to the work context and result in individual behaviour change and/or capacity increase?
⇑
LEVEL 2: LEARNING
Did the client acquire the knowledge and/or skills as per the objectives set?
⇑
LEVEL 1: REACTIONS
Did the client enjoy the training? Was she satisfied with the training?

Source: Kirkpatrick, D. (1994). *Evaluating Training Programmes: The Four Levels*, San Francisco: Berrett-Koehler.

Crucially, this reflection needs to be anchored in events and experience. WEV, like most providers, also carries out a Level 2 'Learning' evaluation of its core programme: we measure knowledge and skills gained in terms of the main learning objectives. This is reflected, for example, in the production of business plans and other requirements for formal graduation from the programme. However, only at Levels 3 and 4 does the 'business' impact of training provision really emerge. Level 3 evaluations explore how well training and other modes of support transfers into increased (behavioural) capacity in the actual 'doing of business'. Level 4 seeks to assess the contribution of training to measurable outcomes such as revenue or growth. It is at these levels of evaluation that insight can be gained into the types of traditional training and support that former clients found more or less useful and importantly, gaps in training and support and the points at which additional provision might have been useful in facilitating business success.

Holistic and Theoretically-Grounded Research Approach

The third main premise of the study is that the effective identification and development of Best Practice requires research that is not narrowly focused on training but rather that takes a more rounded view of client experience and that is theoretically grounded. The research literature on women and career development generally and microenterprise development more particularly have identified a wide range of factors influencing women's economic ventures and their outcomes. Effective research therefore must be designed to take account of these factors—that is, to consider how training interacts with what Doub and Edgcomb[4] call the 'internal environment' (e.g. personal goals, characteristics, personal assets, and business skills) and the 'external environment' (e.g. market sectors, resource availability, networks and social capital) in which women micro-entrepreneurs operate. There is rich theory and research on many of the factors understood to facilitate and constrain women's economic performance; knowledge of this should inform research design, data collection and analysis of evaluation research.

Variation and Overlap

Research capable of informing Best Practice must be attentive to individual difference and to underlying patterns amongst clients and their experiences and outcomes. Exploration of the kinds of enhanced provision likely to be effective over the longer term should not entail a hunt for 'one size fits all' prescription, but explicitly should consider that success has different definitions; individual clients have different aspirations and needs; and contexts differ. Useful research should be capable of capturing and producing rich accounts of individual clients and their experiences since their graduation from traditional programmes. WEV creates individual profiles of a sample of its clients for marketing purposes and for use in attracting funding. Good quality research could systematize these profiles and extend their usefulness as a tool of evaluation and continuous improvement of WEV programmes.

In parallel, analysis also should be able to detect underlying patterns across individuals. In other words, a useful study could also detect 'profiles' or 'types' of client-identifying important issues on which groups of clients will cluster. These 'types' should emerge inductively, however key dimensions likely would include outcomes (growth, subsistence; or closure); individual goals; confidence; personal skills/experience and attributions for critical positive or negative events. Some possible types might include clients with ambitious goals for growth, high confidence, proactive orientation but limited relevant experience and access to networks. Other types may include those with culturally-influenced lower aspirations for their business and low self-confidence, leading to passivity in reaction to business challenges. There may be special issues around clients with disabilities or those with demanding domestic responsibilities. Profiles of this kind would be particularly useful in identifying how clients with particular goals, situations and needs could be targeted for particular types of support. For example, a client who needs to supplement family income and begin earning money quickly, may benefit more from a shorter and simpler programme accompanied by a small start-up loan than from the longer and more in-depth programme.

Qualitative Approach

The final premise is that the particular criteria discussed above as capable of contributing to the development of Best Practice in microenterprise training requires a qualitative approach. There are numerous ongoing quantitative studies of the impact of training on microenterprise outcomes. WEV is a participant in one prominent, large-scale study known as Microtest, mentioned above. The proposed qualitative study is seen as a useful complement to this kind of quantitative research. It will provide richer data, allowing for a more nuanced and dynamic understanding of client experience and the types of enhanced provision that may be useful for different types of individuals and situations.

WEV has collected some qualitative data from clients in the past—for example, open-ended responses to 'suggestion requests' on surveys. However, these data have remained fragmentary and anecdotal and therefore of limited usefulness. A more systematic data collection and analysis can produce useful insight and guidance to use in the design and implementation of the *Thrive in Five*®programme.

Current Research Findings on the *Thrive in Five*®Programme

The goal of *Thrive in Five*® is to support the growth of women-owned businesses by providing customized mentoring, training and support to overcome obstacles, increase knowledge and build confidence. Since its development, *Thrive in Five*® has been consistently examined and refined in order to ensure exceptional client impact and outcomes.

During the programme's pilot phase, WEV conducted interviews with each participant at six and twelve months into the programme to assess the programme's strengths and weaknesses. As a result of these interviews, significant changes were made to the programme's delivery model. Significantly:

1. Much of the services were initially delivered through webinars and teleconferences. Clients much preferred to meet in-person as this was an important step towards building trust and full engagement among participants. As a result, on-line webinars and group coaching were discontinued and replaced with individual coaching, quarterly in-person training and peer group support.
2. Clients indicated that they wanted us to be "tougher" on them (hold them to higher expectations). The most popular part of the programme was the one-on-one mentoring and consulting they received and the accountability it provided. As a result, we increased interaction with the Business Development Specialist (mentor/consultant) from quarterly to monthly.

Today *Thrive in Five*® is a robust and highly effective programme that is making a tremendous impact and WEV has added an additional component targeted towards high growth potential businesses. We continue to interview clients on an annual basis to measure client outcomes and make further refinements to the programme as needed.

Data collected through in-depth client interviews in 2015 show that when compared to WEV's general client population, Thrive in Five® participants show significantly better outcomes overall:

Outcomes	*Thrive in Five® Clients*	*All WEV Clients*
Median business sales	$95,333	$33,000
Median owner's draw	$19,219	$12,000
% of businesses with employees	71%	34%
Jobs per business	4	2
Median increase in household income	130%	82%

Benefits of Research on Domestic Microenterprise

In addition to the obvious benefits of enhanced programme design and improved economic and client outcomes, thorough and thoughtful research in the field can help convince policy-makers to invest more significantly in microenterprise development here at home.

While the United States, through the US Agency for International Development (USAID), has invested in microfinance and microenterprise organizations in the developing world for decades, domestically, the economic and social impacts of microenterprise development are largely unacknowledged. As a result, funding is scarce and local Microenterprise Development (MED) organizations often cannot acquire the resources to sustain and grow their programmes.

The US MED field is not helped by comparisons with international microfinance programmes. In the US, a microenterprise is defined as a business with five or fewer employees, including the business owner, and which requires $50,000 or less to start up. The comparatively greater size of loans, the need for and cost of comprehensive business training and technical assistance, the restrictive regulations governing depository institutions, the significantly lower interest rates charged by US programmes and the cost of doing business combine to impose insurmountable barriers to programme self-sufficiency. High-capacity private donors, instead of investing in the communities where they made their money, choose to invest instead in high-profile international programmes where they get "more bang for their buck" both in terms of programme scale and recognition.

Certainly WEV is not saying that the US Government and private donors should not invest in international MED programmes, only that one does not have to preclude the other. US policy-makers who support domestic funding for job training programmes, corporate and bank bailouts and other subsidies that primarily help large corporations, need to understand and acknowledge the important role that microenterprises play in our economy and fund programmes that support their development accordingly.

There is a distinct difference between the Federal Government and the general public in their perception of what constitutes a "small" business. According to the SBA, a small business is one with 500—and in some sectors—1,000 or fewer employees. The average person on the street considers a small business to be one with twenty or fewer employees. The vast majority of government resources that are invested in "small business" are not really going to small businesses at all; this despite the government's own data indicating that in the twenty years between 1989 and 2009, 82 per cent of the net new jobs were created by businesses with 20 or fewer employees[5].

Programmes under the aegis of the US Small Business Administration which specifically target microenterprises are woefully underfunded. The PRIME programme, which provides funding to MED programmes providing training and technical assistance to low-income entrepreneurs, has been zeroed out of the budget numerous times and then put on life support with small annual appropriations ranging from $2 million to $8 million. The maximum amount of funding the programme ever received was $15 million in its first year due to an appropriation made during the (William) Clinton Administration. At a time when the federal government was begging banks to lend to small businesses and providing $30 billion in capital to community banks to do so, the SBA

Microloan programme received less than $30 million annually in loan capital and around $20 million in technical assistance funds for MED intermediaries. The Women's Business Centre Programme is authorized at $14 million annually with the maximum award set at $150,000. Even for organizations that badly need the funding, the SBA's prescriptive programme structure and onerous reporting and matching requirements make the funds expensive and unattractive. A prohibition on charging fees for technical assistance eliminates an obvious source of matching funds and prevents organizations from earning income and becoming more self-sufficient and financially sustainable. Some microenterprise funding is also available to rural areas through the US Department of Agriculture and to local jurisdictions through Community Development Block Grants. Lack of a coherent and comprehensive domestic microenterprise development strategy adds to organization costs and creates insurmountable barriers to achieving significant programme scale.

US microlenders are also constrained by state laws and cultural norms from charging high rates of interest. Whereas it is common for international microlenders to charge 40 per cent or more (with for-profit microlenders charging as much as 100 per cent), US lenders seldom charge more than 16 per cent, and in fact, are often expected to provide loans at lower than market rates. WEV charges an average 11 per cent interest on its loans. Moreover, US banking regulations prevent microlenders from operating like banks and taking customer deposits. This means that domestic microlenders are constantly searching for capital from banks and other public and private intermediaries. Each investor/lender has different terms and conditions for documenting and tracking loans and drawing down funds which makes operating a domestic loan fund enormously complex and more expensive.

Can This Model be Replicable in Developing Countries?

There are a few key concepts that make WEV successful and that would be applicable regardless of the local level of development:

1. The long-term nature of the programme. WEV provides classroom training for pre- and emerging business clients. Once the business has been established, we provide more individual support (coaching, accountability, consulting), peer learning, and ongoing training in important subjects such as marketing, finance and management. This support is provided for a minimum of one year with no maximum. We have some clients who have participated for more than seven years. The actual delivery method of the material would depend on the literacy level of the clients. Our materials, as written, require high school reading proficiency. For a less literate population, the long-term model might be replicated with changes to the way the information is delivered. The most important aspects of the model are the individual mentoring and accountability, peer group support,, and ongoing education in the more technical elements of expanding and sustaining a business.
2. The commitment to organizational learning through outcomes measurement has been key to programme improvement and development. We look at quantifiable outcomes such as increases in income, job creation and movement out of poverty, but we also measure how well the programme is meeting client needs and expectations. We interview a random sample of clients every year and also follow up at five years. After launching a new programme targeted on growth, we interviewed every participant and made significant changes based on the feedback we received.

Conclusion

While there are many differences between international and domestic microenterprise development programmes, there are also significant similarities. In the US as abroad, the majority of microenterprise clients are women who suffer from disparities in economic and educational opportunities, gender discrimination and cultural expectations to be the family caregivers. It has been the author's experience that the struggle to balance family and work is universal among women. In the short-term, economic development which focuses on women, whether it be microenterprise development or other strategies, pays off in better living conditions and increased opportunities for women, their children and for future generations. In the long run, financial security will allow women greater self-determination and broader engagement in civil society which can bring about meaningful, if not revolutionary, social change which will truly achieve WEV's mission of creating a just and equitable society through the economic empowerment of women.

NOTES

1. Patrice Rosenthal wrote the Research Design.
2. US Department of Housing and Urban Development. "Community Development Block Grant Programme - CDBG/ U.S. Department of Housing and Urban Development (HUD)." *Community Development Block Grant Programme - CDBG/U.S. Department of Housing and Urban Development (HUD).*http:// portal.hud.gov/hudportal/HUD?src=/programme_offices/ comm_planning/communitydevelopment/programmes.
3. HUD (Housing and Urban Development) defines low- and moderate-income for each US county based upon local median income. This method allows for regional differences in cost of living. HHS (Health and Human Services) uses one scale for the entire country.
4. Doub, M. and E. Edgcomb.*Bridges to Success: Promising Strategies for Microenterprise Business Growth in the United States.* (Washington, DC: The Aspen Institute, 2005). 1-79.
5. US Small Business Administration."Office of Advocacy | SBA.gov."*Office of Advocacy | SBA.gov.*<http://www.sba.gov/ advocacy.

10

Pointers to the Future: Revisiting Microcredit as a Strategy for Inclusive Development in a Global Perspective

Patricia Taber

OVERVIEW

The *2014 United Nations Human Development Report* estimated that more than 1.3 billion people worldwide live on less than $1.90 a day[1]. At least half of these are women. Microfinance, in the form of services such as savings and uncollateralized credit extended to the poor, has been lauded as a powerful vehicle for reducing global poverty and empowering women. From its inception in the 1970s with the Grameen Bank in Bangladesh, and other big and small MFIs in South Asia, microcredit continues to be the primary instrument of an expanded number and kinds of microfinance institutions (MFIs), and women continue to be the primary recipients. In countries around the world, businesses, NGOs, governments, and private individuals now provide funds to thousands of domestic MFIs. The outreach to recipients expanded from a few thousand clients in the 1970s to over 150 million by some estimates.[2]

The attention garnered by the impressive growth and international acclaim has invited greater scrutiny by academics, policymakers, and development practitioners in an attempt to determine the direction and scope of economic and social impacts generated by microcredit. With funding for development greatly impacted by the current global economic crisis, the international community has begun to debate the pros and cons of microfinance as the best approach for lifting people out of poverty.

Even though the contributions in this volume reflect further work by the authors in the recent years it is important to recall the original workshop, the debates it generated and insights of the participants which spurred the project to move forward.

The May 28, 2010 workshop organized by the Orfalea Centre for Global and International Studies at the University of California, Santa Barbara entitled: "Revisiting Microcredit/ Microfinance as a Development Strategy for an Inclusive Growth: A Global Perspective," brought together social science scholars and members of civil society involved with microcredit organizations to examine the present realities and future challenges of microfinance as it moves from the margins of the financial system to the mainstream.

Workshop Goals

Assessing progress towards the twin goals of poverty alleviation and the empowerment of women, workshop participants considered these complex issues from the ground-level perspective of the providers and recipients of microfinance programmes in India, Bangladesh, Pakistan, the Philippines, Vietnam, Iran, Egypt, Haiti, Peru and the US. Their analyses examined the ways in which local and global exigencies influence outcomes in the context of social and economic processes that are both increasing global integration and weakening social safety nets. The following are some of the pointers to the future delineated by the workshop participants.

One Size Does Not Fit All

It has become apparent that local and regional differences in the problems faced by women and the poor require different development strategies. "Better-off," or "entrepreneurial poor," may benefit from microcredit for entrepreneurial activities. But for the "extremely poor" microcredit may reduce vulnerability to some degree, however, it is insufficient to lift them above the poverty level. For this latter group there is a need for more flexible financial help to further reduce vulnerability, smooth income and consumption, and simply survive. While microcredit has primarily targeted the entrepreneurial poor, more remains to be done to address the needs of the very poor with services such as savings, micro insurance, and emergency loans.

Speaking to these local and regional differences, Marsha Bailey, CEO and Founder of Women's Economic Ventures, described how single and poor women in developed countries face a different set of obstacles to achieving success on a significant scale than those faced by women in developing countries. While the Grameen peer lending model has proven fruitful among some groups in the developing world, it has not met the needs of low-income entrepreneurs in the US where there is limited public funding or awareness of microenterprise development. As a result, microenterprise groups have had to devise their own individual programmes to serve a variety of constituencies, and struggle to raise a patchwork of funds to support their training and lending programmes. Starting from the premise that more money equals more power, Bailey described how her organization focuses on increasing women's access to capital, which is one of the major barriers to women's economic advancement in the US. She also emphasized the need for business training. Unlike many members of microcredit groups in the developing world, poor women in the US are educated, however, they have no business expertise. In addition, in contrast to the group-oriented approach practised in Asia, the approach in the US is oriented towards the individual.

In Peru, on the other hand, government and non-governmental institutions are involved in attempts to facilitate microenterprise development. There, almost 70 per cent of the urban poor are engaged in microenterprise, 48 per cent of whom are women. Nonetheless, it has failed to become a consistently viable source of income. This is largely due, Brooke Weddle argued, to a lack of understanding about the role that gender plays in this sector. In this, Weddle spoke to an important recurring theme in the workshop: the salience of various kinds of social capital for women. Weddle noted the disproportionate lending to men, even though women actually produce higher returns and repayment rates despite their disadvantages in education, access to credit, and the burden of household labour. She explained how women's more effective use of certain kinds of social capital and microcredit serve to "level the playing field" with respect to economic outcomes. Weddle argued that taking these gender differences into account in microenterprise policy would help women and men in this growing sector to develop more sustainable businesses, and thus increase the economic survival of millions of people in Peru and other developing countries. She pointed out how gender parity would produce significant gains for both recipients and lenders, and provided several practical policy recommendations, among them, educating MFIs about these losses and potential gains, developing programmes and offering incentives to banks that would minimize the barriers that women face, increasing education and training, and tailoring microfinance more specifically to different recipients. The last two points, the need for training, and adapting microfinance to specific needs, were significant themes that emerged in the workshop for both developed and developing societies.

Weddle's analysis is a contribution to one trend in recent decades that has been given impetus by the microcredit movement, and that is the growing realization by governments and development practitioners of the important role of women in successful development. Another significant trend has been the movement of microfinance institutions from the fringes of the financial system to the mainstream. The frontline experience of professionals such as Jean Weidemann, President of the Weidemann Foundation, in bringing these two things together—that is, integrating gender issues into the centre of international economic development and microfinance—provides valuable insight and expertise in the design of microfinance programmes for women as a strategy for women's empowerment, poverty alleviation and inclusive economic growth. Pointing out that economic well-being is connected to all aspects of life, Weidemann offered several suggestions for best practices based on her more than 35 years of experience in

30 countries. These principles and guidelines that have been developed in a broad range of programmes in different parts of the world, included things such as respect for the individual recipients including privacy concerns, lender transparency, the need to include training and literacy education in addition to loans, a focus on sustainability, and a community-based approach that provides different levels of services to different kinds of recipients including the poorest of the poor. Weidemann presented a film about the Fonkoze project in Haiti that provides a variety of financial and social services, as an example of the successful application of these practices[3]. It shows that if everything fails, women's collectives under the subsistence conditions work effectively[4].

The Neoliberal Paradigm

A major point of debate among social scientists is whether the neoliberal development model is the best paradigm for helping women and the poor. As an alternative to top-down development, microcredit is viewed as a way that the poor can help themselves and contribute to economic growth. However, this goal of 'self help' has been critiqued by some who view it as privatization of public safety-net programmes that, as Richard Appelbaum mentioned in his comments, may act to divert resources, as responsibility for poverty alleviation is shifted from the state onto the individual. He cited the example of China where a large investment at one go by the government has resulted in raising millions of people out of poverty.[5] Others argue that education, training, job creation and employment on a larger scale may be more effective than entrepreneurship in addressing the long-term needs of the poor. In a subsequent rejoinder, Jean Weidemann noted that not many countries can provide the social safety nets and real employment that China does, especially where much of the population gains its livelihood in the informal sector. She argued that in countries such as Haiti, where the government functions primarily in the capital city, microcredit becomes even more critical for the empowerment and economic advancement of poor women.

Critiques of the neoliberal paradigm and state interventions have come from a variety of corners. Arguing that microcredit is an important site where the cultural politics of citizenship are waged, Gayatri Menon examined the potential of microcredit both for the state and for women's collectives in extremely impoverished communities in Maharashtra, India. Describing how creditworthiness came to be viewed as the mark of the ideal citizen-subject of the post-developmentalist Indian state, Menon looked at how microcredit is increasingly setting the terms by which the state and development institutions engage, and in effect discipline, the poor. She then went on to analyse the possibilities that microcredit holds for women in community-based savings and credit groups in rural Maharashtra who invest the practice with meanings derived from their experiences of extreme poverty and marginalization. Through their particular practice of microcredit, women in these groups experience a mutual bonding and trust that enables them to work together as a collective in various struggles. Menon found that what is empowering about their practice is the way in which they have sought to configure their credit transactions rather than the credit itself, eschewing the disciplinary potential of credit relations and seeking instead to accommodate as best they can the exigencies of lives lived in extreme poverty. What these groups in Maharashtra show, she suggests, is that if we are to take seriously the contention that microcredit is empowering, then extending the disciplinary model based on establishment banking rationality to the very poor requires radical re-thinking. Her discussion of the personal, social, and political consequences when women come together in groups and lifting themselves from personal conflicts to address their problems was echoed in other papers in the workshop.

The Social Context

Another aspect of the self-help paradigm that is of concern is the social and cultural context in which microcredit programmes take place. Progressives have argued that because poverty is structural, the solutions must focus on providing adequate social infrastructure rather than simply adjusting the conditions of individuals. In recent years a growing chorus of questions has arisen about the efficacy of microcredit, in and of itself, in lifting people above the poverty level on a sustained basis. This argument with regard to the importance of structural conditions also applies to the question of women's empowerment. While Menon's paper showed how the neoliberal intentions of microcredit may be subverted, Soheila Alirezanejad's paper brought up one of the major questions concerning the connection between microcredit and women's empowerment.

The majority of microfinance clients, about 67 per cent worldwide, are women. In some places it is 100 per cent. It is argued that access to financial services that propel women into entrepreneurship can improve their status by opening up new opportunities, fostering increased self-esteem, self-confidence, assertiveness, efficacy in the public sphere, and a greater voice in family and community decision-making. Although several studies, including some in this workshop, have shown this to be true in many cases, the evidence regarding poor women's empowerment through microcredit remains inconclusive. Others have argued that microfinance as an instrument of women's empowerment is overstated and may even diminish gender equality in some instances, since access to credit is not the only determinant of women's power and autonomy. Doubts remain as to whether microcredit and micro-enterprise alone are actually empowering for women, or whether these must take place in the context of larger structural changes in order for women to benefit from their entrepreneurial activities in any significant way. If other structural conditions that disadvantage women remain in place, women do not benefit significantly from the extra work.

This dilemma regarding the larger social and cultural context was clearly illustrated in the case of a rural Iranian bee-keeping project that Alirezanejad described. While the income generated by beekeeping did temporarily have many of the positive effects for women and their families mentioned above, their success did not take place in a vacuum. Once the sources of support and livelihood were destroyed by a combination of environmental and social circumstances, which increased their risk, the absence of cultural and infrastructural support meant that the empowerment the women temporarily enjoyed was not sustainable in the long run. Alirezanejad explained how, although beekeeping is a traditional skill in Iran among older women, the lack of supportive organizations and social institutions caused the disintegration of the group into competitive individual endeavours and schisms based on age and educational levels. External expectations and policies created or exacerbated internal tensions, which frustrated the women beekeeping entrepreneurs' attempts to make more meaningful changes in their lives, thus rendering the new knowledge and skills they had gained of little use to them in the end. In other words, the personal conflicts and lack of trust between educated younger women and skilled older women failed to create the necessary 'social capital,' which was one of the cementing forces in the case that Menon described.

Furthering these ideas in his discussion, Manoranjan Mohanty reinforced arguments that there needs to be flexibility at the local level, and that these programmes need state support that focuses more broadly on social welfare initiatives such as education and training, rather than a narrow focus on savings and credit only. Pointing to the potential dynamism in women's groups that Menon and others in the workshop described, he suggested that unless the socio-political context encourages women to become not only economic actors, but enables them use these microcredit groups as incubators for political mobilization, women may not be able to realize real and lasting empowerment in the society.

In India, this problem of social infrastructural support at the grassroots level has been taken up by the government and NGOs in several ways. One, as Bidyut Mohanty pointed out, is through reservations for women and Scheduled Castes and Tribes in local government institutions (panchayats), and another is through microlending to various women's groups. Speaking to the dynamism and potential for political action of local microcredit groups referred to by Manoranjan Mohanty, Bidyut Mohanty described the 'synergy' that has occurred between women in panchayats and those in microcredit groups in India. While acknowledging certain problems, such as perpetuation of hierarchies and exploitation in some cases, Mohanty argued that these two measures (reservations and microlending) have resulted in social mobilization and empowerment for millions of women, bringing them into the public sphere and active participation in decision-making processes. Mohanty's study once again pointed up the sometimes overlooked effectiveness of certain kinds of women's social capital in these groups—in this case, protective functions, networking between groups, and advocacy lobbying—that produce favourable social and economic outcomes on the local level, and enable women to become active agents in redistributive development and delivery of basic services to the villages.

In Vietnam, too, Le Thi My Hien described how the government has attempted to alleviate poverty through providing a variety of credit and other financial, training, and consultancy services for poor households, many of which are aimed primarily towards women. While it has achieved some measure of success in a few locales, limitations exist in terms of the expertise and infrastructure required to succeed on a larger scale. Le showed how microcredit may function as a stepping stone for poor women in terms of improving both their economic situation, and their social positions. And here again, we see the importance of social capital, and the role that microcredit can play, not only in reducing poverty, but in changing the status of women. Like the women described by Mohanty in India, the formation of client groups and participation in meetings enabled the development of social networks where women could discuss various issues and find support. Through the knowledge and skills provided during their participation in these group and community activities, and through the use and management of capital, Vietnamese women in some programmes have increased their social efficacy and confidence, and gained a greater voice in family and community decision-making.

The question remains as to whether this kind of empowerment can serve as a catalyst for larger structural changes that would sustain the gains that a few women make. In some ways, it can be viewed as a chicken-or-egg argument:

Do women's empowerment and poverty alleviation require the prerequisite of favourable social infrastructural conditions, or can these groups be a force that ramifies through society, creating structural changes? More likely, as Mohanty and several other workshop participants' research suggests, it is most effective as a synergistic movement with the two working together towards change. It appears that one is not likely to succeed without the other.

Le Thi My Hien pointed out that in Vietnam, as elsewhere, social, political and infrastructural support will have to increase before the majority of poor women can reap the potential benefits of microcredit. The challenge as she saw it is how local semi-formal microcredit organizations can be integrated into the larger formal sectors while retaining their local characteristics and control.

The importance of the social capital and support that women gain through participation in groups was again demonstrated in a somewhat different context in Annapurna Pandey's description of widows and battered women in Puri, India who have chosen to live together in a collective, supporting themselves and each other through micro-enterprise. Given the social conditions for women who lose or who leave their husbands in India, this cooperative provides a safe and meaningful haven for these women, and their entrepreneurial activities make it a viable alternative to what might otherwise be a miserable life. Pandey also brought up several problems related to women's involvement in microcredit and local politics, and the question of if, or to what extent, it can actually benefit women. Again, the social context can be determining. What the poor widows and battered women in this group have done it seems, is to effectively "opt out" of that context, and with some financial help from outside sources, carve out a space in which they can flourish. Again, the importance of the social came to the fore in Pandey's description, not only in terms of emotional and economic support, but in terms of the platforms these groups provide for formulating critiques of the system itself.

A question arose during discussion regarding the

entrepreneurial success of the Puri widows' cooperative vs. the failure of the Iranian bee-keepers. Although both these projects took place in an environment in many ways not conducive to women's empowerment, Pandey's work suggests that perhaps the success of the Puri women's collective was due to their group coherence vs. the disintegration into factions and individual endeavours experienced by the beekeepers. Also, as Alirezanejad pointed out, members of the widows' cooperative did not have the kinds of social and familial obligations and claims on their energies and earnings as the beekeepers. It appears that their minimal expenses and the power of concerted action enabled the Puri group to achieve sustainable success. Discussing the economic aspects of these enterprises, Aashish Mehta highlighted the risk component involved, noting that the beekeepers may have lost out because they did not account for the uncertainty involved in their micro enterprise. The Puri group, on the other hand, pursued a less-risky business plan by choosing a sure-selling favourite snack sought by the pilgrims who flood into the famous sacred city of Puri all year round. Eileen Boris noted that the consequences of microcredit cannot be judged solely from an economic perspective. Cultural and social consequences must be taken into account as well in judging the impact.

Global Capitalism

Describing neoliberalism as an ideology that rests on the idea that human welfare is best served by the withdrawal of the state from welfarist policies, Lamia Karim addressed the concern that microcredit programmes operating under the logic of neoliberal capitalism may supplant not only social welfare programmes, but other aspects of sovereignty formerly in the domain of the state. In her ethnographic study in rural Bangladesh, one of the birthplaces of the microcredit movement, Karim described how global capitalism operates at the grassroots level of home and community through the microcredit policies of NGOs that act as a "shadow state." She focused on Bangladesh's Grameen Bank, which boasts a 98 per cent loan recovery rate and is celebrated by many worldwide as a magic bullet for the poor.

Examining some of the tactics behind NGO loan recovery programmes, Karim showed how traditional concepts of 'honour' and 'shame' among poor women are manipulated to further capitalist interests. Discussing the predicament of postcolonial governance, she described the ways in which developmental NGOs with economic ties to Western capital, target poor people with much-needed services that the state has failed to deliver, thus linking together economic, political, and social life through their microcredit programmes. Karim argued that as a result, NGOs and multinational corporations become connected to the rural poor in ways that make them economically and socially dependent.

Karim acknowledged the Grameen Bank's role in introducing new forms of social identity among rural women, and the creation of a space in which women can speak without men dominating the discourse. She also agreed that grassroots mobilization may unleash new political potential. But in the groups she studied this potential remained inhibited by the financial imperatives of NGO microcredit institutions that acted to depoliticize this energy through various mechanisms, including the use of shaming as an instrument of social control. Karim's analysis centred on the intersection of the microcredit model with local patriarchal norms and cultural practices, particularly manipulation of the code of family honour that rests on women, often to their detriment. She described how this intersection creates a system that depends on sometimes brutal self-policing by the women in the local microcredit groups in order to avoid the shame and family dishonour that would come with default. Karim characterized the "toxically synergistic" combination of kin obligations and collective responsibilities as operating within what she called an "economy of shame" that results not only in further impoverishment of the neediest families, but in a gradual disintegration of the community, while absolving NGOs of responsibility. The national pride fostered by the ostensible success of the Grameen Bank on the world stage, together with the hegemony exercised by NGOs, enables them to neutralize dissenting voices.

During her critical discussion of the claims by Yunus and

other Grameen model advocates that microcredit reduces poverty, Lamia displayed a photo that showed the descendants of the bank's first borrower, Sufia Begum, continuing to live in poverty. In addition, Karim found that 95 per cent of the loans to women were used by male relatives, that wealthier clients often used poorer women as proxy members, and that the most widespread and profitable business from microcredit was the practice of usury by women who adopted the norms of traditional moneylenders, including high interest rates, which brings many more poor people "inside the web." Lamia argued that microcredit has thus helped primarily middle-class women who charge exorbitant rates of interest and send their sons to the Middle East. Husbands are often the ones who take the products to the weekly markets, thus depriving women of direct access to the money to which they are entitled. Thus, the question of women's empowerment becomes dubious. However, Karim did not totally reject microcredit, suggesting instead a different kind of investment targeted more specifically towards poor women[6].

The question of whether neoliberal capitalism is the best paradigm for helping the poor and empowering women was addressed from a slightly different angle by Stephanie Santos in her analysis of the situation of indigenous women in the Philippines who were ousted due to construction of a dam. Instead of viewing state interventions as a better alternative to individual 'self-help' schemes, Santos argued that societies with traditional social structures based on communal sharing are actually harmed by what she termed, the "development aggression" of states who attempt to impose a Western or nationalist neoliberal development model that demands a certain form of economic citizenship. In the process, women have been dispossessed of their ownership of land and turned into mere retailers of products. Performing close readings of the principles of microcredit espoused by Grameen to study microcredit as part of the growing financialization of the world, Santos argued that microcredit serves as one of the ways that women may be rendered as the "new subalterns," who are geographically but not socially mobile[7].

Echoing some of the points raised by Menon, Santos showed

how development is often a site where cultural politics are contested, and how women may imbue it with different meanings based their experiences of marginality and struggles for survival. She described how some women-centred coalitions in the Philippines are reconceptualizing development paradigms in non-developmentalist, non-nationalist, and non-Western terms. And in an analysis similar to Karim's, Santos described how marginalized populations such as the indigenous women she studied, may become fodder for nationalist development discourses centred around neoliberal programmes like microcredit. She argued that in this way, microcredit programmes may co-opt the subjectivities of poor people as economic rather than cultural citizens, thereby reproducing the global economic order. Santos described how the neoliberal state apparatus in the Philippines has disrupted indigenous women-centred knowledge, ignored women's important roles in sustainable agriculture, and caused the disintegration of independent socio-political systems of mutual support and community integrity that have protected women and children from various forms of violence. She emphasized the need to view women as knowledge producers rather than trying to force on them a neoliberal economic subjectivity and citizenship defined simply as producers and consumers.

The primary objective of microcredit is, ostensibly, to promote the generation of income among poor households, thereby alleviating poverty. But, as several workshop participants demonstrated, the extent to which microcredit and microfinance actually benefit the poor, and in what ways, is a much debated subject. Several researchers have lamented the dearth of reliable macro socio-economic data, and reliance instead on anecdotal evidence regarding poverty alleviation. Others have pointed out the need to distinguish among different levels of possible social and economic effects: for example, individual agency for women, family and household resources and relations, changes in the community and society, and at the level of state governments in terms of legal and structural changes. Questions remain about methods of ascertaining and measuring relevant criteria. The view currently gaining currency is that providing financial services for the poor, rather than a magic bullet, is only one of many components of poverty that need to be addressed. The fact that local markets can only sustain a certain number of micro-enterprises before they become saturated and therefore unprofitable has led some observers to argue that education, training, job creation and employment on a larger scale may be more effective in addressing the long-term needs of the poor.

Another problem in assessing the effectiveness of microfinance that was brought out in several papers was that of distinguishing among different types of poor. Studies have shown that different groups need different financial services. For example, the "better-off," or "entrepreneurial poor," are those who can benefit from microcredit for entrepreneurial activities. The "extremely poor"—defined by the World Bank as those who live on less than $1.25 a day—who lack economic security and even the ability to meet basic necessities such as food, shelter, and clothing, require different development strategies.

Analysing quantitative data collected in several impact assessments, and evaluating the methods used to measure impacts, Laila Fahimuddin addressed these broader questions regarding the efficacy of microfinance for poor women in Punjab, Pakistan. She described how, since 2001, Pakistan has placed a national focus on developing microfinance programmes as a poverty alleviation and gender equity strategy. But while foreign aid continues to pour into microfinance projects, the impact it has had on these goals is unclear. Critiquing the approaches used in impact assessments for three types of microlending institutions: an NGO, a bank, and the National Rural Support Programme, Fahimuddin examined who microfinance institutions target and how effective they are at economically empowering women. Her analysis included questions regarding the poverty level of people targeted for microfinance programmes, whether lending based on social capital works to include or exclude the poor, and whether the structures of microfinance NGOs, banks, and the National Rural Support Programme have had differential impacts on women's ability to develop socio-economic capital. Describing what she called a "hierarchy of poverty," her analysis suggested that the Grameen model of microfinance instituted in Pakistan has mostly been effective in empowering the marginally poor, while excluding or extorting the poorest of poor. In terms of its impact on women's empowerment, Fahimuddin did not find any significant difference between borrowers and non-borrowers. However, there appeared to be some difference in terms of health benefits, since the children of the borrowers received vaccinations, while the non-borrowers' children were not vaccinated.

Jayne Lee described what she viewed as an example of a successful microfinance project in Cairo, Egypt that apparently works on these different levels of poverty. The Village Savings and Loan (VS&L) programme she visited in Dar es Salaam offered a way for both the poor and the very poor to manage their household cash flow more efficiently and flexibly, and to invest in income-generating activities that secure and stabilize cash income. Lee described the various aspects of the programme that facilitated this success, including local control. Each savings and loan group developed their own rules with regard to membership, duration of cycles, and protocol. Each group had a cash box with a padlock on three sides. The keys for the padlocks were given to three different individuals, and the cash box entrusted to a fourth. Each member also had a booklet in which to record participants' savings, contributions and loan amounts that was written in a simple format so that illiterate members could easily participate. From the participants' point of view, these informal all-female microfinance groups were regarded as successful both in terms of solidarity, and because members benefited from the savings component. However, Lee noted that interest rates were set too low for the loans, so each woman did not receive much more than her savings deposits at the end of the cycle. As with Karim's study, Lee also found that women in these microfinance groups are often just the financial conduits for men who are the actual beneficiaries. For example, loans may be used for such things as investment in sons' or husbands' businesses. Lee said that because of the relative success of the VS&L model, there is interest among some larger NGOs, such as Plan Egypt, to start VS&L groups in Mansheyat Nasser, the largest scavenging and recycling community in Egypt. This community is also the largest female group-owned industry in Egypt, but there are currently occupational hazards that need to be addressed[8].

Discussion following the final round of presentations brought up two major issues. One, as Phil McCarty emphasized, was the integral connection between microfinance and women's empowerment. He argued that one could not be successful without the other. He also pointed out that the fact that formal financial banking institutions are vying with each other to enter into the microcredit sector proves their economic viability in terms of investment. A member of the audience, Marty Jenkins, whose positive assessment of microcredit was based on personal experience with Muhammad Yunus and microcredit projects in various parts of the world, took issue with some of the critiques raised in the session. He felt that saying that the Grameen model of microcredit was lauded as a silver bullet was essentially a straw man, since he had never heard it referred to in that way by Yunus or anyone else in microfinance. He was particularly mystified by Karim's portrait of the descendants of Sufia Begum as living in poverty, and especially the contention that her daughter, Sukhia Khan, had died in poverty, since he had visited them subsequent to the alleged date of death and found them very much alive and living relatively well. While acknowledging that these programmes may not be perfect, he wondered what anyone might propose as a better method for alleviating poverty.

Conclusion

Poverty alleviation and the empowerment of women are two crucial issues confronting governments and development agencies around the world today. They have become arguably even more urgent in the face of current economic and environmental conditions exacerbating the hardships of many of the world's poorest people. Since Muhammad Yunus's successful experiment in Bangladesh in the 1970s, microfinance, and its principal instrument, microcredit aimed primarily at women, have grown in scope and scale. Today various mainstream entities, including commercial and state banks, internet-based organizations, and insurance and credit card companies, have joined the microfinance bandwagon, offering poor people access to basic financial services. While microfinance will undoubtedly continue to play a vital role in socio-economic development, certain questions regarding both the efficacy and ethics of various applications of this approach need to be critically reevaluated. Analysing cases from different parts of the world, workshop participants addressed these issues at the intersection of local populations and global forces. These on-the-ground analyses by investigators coming from both social science disciplines and microfinance organizations are an essential component in assessing the way forward for policymakers and development practitioners as they grapple with the very difficult and integrally related problems of poverty alleviation and women's empowerment.

What the diverse views and data presented in this workshop indicate perhaps more than anything, is the immense complexity of the issues and problems, both economic and non-economic, inextricably imbricated with microcredit that affect its ultimate success or failure in bettering people's lives. Microcredit has so far not been able to everywhere meet all of the needs of the poor. While some projects appear to be achieving the stated goals of poverty alleviation and/or women's empowerment, other results appear mixed at best. Although access to credit can be a catalyst for positive socio-economic change in the lives of the poor and disempowered, and especially women, there was general agreement that credit alone is insufficient for poverty reduction on a macro scale. This is because, in addition to simply giving loans and providing savings to women and the poor, many other aspects are involved. The social and cultural contexts are critical factors in the equation, as are infrastructure improvement and equitable access to things such as healthcare, the legal system, sanitation and safe drinking water. Although far from having been perfected, most agree that in conjunction with many other factors that must go along with it, including adequate support, education and training, larger structural changes, local control, and a consideration of gender differences, microcredit has the potential to be an effective measure. The way in which programmes are implemented is also an important factor. As the number and types of microfinance providers proliferate, care must be taken to ensure that women and the poor are not exploited by practices such as excessive interest rates and abusive repayment tactics.

What is clear is that microfinance in various forms may have the potential to help the poor and empower women, but there are still many problems that need to be addressed before it can fulfil the promise of sustained and substantial social and economic effects. The participants in this workshop drew attention to areas in need of attention, and made suggestions for possible solutions. They showed how programmes in some places have had positive results, while pointing out how strategies must be adapted and modified to take account of local class, gender, cultural, and regional differences. As with any endeavour as complicated and daunting as poverty alleviation and gender equity, working out the best combination of approaches for different groups of people will take time and energy on the part of many different institutions and individuals. Interrogating assumptions, drawing on lessons learned from both successes and failures, and approaching the problems from many different perspectives, this workshop was one such effort in the movement toward that goal.

NOTES

1. United Nations Development Programme. "Sustaining Human Progress: Reducing Vulnerabilities and Building Resilience." Human Development Report, 2014. http://hdr.undp.org/sites/default/files/hdr14-report-en-1.pdf. $1.25 per capita was used for the poverty line in 2005. It later changed to $1.90 in 2015 to include the variations in the cost of living. This line also includes the cost of basic food, clothing, and shelter in tune with the Sustainable Development Goals (SDGs) – the number one goal of which is 'eradication of extreme poverty by 2030.' http://www.worldbank.org/en/topic/poverty/brief/ global-poverty-line-faq
2. However, the number of loans to beneficiaries has varied over time,

and in recent years it has been affected by a crisis in the MFI sector, resulting in some reductions in their activities.

3. Unfortunately, she could not finalize her paper due to work pressure in Haiti.
4. Addendum added after presentation: "It should be remembered that Haiti had experienced a severe natural disaster—an earthquake—in 2010, and the entire economy, society and political system had been destroyed. Since the United States was the country nearest, voluntary organizations from the US rushed to provide relief on humanitarian grounds. Apart from the short term relief, many thought of long-term measures such as organizing women's self-help groups to generate some additional income. Since at that time, Yunus's Grameen Bank was still working without any blemishes, some voluntary organizations adopted that model. Under similar circumstances, but somewhat personalized, widows of Annapurna Pandey's case study were neglected by their family members and by society as a whole, since they were considered inauspicious. Being rejected by the society, they tried to lead a life of dignity and did so by a labour of love. They only needed a couple of thousand rupees to begin with in order to lead a happy life."
5. Addendum: "However, he did not point out whether those large groups of people could live happily in a sustainable way once the government withdrew. The latest statistics show that the poverty ratio has declined considerably, but is much higher than that of India. Nonetheless, the recent data shows the stubbornness of the poverty ratio, and hidden poverty is still prevalent in China. The Gini coefficient of inequality in China is also much higher than that of India": 46.9 for China in 2014, 33.6 in 2012 for India (CIA World Factbook 2015. https://www.cia.gov/library/publications/the-world-factbook/rankorder/2172rank.html.
6. Marty Jenkins contested the claim made by Lamia, showing another photograph of Sofia Begum, whom Lamia claimed to be the first beneficiary who died in penury. Mr. Jenkins, on the other hand, said that he visited Sofia Begum in 2007. She had not died in poverty, and was found to be living in a relatively good house. We have reproduced his mail and the blog in the appendix.
7. Unfortunately she also could not finalize her paper owing to some other preoccupation.
8. She was another dropout from the original group.

Appendix:
Sixteen Point Decision of Muhammad Yunus

1. We shall follow and advance the four principles of Grameen Bank: Discipline, Unity, Courage and Hard work – in all walks of our lives.
2. Prosperity we shall bring to our families.
3. We shall not live in dilapidated houses. We shall repair our houses and work towards constructing new houses at the earliest.
4. We shall grow vegetables all the year round. We shall eat plenty of them and sell the surplus.
5. During the planting seasons, we shall plant as many seedlings as possible.
6. We shall plan to keep our families small. We shall minimize our expenditures. We shall look after our health.
7. We shall educate our children and ensure that they can earn to pay for their education.
8. We shall always keep our children and the environment clean.
9. We shall build and use pit-latrines.
10. We shall drink water from tubewells. If it is not available, we shall boil water or use alum.
11. We shall not take any dowry at our sons' weddings, neither shall we give any dowry at our daughters' weddings. We shall keep our centre free from the curse of dowry. We shall not practice child marriage.
12. We shall not inflict any injustice on anyone, neither shall we allow anyone to do so.

13. We shall collectively undertake bigger investments for higher incomes.
14. We shall always be ready to help each other. If anyone is in difficulty, we shall all help him or her.
15. If we come to know of any breach of discipline in any centre, we shall all go there and help restore discipline.
16. We shall take part in all social activities collectively.

Source: Yunus, M.B. *Creating a world without poverty: Social business and the future of capitalism*. (Public Affairs, 2007).

Bio-Notes on Editors and Contributors

Editors

Bidyut Mohanty, PhD, is Head, Women's Studies, Institute of Social Sciences (ISS), New Delhi. She is a visiting fellow in Orfalea Centre, in the Department of Global and International Studies, University of Santa Barbara, California (UCSB). From 2007-11 she taught a course on 'Women, Culture and Development at UCSB. At ISS she has been engaged in research and training of elected women representatives at the grassroots level for over 20 years. Her publications include several edited books, among them: *Women and Political Empowerment (Annual volumes from 1995 till 2006)* and *Local Governance: Search for New Path* (New Delhi, Concept, 2011) (ed.) *Panchayats, Women and Health for All* (New Delhi, Concept, 2014).

Victor Faessel is Associate Director of the Mellichamp Initiative on 21st Century Global Dynamics at the University of California, Santa Barbara. Major publication initiatives have included Managing Editor of the *Encyclopedia of Global Studies* (H. Anheier and M. Juergensmeyer, eds., Sage, 2012) and of the online journal *global-e*, formerly as assistant editor of English-language publications at the Centre for Interdisciplinary Study of Monotheistic Religions (CISMOR) at Doshisha University in Kyoto. PhD (2004) in mythological studies with research and publications on the potent public life of myth and cultural imaginaries as they confront processes and challenges of globalization.

Contributors

Annapurna Pandey is a senior lecturer and teaches Cultural Anthropology at the University of California, Santa Cruz. Dr. Pandey PhD in Sociology from the Jawaharlal Nehru

University, and was a Post-doctoral fellow in Social Anthropology at Cambridge. Her research interests are women's activism, their economic and political empowerment in India; and women's identity making in the Odia Diaspora in California.

Brooke Weddle Ricalde PhD, University of Virginia, Charlottesville, VA. Consultant, Grameen Foundation, Washington, DC 2005–2007. Designed and implemented first multi-country impact assessment of financial inclusion targets set by the Microcredit Summit Campaign. Presented results at the 2006 Global Microcredit Summit in Halifax, Canada. At present, Dr. Weddle is the *Global Head of Services and Leader of Client Services, Americas.*

Gayatri A. Menon PhD, Cornell University, USA, serves as an assistan Professor, School of Development in Azim Premji University, Bengaluru. In 2013 she was an Honorary Research Fellow, Effective States and Inclusive Development Research Centre, University of Manchester. She has recently conbtributed an article 'Gender and Inclusion: Lessons from the Basic Services for the Urban Poor Submission of the JNNURM,' in *State of the Urban Poor Report 2015*, with Diana Mitlin and Sundar Burra. Edited by Om Prakash Mathur, OUP (2014).

Lamia Karim, Associate Professor, University of Oregon is a cultural anthropologist with a focus on political anthropology. Her primary area of research is Bangladesh in South Asia. She is the author of the much-acclaimed book *Microfinance and Its Discontents: Women in Debt in Bangladesh* (University of Minnesota Press, 2011). Her pioneering work on gender and development has received multiple fellowships and grants, including a fellowship at Humboldt University, Berlin, two Rockefeller Postdoctoral Fellowships, the National Science Foundation, etc.

Le Thi My Hien got her masters degree on Gender and Development in Asian Institute of Technology, Thailand in 2004. She was a community worker for more than 20 years, since 1991 and had chance to work with many microcredit groups, particularly with women's credit groups in urban communities. At present, she is a lecturer in the Open University teaching Gender and Development, and

Community Development.

Hien, 2010 'Community Saving-Credit Programme: A Sustainable Development Approach' *Journal of Science* (Ho Chi Minh City Open University), Vol. 1 (16), pp. 14-21 and conducted various researches on gender. She also works as trainer giving trainings on microcredit for community projects.

Mahlyah Laila Fahimuddin is a researcher, community organizer and policy advocate. Over the past ten years, she has specialized on education reform issues in California and the US, with a focus on access and equity in higher education, K-12 school finance, racial inequality, freedom of expression, and structural violence in public schools. Fahimuddin holds a BA in international development studies with honours from the University of California, Los Angeles.

Marsha Bailey, President, CEO and Founder of Women's Economic Ventures with over 25 years of experience in women's business development and microlending. Under her leadership, WEV has become nationally recognized for its innovative business education and consulting programmes. She currently serves on the National Women's Business Council, the Alumni Council for UCSB's Department of Communication Studies and is Chair of the Board of the Association of Women's Business Centres. Bailey earned her MA in Communication from UC Santa Barbara.

Patricia Taber is Sociocultural Anthropologist and currently a Visiting Research Scholar and Lecturer in the Department of Anthropology at the University of California, Santa Barbara, where she received her PhD in 2005. Her specializations include South Asia, social theory, psychological anthropology, and feminist theory, with a special interest in the middle classes and urban South India.

Soheila Alirezanejad was a visiting scholar at the Women's Studies Programme at Boston University (Spring 2010). At present she is an Associate Professor of Sociology at Faculty of Humanity, Islamic Azad University, Garmsar Branch in Iran. She has contributed many research articles to reputed journals.